About the author

Marcelo Svirsky is a lecturer in international studies at the School of Humanities and Social Inquiry, University of Wollongong. He teaches subjects in international studies and researches on Middle East politics and continental European philosophy; his focus is on social transformation, activism and revolutionary action, and on bilingual education.

AFTER ISRAEL

TOWARDS CULTURAL TRANSFORMATION

Marcelo Svirsky

Zed Books
LONDON | NEW YORK

After Israel: Towards cultural transformation was first published in 2014 by Zed Books Ltd, 7 Cynthia Street, London N1 9JF, UK and Room 400, 175 Fifth Avenue, New York, NY 10010, USA

www.zedbooks.co.uk

Set in Monotype Plantin and FFKievit by Ewan Smith, London NW5
Index: ed.emery@thefreeuniversity.net
Cover design: www.roguefour.co.uk

A catalogue record for this book is available from the British Library
Library of Congress Cataloging in Publication Data available

ISBN 978-1-78032-613-9 hb
ISBN 978-1-78032-612-2 pb

CONTENTS

FIGURE AND TABLES

Figure

Tables

ACKNOWLEDGEMENTS

First and foremost I am deeply indebted to my family, not for having provided me with the time and space to isolate myself and keep on the work of thinking and writing, but precisely for the opposite, for sharing that time with me. For about two years I have been discussing the ideas in this book with my partner in life Michelle and my three children Dekel, Tomer and Gefen. During the time of writing of this book, I have regularly been adding to our family meals my own dish of questions. I was never disappointed. Something always came out of our debates. Mostly, I found myself in the middle of dinners running from the kitchen to my computer to type out the brightest points they raised. Many arguments in this book are the direct reflection of those conversations. I owe the title of this book to my son Tomer, who suggested it when I first discussed with the family the idea of writing a book about how everyday life in Israel confirms the kind of society we need to put behind us. For him, apparently, it was clearer than for me, that I was not talking about Israel, but about its *after*.

I am privileged to have very special friends and colleagues with whom I am able to discuss my work. In our neoliberal academic age, this should indeed be seen as a privilege. Over a few years now I have benefited from having Ian Buchanan as such a friend and colleague. Our weekly conversations are a sort of laboratory of thoughts, and also a great pep pill for my research that has helped me to refine important ideas in this book. It seems to me that Australian weather has boosted this collaboration.

If the book has achieved some degree of consistency, the reader should blame the insightful observations and comments of Aura Mor-Sommerfeld, Ronnen Ben-Arie, Swati Parashar, Tim DiMuzio, and my partner in life Michelle Svirsky. They carefully read previous versions of the chapters and suggested corrections that truly helped me focus my thoughts. This book offered me a wonderful chance to actualise my commitment to feminism in writing, something that has been shamefully missing in my previous works. My dear friend Swati Parashar is the one who helped me to tread this camino. Similarly, I am grateful to Christopher Muller, Rela Mazali, Lorenzo Veracini, Yoav Haifawi and Ika Willis, who contributed comments, materials and critical notes. I would also like to thank Tal Haran, who copyedited the final manuscript before its submission to Zed Books under a stressful timeframe and also contributed to this text with her own comments and adjustments. To Judith Forshaw, Zed Books' copyeditor, I owe the colossal work of making this text digestible for the native English speaker without losing the stormy spirit of my own non-English background. Deep thanks go as well to Zed's anonymous reviewer whose comments were of great significance and helped correct and polish the last version of the manuscript.

Lastly, I am indebted to the Institute for Social Transformation Research (ISTR) at the University of Wollongong which granted me a Book Completion Grant during the first half of the 2013 academic year, a support that empowered me with the greatest of all academic resources, time. ISTR also assisted in the completion of this book with financial aid for copyediting.

A STATEMENT

Israel was a bad idea from its inception. At the time the well-integrated lives of Jews in Muslim societies were completely disregarded by European Zionists, the good intentions of securing in Palestine a home for the persecuted Jews were at one stroke ruined the moment Zionism required the dispossession of the Palestinians from their ancestral home. A national home to be established instead of a native home is always a bad idea. After a century of continuing dispossession and warmongering, Israel's suicidal policies and ways of life have pushed the region into existential instability.

Crutched by all sorts of fundamentalists – the American government, evangelists of all kinds, European orientalists and Jewish diasporas stuck in the past – Israel refuses to recognise the truth of its situation. Consuming the last drops of holocaustic fuel, it runs on air like a maniac. It fires missiles and bombs at civilian populations, it destroys homes and erects separation walls everywhere, as if to say 'I will take you all with me' in a Samson venture: 'Let me die with the Philistines.' On the backs of its Jewish citizenry faithfully carrying out the unsustainable mission of a Jewish exclusivist region, Israel refuses to give up on its endeavours. No negotiation of land, borders or sovereignty can divert us from the suicidal track on which Israel has placed life; the time to reconstruct and adapt Zionist modes of being has expired. No golden path, no negotiations, no balance of interests, no place for a healthier Zionism.

Jewish-Israelis must realise that Israel compels them to an unsustainable form of existence. They must realise that the ways of life described as Israeli wreck their lives in vain. Once they – we – realise it is over, we shall all be liberated from the problem of trying to fix the system of anti-life called Israel. Nothing can be fixed in a political project that deprives the life of its beneficiaries as well as of its victims, Jews and Palestinians. Once we realise it is over, at that very specific moment old political allegiances will be put behind us. Once we realise it, we will understand that we must now make a new beginning. That very specific moment is the moment of *after* Israel. This is why the most important political project is the cultural project, that of taking away our bodies from the characters, the identities, the practices, the associations and the ways of thinking that together make this Zionist century of ours. By the time Israel would have been celebrating its centenary, another society will be in place from the Mediterranean Sea to the Jordan River. The very same people of today and their children, those we naturally identify as Jews and Palestinians, will be invested in constructing their shared life away from the assumptions that Zionism has forced on the region. *After Israel* means exactly that.

Edward Said identified in 1998 that profound contradiction of Jewish-Israeli intellectuals, bordering on schizophrenia; in spite of their understanding of Zionism's wrongdoings to the Palestinians, in spite of their recognition of the fundamental incongruity between Zionism and democracy, there are still enough Zionists to refuse to surrender their privileged and oppressive ways of existing (Said 2003). In fact, most Jewish-Israelis show a benign quota of self-criticism as regards the oppression, marginality, exclusion, discrimination and inequality that nurture their privilege. But they have no intention whatsoever of fundamentally changing their lives or putting an end to the impoverishment of life they cause. The problem is that Zionists do not understand their oppressive ways of life as conveying a morally problematic existence, nor have they perceived their own ways of being wretched and insecure for themselves. It seems they can live with this state of affairs without major distress or discomfort. This is in fact what knits Jewish-Israelis from all streams and strengths together – from the blunt right-wing to the weak-willed left, from the more fanatic religious nationalists to the hypocritical secularists, oriental and occidental Jews, Ethiopian and Russian, women and men. But Jewish-Israelis must realise the unsustainability of their way of life and redirect their lives into the construction of new shared horizons with the Palestinians.

Any serious attempt at changing that collective political attitude must engineer the means by which Jewish-Israelis can be re-affected in regard to their perception of their modes of being. A book can offer merely a textual exercise to induce that stimulus. The strategy used in this book is to generate a reflective attitude that may re-affect Zionists by means of exploring how they become the protagonists of privilege and oppression. In other words, *I explore here how Jewish-Israelis become Zionist subjects.* We thus engage in a critical exploration of social training, how Zionist characters and behaviours are constituted in various spheres of social life. For that purpose, each chapter focuses on a specific form of subjectivity that has become dominant in Jewish-Israeli society. This book investigates four forms of subjectivity: *the hiker, the teacher, the parent* and *the voter.* In order to make it productive, however, the exploration is carried out by intersecting the tales of subjectivity with the forces of profanity. These are the acts, practices and affects that patiently crumble and disintegrate Zionist logics and common sense. These are our *vehicles of transformation.* With the help of the textual intervention of already existing dissident mentalities and practices, the chapters investigate how Zionist characters are formed, and consequently deformed. Thus, I am not assuming that Zionist ways of being are naturally given. On the contrary, I adopt the idea that these ways of being are produced and protagonised. The point is that everything that is produced can also be fractured through the production of new modes of existing and new ways of being. The challenge that the stories about the processes of gestation of Zionist characters puts before the reader may release minute emotional thunderstorms and eventually induce a relocation of affect regarding how Zionists feel about their ways of existing. Individual transformation – through a collective effort – is eventually what is needed to go beyond the Israel we all know.

I am aware that texts on Israel and Palestine are inclined to engage with political solutions, not with cultural transformation, as if a negotiated exchange of land, borders and sovereignty will save us. But no political solution can provide the cultural marrow that is utterly necessary to substantiate a thorough transformation of ways of life – without which new forms of Israeli domination will be forced on everyone who falls under the new series of arrangements of land, borders and sovereignty. This is why there is a vital need for another answer, one that takes society, culture and politics into account. It is time to understand that formal institutions and policies cannot be changed in isolation from a radical transformation of habits, identities and dispositions. The ways of life and the modes of being shaped and woven during the Zionist century must go. *This is because these ways of life and these modes of being are the continuous war waged against all the inhabitants of the region.* Overcoming these ways of life and these modes of being is to *after Israel.*

The analyses in the six chapters that follow are based on the processing of fieldwork performed in Israel during 2012 and 2013. The ideas stem from the intersection of several elements, chiefly the evaluation of individual and group interviews with activists, the study of legal documents, introspection into social practices, educational policies and cultural and political events, all aided by theoretical literature. In each chapter, the presentation of ideas does not follow a formal or strict academic script. More precisely, the ideas appear and disappear as in a collage, so the chapters can be approached as miniature essays, each on a different topic. Sometimes just a few pages suffice to make sense of something for the reader. Different objects, forms and types of expression are pasted together to form images, although it is up to the reader to see where an image starts and when another is already overlapping it. All in all, the images in this book share a resemblance; in a way, they create a family of images, or an assemblage of images trying to convey an affective text.

For those who prefer to skip the theoretical conceptualisation that wraps the contents of this book, I would suggest starting the reading at Chapter 1: 'The Hiker'. On the other hand, it is my opinion that 'theory' is never just theory, but provides the necessary language with which to read and comprehend. The alternative thus, is perhaps to leave the 'Introduction' for the end.

This book is dedicated to the peoples living in the region that extends from the Mediterranean Sea to the Jordan River and to those who have been expelled from that region since 1948 and for whom I wish their return.

'At any rate, each chapter of this book attempts a diagnosis of the cultural present with a view towards opening a perspective onto a future they are clearly incapable of forecasting in any prophetic sense.'
(Fredric Jameson, *The Seeds of Time*, p. xiii)

INTRODUCTION

The preservation of the texture of a particular social order is
confused with the preservation of the social order as such ...
(Félix Guattari, in *Molecular Revolution in Brazil*, 2008)

We begin with an upsetting fact: in most cases, knowledge revealing past and present-day injustices does not trigger unambiguous
responses. In the face of accounts that explain how oppression affects
real people's lives, some might expect shock and a change in current
perceptions and sensitivities about society. Commonly, however, one
faces disappointment – and all the more so when our own stories as
victimisers are at hand. In the case of foreign stories, we can afford
to develop some sympathy for the distressed, and as victims we are
reluctant to give up our obsession with the narratives of our past
miseries, which eventually become instruments of paranoia. All in
all, society prefers to have its own wrongs go unnoticed, unheard.
At best, these accounts are incorporated only to be rejected as mere
tales spun to serve the wrong ideology.

Oppression in Israel past and present is a case in point. Look
at the substantial academic industry of knowledge informing us
of the ways in which Jewish privilege in Israel has been hewn and
maintained through the ethnic fragmentation of life – the way in
which the Palestinian people has been dispossessed of its right to
have rights, particularly after the violence of 1948 that constituted,
and led to the constitution of, the State of Israel. However, despite
all the incriminating archival evidence, statistical indicators and new
understandings of power relations, one cannot help but wonder how
perpetrators' minds manage to accommodate every piece of information detailing their participation in the production of oppression. 'No
whispering in their hearts' causes any discomfort (Reynolds 1998).
No disaster is seen as such: neither the colonisation of Palestine,
the 1948 Nakba, nor the occupation of the West Bank, Gaza and

East Jerusalem since 1967, nor the persistent structural exclusion of the Palestinian citizens of Israel. As Ariella Azoulay recently noted, Jewish-Israelis are trained by the regime not to identify the disaster, not to 'perceive themselves as those who inflict such a disaster or are responsible for its outcome' (2013: 549–50), nor much less to recognise the disaster as their own, even though it is the disaster that explains their privilege.

At first sight, the fact that colonialists do not question their source of power and privilege should not surprise us. Intriguing, though, is the way this inability is constructed in the first place. In other words, what is it about the oppressor's collective mind that turns this inability into a habit of produced and re-created neglect? In order for us to acknowledge our own involvement in the oppression of others, then, and to understand how it vitiates our life by substantiating our privilege, educated information and analyses of the consequences of that oppression – and the costs we force its victims to pay – are just not enough. At certain moments, evidence, testimonies and reports to the Israeli public of how it is implicated have aroused some concern. Some Jewish-Israelis are still truly concerned. But, from a bird's-eye view, Jewish-Israeli society seems to have success-fully inoculated itself against moral and political reflection; thus, owing its existence to Israel's acts of oppression on the ground, the industry of knowledge about Israeli oppression whirls on without arousing moral concern. That discursive production has become a genre that is taken for granted and that few still bother to notice, an imploded star, a black hole: as far as Jewish-Israeli society is concerned, these narratives do not take off but are drawn into and trapped in the smoky rooms of radicals. Deleuze and Guattari would have defined this discourse on Israel's oppressive traditions as a line of flight that has failed – a resistance with radical aspirations that has self-aborted. In other words, although that knowledge is important in order to understand power relations in the region and potential transformations, the narrative about Israeli oppression has become a 'tale' without Jewish-Israeli listeners.

So, to help people listen and to inspire them to think and feel change, mere exposure to accounts of oppression that point them out as the villains is just not enough. People erect mental, emotional and discursive walls to protect themselves from having to account for their actions. For Jewish-Israelis, assuming that responsibility would mean stressing inadequacies in their self-image, as well as risking the loss of privilege, so some Jewish-Israelis minimise the significance of the anguish they are accused of causing while others busily justify their actions. Strategists of the Zionist left love to temporalise their apathy, claiming that a proper Palestinian partner has yet to appear. And there is a second problem: narratives of oppression present the oppressors with the horrors of the given as if they were not its perpetrators but rather subjects who are already equipped and fit to change their given. But they are not. In their present constitution, they are equipped and fit to reject the reformatory hopes of the narratives of oppression. In other words, it seems to me that narratives of oppression fundamentally dissociate between the horrors of the given and the historical and cultural particularities of their audience. In all honesty, the disillusion of their narrators is a sign of their own blindness. Traditional scripts on oppression seem to assume that there is little connection between the processes by which real practices become oppressive and the processes by which the subjectivities performing these practices are constituted. We need new mediators between our perception of reality and the ways in which that perception affects us on our path to action (Deleuze 1995). Far be it from me to claim that it is no longer crucial to keep recording the present and conceptualising the practices of oppression we create and entertain. But if we do aim to affect Jewish-Israelis in their own transformation, this intellectual work needs new allies, new mediators.

But who is the subject, the Jewish-Israeli? It is necessary to clarify that a single, unified Jewish-Israeli group or identity does not exist. The Mizrahi–Ashkenazi racial fissure,[1] the secular–religious division, the self-ghettoisation of Jewish and non-Jewish immigrants from the former Soviet Union, the cruel racism against Ethiopian Jews, and the gendered processes that still assemble the militarist Zionist machine are anything but a testimony of Jewish homogeneity in Israel. It is widely acknowledged that white Zionists have shown their oppressive talents not just towards their exterior others but towards their interior others as well. As Ella Shohat put it, Zionism has created not only external victims but also Jewish victims, the oriental Jews (1988). Thus, Jewish communities in Israel might be distinct not just for their celebrated identities and traditions, but also, and more importantly, for their position in the historical matrix of wealth and marginalisation. However, white Jewish dominance has never ended at the material level. Without a shred of integrative intention, white Zionism has always demanded full ideological and organisational submission from the moment it established itself as a colonising enterprise in Palestine. This was the case in relation to the Sephardic Jews living in Palestine at the time when European Zionists launched their colonising project (Chetrit 2010; Giladi 1990) as well as in relation to the immigrant Jewish communities that arrived in Israel from Muslim countries in large numbers during the 1950s and 1960s – and that incrementally formed the post-1948 Jewish society in Israel. So, for instance, the desire to have a greater share of society resulted in the Mizrahim[2] developing loyalty to the Zionist project despite their relegation and the consistent and persistent discrimination against them from the outset (Chetrit 2004; Hever et al. 2002; Shenav 2006; Shohat 2006), orchestrated by the white culprit who fabricated the de-Palestinisation of the country during 1948. Therefore, it is right to ask how I can claim to have 'the Jewish-Israeli' as the protagonist of my stories.

Moreover, at first glance, the reader might feel that my issue here is only with the lives of the rank-and-file middle-class Ashkenazim.[3] A book written by a white for whites. I can already visualise the complacent smiles on the faces of racial profilers of all sorts, racists and radicals alike. It would be easy to infer from the term 'Jewish-Israelis' that my concern, conscious or not, is just about white middle-class Ashkenazim. But this would be true only if the contemporary and dominant Zionist beliefs, commitments, practices and political dispositions – the very soul of Israel's machine of deprivation of life – were the monopoly of Ashkenazi Jews. Despite the fact that Ashkenazi families (however demographers would like to define this category today) are the main material beneficiaries of

Israel's machine of deprivation of life, the dominant Zionist beliefs, commitments, practices and political dispositions that make up this machine are not their exclusive monopoly – regardless of the variety of historical, economic, political and social reasons that brought and bring the different Jewish communities to commit themselves to Zionist practice. It would therefore be senseless to overlook the fact that anti-Zionist politics and practices in Israel do not enjoy the massive support of Jews of Soviet 'descent', nor of Ethiopian Jews or of the various other religious communities. It should also be noted that, as Sami Shalom Chetrit states, '[m]ost Mizrahim today are, unfortunately, of the new generations who believe that being a proud Mizrahi is waving a bigger Israeli flag than the Ashkenazim wave' (Krawitz 2009). It is true that, in a historical attempt to shrink the gap of differentiation that marginalised them as second-class partners of the white Zionist project, most Mizrahim found themselves embracing Zionism's most horrific beliefs and behaviours. The point is that 'all Israeli Jews are implicated in and must take responsibility for the colonisation of Palestine, even though ... as Shohat ... argues, Mizrahi Jews were, and are, Zionism's Jewish victims' (Lentin 2010: 10); therefore it would be thoughtless to overlook the fact that in our contemporary society most Jews in Israel *actively nurture Zionist politics with their minds and bodies*. The pro-Palestinian sympathy of some small fringes within the ultra-orthodox Jewish community, certainly in Neturei Karta, says very little regarding the consensual participation of the vast majority of the heterogeneous Orthodox community in the official Israeli political system at both the national and the local level. Then perhaps it is incorrect to claim that Orthodox Jews are Zionist ideologues or believers, but most of them are undoubtedly Zionist practitioners – they practise Zionist settler-colonial politics. This is, I believe, the readership of this book: *Zionist practitioners*, the Israeli Jews who have made Zionist practice their way of life, regardless of their historical or political reasons for doing so. However, a vivid and appropriate anti-Zionist challenge should find ways to assemble the fragments in the histories and the present contexts of these Jewish communities that can boost the collective struggle of Palestinians and Jews to *after Israel*. If I have not achieved this aim here, at least to some modest extent, this is a fault I hope to correct in my next works.

As I have said, my issue here is with the broad and heterogeneous array of Zionist practitioners, not with a particular set of ethnically or racially identifiable subjects. I am therefore focusing on the phenomenology of particular modes of being, namely *the assemblage of Zionist modes of being that nurture the deprivation of life of all the inhabitants of the region.* Even if these modes of being have evolved through their internalisation by the distinct Jewish communities in Israel for extremely different and even contradictory reasons and motivations, as previously mentioned, this heterogeneity has not prevented so far the consolidation on the ground of Zionist practices shared by most Jews in Israel. Quite the opposite, if you ask Palestinians. Let me explain again: there is no one whole and unified Israeli Jewishness, and Zionism, as a historical political project, was manufactured by and for Ashkenazi Jews, so to a large extent Zionism in this sense 'cannot be used as a totalizing concept for all Jews' (Abdo 2011: 34).[4] As Ella Shohat maintains, Zionism was never a liberation movement for all Jews, despite the fact that 'Zionist ideologists have spared no effort in their attempt to make the two terms "Jewish" and "Zionist" virtually synonymous' (1988: 1).

Despite this, it is essential to establish that Zionism is not only a historical political project but *a series of contemporary practices.* What I address in this book, therefore, are those who engage in Zionist practices, the *Zionist practitioners.* While I am aware of and in total agreement with the Mizrahi critiques that reject the attempt to conceive Zionism as the national movement of all Jews (see, for example, Hever et al. 2002; Lavie 2005; Nimni 2003; Shohat 1988),[5] I claim that the momentous gains of this scholarship cannot obscure the Jewish rainbow of real Zionist practitioners making Israel the kind of settler society it is. Can we firmly state that Israel's Zionist ways of life are supported and practised only by white, male, secular Jews? Can we claim that in spite of the anti-religious cargo East European Jews brought with them to the colonisation of Palestine, the Jewish religion has no part in the Zionist settler-colonial practice of dispossession? Of course not. It would be insane to claim that. My approach is not ethnic-centred but practice-centred: when I refer to the 'Jewish-Israeli' I am not assuming a unified Jewish ethnic subject condensed by a homogeneous set of histories and interests coiled around Zionist ideologies; rather, I am referring to those people who walk through their lives enacting Zionist practices, thus becoming Zionist practitioners. So, this heterogeneous category of subjects is created by participation, not by racial, ethnic, gender or religious affiliation. In short, we cannot hide our complicity with Zionist practices behind the colour of our skin.

I certainly claim that a confident Zionist anti-Palestinian consensus exists across large segments of Jewish society in Israel, coexisting with the internal heterogeneities and escapes (the non-consensual behaviours and ways of thinking) of this society. For whoever looks for the accomplishments of the Zionist melting pot, this is exactly where to find them. *The melting pot of hatred.* As Edward Said (2001) put it:

> The core idea is that if Jews have all the rights to 'the land of Israel', then any non-Jewish people there are entitled to no rights at all. It is as simple as that, and as ideologically unanimous.

Let me dare to correct Said and say that, more than being ideologically unanimous, *it is practised unanimously.* Here, I am addressing this consensus in its more general patterns, and, where relevant, the discussion brings forth the historical and political distinctions that bring to the surface the internal heterogeneities of Jewish society in Israel. By more general patterns, I mean the patterns that make Israel the kind of state and society that structurally imperils not only the lives of Jewish-Israelis and Palestinians but increasingly incites the world to support political instability, large-scale conflicts and wars.

Therefore, the fact that my stories have 'the Jewish-Israeli' as their protagonist does not mean at all that I am unaware of the many historical and contemporary embodiments of that category. The Jewish-Israeli of my stories is not one, nor does he belong to a set ethnic category of Jews. The Jewish-Israeli of my stories is the Zionist practitioner and should be read in the plural, as the disparate collection of individualities that populate the locus or plane of existence in which the Zionist modes of being that nurture the deprivation of life converge, however significant the internal heterogeneity of the collection itself. In this sense, the verb 'to *after Israel*' means reviving the Zionist/Jewish distinction by disengaging from the practices that blur it.

§ As I was saying, exposing oppression in its full horror, trying to explain that military occupation, discrimination and segregation are unjustifiable, and showing that Zionist policies towards the Palestinians perpetually defer any actual resolution have all proved futile in the effort to affect most Jewish-Israelis and drive them to change. These texts mostly fall upon deaf ears. In this book I offer another approach to cope with that inability to perceive privilege in terms of the oppressive practices that secure it. I ask how, as Israeli Jews, we have become the protagonists of such horrible stories. These stories have not been repressed in the Israeli public sphere to such an extent that their voices have been lost; in fact, knowledge of these stories is widely accessible. Yet there is an excruciating gap between that reality and the emergence of transformative impulses to change things. Without guessing how many protagonists need to become 'race traitors' and which alliances need to be forged in order to reach a critical mass that might generate change, it is safe to assume that invitations to consider social transformation are thought unnecessary as long as we do not see ourselves as the protagonists of horror stories.

Let me explain. As has already been said, the Jewish-Israeli society is a very diverse society, and yet most of its members are strongly knitted by a compulsion to uphold the Zionist project of the Jewish state. This commitment is expressed in terms of the kind of practices Jewish-Israelis perform, in the sort of beliefs and dispositions they hold, and by way of the discourses they voice. In this society, there are Jewish-Israelis who at times reflect on the sort of beliefs they were trained to hold and examine the practices they are required to perform as part of the Zionist collective. Others are truly aware of the oppressive character of their beliefs and their practices, yet they embrace them as their preferred way of existing. Such awareness may lead to attempts to exit the Jewish-Israeli collective way of life, but only a small minority opt for that. The majority of Jewish-Israelis do not critically reflect on their lasting commitment to their collective beliefs, ideas and practices and hence they do not take notice that these are vehicles of privilege and oppression. In other words, most Jewish-Israelis choose, unconsciously or not, to live in peace with the misery they cause. For them, these beliefs, ideas and practices are just their obvious ways of existing in this world, as much as it is normal for them to have their public spaces crowded with armed soldiers, or have their bags and bodies regularly checked by security guards. In fact, most people do not go about questioning their ways of being (Pease 2010).

Furthermore, most people tend to protect their ways of existing from critique. In a society such as that of the Jewish-Israelis, this protection has many sources of legitimation that also help reinforce the cohesiveness of the political community. True, in recent years a sharp right-wing radicalisation has been taking place in all strata of society and many Jewish-Israelis are no longer really concerned with explaining or justifying their deeds. Today, most non-receptive reactions to critique fluctuate from 'leave me alone, this is how we live here' to 'leave me alone, this is how we *should* live here'. The implications and consequences of their deeds on others just do not sink in. Oppressive deeds have been made routine and their con-sequences ignored. To do this, Jewish-Israelis have developed a sort of 'Teflon coating' that prevents those oppressive implications and consequences from effecting them to change. Their Teflon coating keeps their sense of themselves defensible by erecting discursive and emotional mechanisms to help them come to terms with any critique of their actions. As a result, they can go on with those actions without interruption.

How can we pierce that protective shield and effect Jewish-Israelis to abandon their oppressive practices? Given the failure of the nar-ratives of oppression, I suggest focusing on the processes by which Jewish-Israelis become Zionists, rather than focusing on the visible oppressive practices Jewish-Israelis protagonise in their relationships with others, particularly with the Palestinians, or on the lethal and depredatory consequences of these practices. This means focusing on the ways in which *Zionist subjectivities* are constituted as such. This is about studying processes of subjectivation, the minute moments of everyday life through which people are constituted and constitute themselves as subjects – becoming individuals with particular ways of thinking, doing and feeling, and with predictable predispositions to interpret the world in determinate ways. Following Guattari, these processes, with no definitive goal and endless in character, create our *existential territories*, namely the spaces to live in that we construct and reconstruct in our interactions with society: minds and bodies, lifestyles and occupations, friends and relationships with others, leisure activities, political dispositions and so forth (1996: 125, 196).

Why should we study processes of subjectivation? Simply because these processes, by forming our social characters and habits, cast us in a central role in the very acts of oppression we take part in. In other words, these processes of constitution that make Jewish-Israelis into Zionists hold the key to understanding how Jewish-Israelis develop the necessary disposition to oppress. In the context of Jewish-Israeli society, studying processes of subjectivation helps to reveal the inherent interconnections between the vibrancy of oppressive practices and the constitutive subjectivation processes through which these practices become wilfully animated. Processes of constitution of subjects need to be understood as processes that involve relations of production – of subjects. In the course of these relations of production, the cultural and material core that *animates* society is produced.

The point of socialisation is that the particular patterns of relations of subject production are present in their effects – in the characteristics of the subject's behaviour, beliefs, modes of life and dispositions. Hence, because of this link between the two realms, by examining the relations of subject production we might be able to shape a critical attitude towards both these relations and their effects. However, it is extremely important to conceive the relations of subject production and their effects as *not being relations of perfect agreement*. If not, we will be seeing experience as a mere reproduction of subject production, and therefore no escape from our despotic identities will be possible. In line with the Deleuzian–Guattarian approach of how subjects are constituted, I adopt the position according to which a 'subject ... is as much the product of self-invention, as it is the con-sequence of a conformity to existing structures' (Buchanan 2000: 86). Subjects are constituted in ways that both transcend the given and conserve themselves in the given. In other words, I adopt the activist position according to which subjects might go beyond their given conditions of life – a subject can transcend itself – and reconstitute their subjectivities by creating and incorporating dissonant meanings, interpretations and practices that stand in disagreement with the patterns embedded in the dominant relations of subject production.

To the tales of oppression I suggest adding *subjectivity tales*. These tales will close the gap that exists between how Jewish-Israelis perceive their socialisation into becoming part of the Zionist collective and how they perceive their participation in practices that factually cause oppression. Simply put, most Jewish-Israelis are unmindful of the ways by which socialisation makes them into oppressors. My claim is that by looking into the production line of ourselves, we might be able to identify the nuts and bolts of our oppressive characters and habits, those protagonising in acts of oppression. The question I ask is what is it about the construction of Zionist collective characters and ways of life that has Jewish-Israelis wilfully playing those oppressive roles.

However, my aim is neither an introspection of processes of sub-jectivation for the sake of witnessing our submission into becoming oppressors nor to moralise. The aim is experimentation. My sugges-tion is to stimulate a *critical look* at the various ways by which one becomes a Zionist practitioner in Jewish-Israeli society. What do I mean by critical? On the one hand, I am interested in the processes that render Jewish-Israelis so willing to accept the role of actively producing misery for others; I am interested in how their disposi-tions become dominant behaviours, and how these dispositions are shaped by and play a role in the maintenance of asymmetrical ways of life and the substantiation of privilege. From this perspective, the mundane is animated by *normative social figures*, their dispositions and habits. These normative social figures crystallise the processes of Zionist subjectivation in the different social spheres. On the other hand, I am no less interested in the ways in which the roles these figures perform are defied by emerging alternatives, by *acts of profanation*. One can only profane the sacred, and nothing is regarded more sacred in our lives than our normative characters, identities and dispositions. Their survival depends on their ability to prevent inventiveness and creativity (Guattari 1996: 215). Profanatory processes, on the other hand, manufacture new and singular modes of existence that wrest us from the current attachments that fix our bodies to specific social practices and political dispositions at particular times. Taken together, this exercise problematises the constitutive conditions of the beliefs, understandings and perceptions of subjects with regard to the given in an attempt to change this bundle – while keeping in mind that the self is no more than the ways in which the components of this bundle are related (Bell 2009: 43). Simply put, the textual exercise aims at problematising the circumstances behind processes of subjectivation and the conditions of the relations of subject production.

The contribution of this book is to stage *images* that intersect these two interests. To put it in Chris Weedon's (2004) terms, my goal is to delve into how culture *produces and challenges* subjectivities in Jewish-Israeli society. The critical aspect is a result of reading our own processes of subjective constitution through the lens of existing profanatory practices. Images of this sort, I assume, invite us to critically reflect on how we form and conduct our lives and, consequently, urge us to intervene in our own mode of life in order to alter its current course.

I name the reading I suggest *critical protagonism*. This is the process by which subjects recognise situations, practices, thoughts, emotions, discourses and tasks *as parts of their being, as their existential organs*. They do so through the critical images created by text – whether written or lived. Crucially, they recognise the minute moments in which they are constituted as the subjects they are. In viewing the images that the text supplies, they identify the practices in which they participate and the characters they feel comfortable with; they anticipate how a particular narrative will unfold; they are shaken by an unexpected feeling of shame in the face of images that only now become disturbing; or they compulsively repeat their ardent political support out of their most habitual forces. However, I feel obliged to warn the reader that the notion of recognition I use here has a strong antithetical charge when related to a celebration of identity. Critical protagonism is not about recognising a unified self in order to glorify it – quite the opposite. The kind of recognition I suggest should induce critical reflection, re-evaluation, and eventually transformation, not masturbatory self-celebration. More precisely, by targeting our affective capacities and not just our rational thinking, the text here, in line with Papadopoulos, moves us towards '*dis*identification and imperceptibility' through a process that entails 'refusing who one is supposed to be' (2008: 156).

In order to recognise some of our individuated selves and their functions as protagonists of oppressive subjectivities, to recognise the violence in our own constitutive processes, it is not the voice of oppression that a critical text needs to illuminate. As stated above, to urge a critical reading, the analysis of oppressive processes of subjectivation needs to be combined with the challenging viewpoint produced by acts of profanation that help us see and feel things differently, hence enabling the protagonists to step outside themselves and embark on new projects. As Foucault put it, this consists of using profanation 'as a chemical catalyst so as to bring to light power relations, locate their position, find out their point of application and the methods used' (1982: 208). Ultimately, I am asking the reader to engage in Rela Mazali's exercise, to look underneath their house, to ask themselves about its foundations as well as to pay more attention to its cracks (2011).

The textual exercise here is my version of Brecht's estrangement or alienation effect (1964), the technique used to make us see the everyday in its historical light as an invitation to change our hearts. Seeing life in its historical light means perceiving its moments as historical constructions that involve the active, though not always conscious, participation of individuals – namely as a specific production under particular conditions. For those who dutifully believe that 'our life is what it is supposed to be', or for those who believe with some resignation that 'changing reality is beyond our reach', the textual exercise here aims first and foremost to enable the cognisance that subjects are actively – consciously and unconsciously – involved in the production of their modes of being and ways of life. We cannot deny our complicity in the production of the self we are; in other words, blaming parental genetics for the kind of person we are reveals only the passive characteristics of our agency, not the lack of it. For the purpose of illuminating the personal and collective historical aspects in the constitution of our subjectivities, it is crucial to challenge the organic image that we have of our way of life by stripping from it its self-evident quality, and to do so only for the sake of presenting the parts and elements of this image 'as objects with which we have relations' (Buchanan 2000: 160). Of course we have relations with them! These are the parts and elements that, when assembled, constitute the mouth that voices political allegiances, the hands that beat and shoot, the ears that refuse to listen, and the back that rests on the stolen soil.

Coming to terms with the fact that the selves defined as 'we' have intimate relationships with certain parts and elements of our way of life means *protagonising*, or historicising, for it is an effect that 'makes us aware that our spatial habits are tied to a conventional *ordering of elements in space* and that such an ordering is not naturally occurring, and far from being immutable, is entirely contingent' (ibid.: 160, emphasis added). Importantly, the historicism that the text sets out makes us aware of our own historical coordinates, our ordering in space as it is constructed through time. These are the coordinates of the Zionist collectivity, its positioning in time and space in relation to universal ethical axes such as relating to others, heterogeneity versus homogeneity, uniformity versus pluralism, and so on. Therefore, we cannot shake off this evidence as just another set of tales: once these coordinates are known they cannot become unknown. This is the moment of *after Israel*.

Seen through profanatory lenses that challenge the ethical time-space positioning of the Zionist collectivity, a reading of the formation of Zionist subjectivity reveals the innate connections between this formation and the acts of oppression that Jewish-Israelis perform to maintain their privilege. Importantly, this reading restores to op-pression the affective powers to which oppressors are immune, thus inducing judgement and a decision to re-evaluate life. The subjectivity–profanation images provide *evidence* that the ways in which we constitute ourselves and live our lives in Jewish-Israeli society are also *the coordinates of our oppressive actions*. Ultimately, the text leads us to reconnect ourselves as the very protagonists of actions that seriously impoverish life in the region, to accommodate the knowledge it reveals and to change how we see things, experiencing what Buchanan calls 'revelation' in the process (Buchanan 2013).[6] This process might take different paths and enact itself through distinct emotions according to different subjective positions. In no way do I mean to prompt guilt; rather, my hope is that the text will have a positive effect on the reader. Other than guilt, there might be shame, discomfort, disgust or anger. Shame and guilt differ in that shame lacks a clearly defined object. While guilt grips the subject by affixing its reaction to a particular offence and hence losing the reality of the conditions that facilitated that offence, shame overwhelms the mind and body and necessarily leads to a process of re-narration of self. In contrast, guilt, like fear, reaffirms our image of ourselves and of others because it necessitates recognisable selves that can accuse and make those selves answerable. Guilt is thus more conservative as it affirms hierarchies and constellations of power, whereas shame is creative and involves re-narration and a renegotiation of power relations.[7]

In the process of revelation, profanatory texts play a vital role. They intersect with the narratives on subjectivity formation and in so doing create a space, a sort of textual territory, where the political change of heart can take place. For that reason, it is never enough to stress the significance of the acts of silent dissidents and extrovert activists who, in their actions and discourses, make bodies, minds and environments deviate from present trajectories, compositions, dispositions and relationships. We cannot see ourselves as the protagonists of oppressive subjectivities unless our bodies are touched by profanatory forces, coming either from our own exploratory initiatives or from the outside. It is not that the text here completely disconnects itself from the measurable output of oppression, but its images focus the reader on the mundane ways in which he or she tends to become a protagonist in the production of that oppression.

This is important because, in their hearts, Jewish-Israelis do not feel that criticism of the oppressive practices in which they take part is related to the oppressive ways by which they become Zionist practitioners, unfolding Zionist subjectivities. For them, the way others see these practices does not represent the political community of which they feel themselves to be a part. Eventually, the idea of the textual exercise proposed here is to close the gap between how subjects perceive the formation of themselves and how they perceive their deeds. Collapsing this gap is about revealing the reciprocal causative relationships between the daily and mundane processes of subjectivation on the one hand and, on the other, the practices we participate in as fully fledged subjects proclaiming to the four winds 'I'm this, I'm that', including those oppressive practices that impoverish our lives and the lives of others. Collapsing this gap is key to undermining the source of detachment and relief Jewish-Israelis rely on to continue doing what they do in order to reap their privileges on the basis of oppression.

§ As a way of understanding and responding to the question of how Jewish-Israelis become protagonists in oppression stories, this project undertakes a study of some of society's fundamental social figures in the production of the settler-colonial ways of life that animate the present. Every society, colonial or otherwise, has an array of possible normative social figures or characters who make up its cultural texture and are essential in the constant reproduction of power relations. Israel is no exception. Here, I intend to focus on a series of Zionist figures – *the hiker, the teacher, the parent* and *the voter*, corresponding to the social fields of leisure, education, family and politics. Each plays a key role in the functioning of the Zionist organism; they are among its vital organs. The idea behind the intro-spection into these figures follows Brecht's estrangement effect: to break up a given and self-evident reality into its constituent elements and relationships to intensify their historicity in the eyes of the reader (1964; Buchanan 2000: 160). Here, I aim to break the banality of that reality by prying into a collection of minute moments and experiences in the lives of normative Zionist social figures, as well as into their various relationships. Hence, as an addition, or perhaps as a challenge, to the discourse on Israeli oppressive practices that assumes an impersonal whole that perpetrates actions, I suggest evoking the everyday instances that form the matter and soul necessary to carry out the functions of oppression that the Zionist regime depends on for its survival. However, each of these normative social figures represents a *range* of behaviours, beliefs and dispositions and not a clear-cut persona, so different parts and viewpoints in my stories will appeal differently to different Jewish-Israelis, to different Zionist subjectivities. Let me now briefly introduce the Zionist sociological figures elaborated in the following chapters.

The hiker: in no way does Henry Thoreau's relationship with nature lie at the root of Zionist hiking – Thoreau's walks in the countryside have the great benefit of teaching participants to appreciate nature beyond any instrumental value. In contrast, since the early days of European Zionist immigration to Palestine at the end of the nineteenth century, hiking has been shaped as a strategic political practice that converts every encounter with nature into an occasion to immerse participants' bodies in selective stories of the land. The physical activity of walking builds up a corporeal bond with the soil one treads, a bond that is fully exhausted during one's service in the army. Israel teaches us not just to saunter, but to familiarise ourselves with nature by subjecting its wilderness, landscapes, colours and smells to a particular political ideology. Zionist hiking is a military practice that turns land into territory. Walk forth and conquer.

The teacher: in all societies, education is the piecemeal business par excellence of constructing consciousness and setting the course of the mind. What distinguishes the role of the teacher in Jewish-Israeli kindergartens and schools, however, is that it serves a settler society in arms. The teacher's role is to set the course of the mind in ways that foster uncritical action, indispensable for the long journey that prepares young people to continually carry out the tasks of fortressing Israel. As the French philosopher and activist Félix Guattari states about the role of subjectivity manufacturers as teachers in the production of individuality: 'We are the workers at the tip of an industry, an industry that furnishes the primary subjective matter for all other industries and social activity' (1996: 123). There are essentially three means of doing this: first, an all-pervasive nationalist discourse in curricular and extracurricular activities; second, blatant complicity with the army, ranging from an official open-door policy for army representatives to enter schools and preach war, to various forms of educational events, including military training inside high school – all establishing the inevitability of soldiering; and third, fortressing Israel in the school system through teaching that internalises Israeli ethnocracy as democracy.

The parent: there is nothing more disturbing about Israeli society than the role played by most Jewish parents. Above all else, they are the Abrahamic immolators. There is no easy way to put it, but we need to ask how a modern society comes to socially reward progenitors for encouraging and demanding their sons and daughters to become soldiers in an army that risks their lives and trains them to actively deprive others of life. It is that 'handing over' of the children, that betrayal, that must be questioned. Undoubtedly, without the teacher's preparatory role, few parents would let national pride overrule their natural concern for the fate of their children.

The voter: what is the image of democracy if not that of the voter? Although we can safely assume that the inequality suffered by Palestinian citizens and the violence exerted against the regime's Palestinian non-citizens will continue to be legalised by the Israeli parliament, and that the political persecution of dissidents will intensify in the years to come, the right to vote and the representative system are precious to the Israeli political system because their periodic manifestation in elections streamlines the common belief that 'despite all difficulties, Israel is a vibrant democracy'. Literally whole libraries have been published that comprehensively demonstrate Israel's non-democratic character, despite its democratic procedures.[8] We shall, then, abandon that indulgence right here. The question that interests me relates to the potential energy – contained in the procedure of voting – to redefine the image Israel wishes to maintain as a democratic polity. I am interested even more in the potential of new uses of that procedure to begin working on some aspects of the foundations for a new political community *after Israel*.

The abstraction of these roles as sociological figures unveils the functions they serve in the Zionist apparatus; these functions help explain the inability of their actors to question their privilege, and their willingness to participate in the production of misery that makes Israel a pariah state. The study of sociological figures is a study of processes of subjectivation, namely *how people become, but also resist, the sort of subject they are trained to become.* Hence, in line with Mansfield, I adopt the view that subjectivity 'is primarily an experience, and remains permanently open to inconsistency, contradiction and unselfconsciousness' (2000: 6). Subjectivity is an always contested construct in which transitory relationships and qualities are established and abolished. Only when processes of subjectivation achieve a high degree of stability does the very process of change become invisible and seem inaccessible, as if all we have left are just dominant subjectivities. But in their essence, these are processual phenomena, plural and dynamic constructions. Hence, despite the representative face people use to show and take pride in, behind and beyond that face, subjectivity always bubbles as 'a double movement, on the one hand of closure and on the other of opening' (Guattari 1996: 216). As Guattari warns, it is thus wrong to determine that subjectivities are constituted by 'a dominant factor that directs other factors according to a univocal causality' (ibid.: 193). Rather, they are constituted and destituted by a multiplicity of forces even though all dominant subjectivities develop by preventing inventiveness and creativity (ibid.: 215). Therefore, the work interactively invested by society and individuals in sculpting human lives, surroundings and the relations between them is in a state of constant tension with inner impulses, external motivations and situational opportunities resisting that modelling, and collaborating to pursue instead exploration and experimentation that leave habitual attachments behind. In this context, it is easy to see why the concept of resistance commonly attributed to emancipatory acts is simply incorrect. In the struggles over subjectivity, resistance is offered by reactionary forces keeping dominant identities and ways of life together, whereas *profanation* is carried out by those forces aiming to dissolve the consistency and pervasiveness of privilege (Agamben 2007).

A field of forces arises here, between stable subjectivities and transformations, or between stable subjectivities and new becomings. However, we should not understand these two terms as purely oppositional. Rather, from the perspectives of both its genesis and its disintegration, subjectivity is reliant on becoming. It cannot be otherwise. To explain one, we need the other, in both directions: to explain how dominant subjectivities emerged historically (becomings in the past), and also to explain how their produced stability and consistency are always under threat (becomings in the present). The field of forces that extends between stable subjects and lurking becomings is complex and heterogeneous; it is within this field that our lives evolve and change. Then, to add to Guattari's definition, I would say that our existential territories arise and decline within the fields of struggle between subjectivity and becoming.

Attempts at reconstructing subjectivities have the great benefit of making visible the very existence of the process of reconstruction itself, or the promise of new forms of organisation; in so doing, they defy and even ignore the arrogance and absurdity of final identities. However, these attempts are worthy of praise insofar as their intervention remains pure mediality, as means without an end (Agamben 2000). Their action surely has political purposefulness (moving life beyond Israel), but no fixed purpose (the identity of the new society). This is how I suggest understanding the notion of the *after*. To '*after*' the kind of society Israel *is* in the present, we must embark on a series of processes that divest themselves of and diverge from the roles being performed by the dominant social figures and from Israel's national projects and explore other ways of existing. For contemporary Jewish-Israelis, these interventions are problematic precisely because they create their own praxis and their own subjectivities, sliding Israel into its own *after*. But these interventions are also an opportunity to experiment and practise alternative relations to life informed by attitudes and emotions removed from their settler-colonial attachments. It is not farfetched to expect that Jewish-Israelis would prefer to abandon their leading role in oppression stories and become the protagonists of other narratives.

§ The making of subjectivity involves affixing particular meanings and interpretations to 'things' such as myths, rites, ideas, events, passions and substances, in so doing producing zones or fields of attraction within which bodies orbit and incrementally acquire new corporeal, cognitive and affective capacities and qualities. These 'things' thus become referents or centres of subjectivation, points of signification around which life is organised and given sense. Thus, the relation between a 'thing' and a social sphere effectuates particular 'uses', which in turn beget social functions. Social life is created through orbiting, its meaningful practices, its zones of thought, its hopes and its expectations. Significantly, the forces that bring about the possibilities to enter into orbit are not exempt from bringing about escapes. Immanence is precisely that double substrate.

The significance of profanatory acts resides in their destabilising effect on the dominant roles of centres of subjectivation or reference. Specifically, they destabilise the authority of those myths, ideas, events, passions and substances around which society coils our minds. The Jewish holocaust, for example, is one such organising centre of subjectivation in the Zionist organism. Zionist politics have appropriated the Jewish holocaust in ways that prevent all universal interpretations – of this there is no doubt (Evron 1981; Massad 2002; Zuckermann 2002). As Boaz Evron rightly put it thirty years ago: 'Two terrible things happened to the Jewish people this century: the holocaust and the lessons learned from it' (1981: 16). Anti-humanistic manipulations of the holocaust have pervaded and continue to envenom social life in Israel, even in the most ordinary situations. Let me cite just one ritual as an example. It is not unheard of for holocaust survivors to send for the adolescents in the family, once they have been recruited into the Israeli army, to see them 'exhibit' themselves all uniformed and armed. It is hard to tell whether the perverse pleasure triggered by the image of the young Jewish warrior satisfies a compulsion for retribution or a nationalist introjected appetite, or perhaps both. Either way, such a pleasure problematises the social field by allowing the military bond to regulate individual relationships within the family. In the foreword to Lyotard's *Heidegger and the Jews*, David Carroll states:

The 'lesson' of the Shoah becomes: Let us ensure that what happened to the Jews and gypsies of Europe will never happen in the future, or in the case of Israel, that it will never again happen to Jews. In that light almost any action against any 'enemy' can be justified. What appears to have been learned is that it would even be better to support an authoritarian, totalitarian police state than to side with the victims of its injustices, or, put even more brutally, that it is better to be on the side of the persecutors than the persecuted as if this were the only alternative one had (1990: ix).

More than half a century after the events, it is safe to claim that the memory of the holocaust has played, and continues to play, a central role in justifying the omnipresence of military logic as the '[one alternative] single option' society must follow. This function of the holocaust fascistises other social fields as well, particularly education. Undoubtedly, the most appalling educational activity organised by the Ministry of Education in Israel since the late 1980s is the Trip to Poland for high school seniors, in which they are compelled to visit Auschwitz and participate in the March of the Living ceremony. In theory, the trip is supposed to foster both national and universalist understanding of the holocaust, but in practice it is conducted in ways that magnify the former at the expense of the latter. Importantly, studies have shown that the trip encourages positive attitudes towards the army, which in turn fuel aggressiveness towards the Arab world in general and the Palestinians in particular (Lazar et al. 2004; Segev 2000). However, the trip is not accessible to all students; its cost (US$ 1,500) bars the poor. As a result, the delegations comprise 86 per cent of students from the higher socioeconomic echelons.[9] In other words, these delegations are mainly white, mostly students from Ashkenazi homes, and therefore the trip re-enacts social differences. This is not surprising. Goodman and Mizrahi have shown that racial and socioeconomic divisions between Ashkenazim and Mizrahim are reproduced through the teaching of the holocaust, among other means (2008). According to Goodman and Mizrahi, different teaching and memory techniques are used in different schools;

so, for instance, while in predominately Ashkenazi classes these techniques incentivise an active attitude on the part of the students in relation to the national ethos (encouraging students to share their families' European memories), a passive attitude is induced in predominantly Mizrahi classes, where students are taught how to understand the holocaust. Hence, 'hegemonic national memories are still processed differently by dominant and peripheral subgroups', namely the memory of the holocaust is used 'as a specific medium for social positioning and privileging' (ibid.: 108). Differentiation of education in Jewish-Israeli schools has its historical roots in the late 1950s, the time when the 'educational elite opted for the official institutionalization of differential education', introducing 'lower-level educational programs constructed specifically for Jews from Arab lands, and designed to limit the extent of scholastic failure, at the cost of giving up the vision of full educational achievements for all the new pupils' (Swirski 1999: 175–6; Yonah and Saporta 2002). This should be seen in direct association with the racial division of labour that trapped Mizrahi communities in the lower ranks of society (Swirski and Bernstein 1993). As I will discuss in a moment, this state of affairs demands that Mizrahi interventions are considered as an alternative lens through which to interpret the ways in which the holocaust is articulated in Jewish-Israeli society.

§ The tragedy of the Jewish holocaust thus found no relief or emotional expiation in the figure of the Jewish state, but rather its extension – also expressed in the inverted relationship established between the holocaust and the ethnic cleansing of the Palestinians in 1948 (the Nakba), perpetrated by Jewish forces just three years after the liberation of Auschwitz (see Pappe 2006). As this case shows, there is an intimate historical relationship between how 'things' become referents for subjectivation and the cultural texture of a society. The point here is to grasp these relationships as the objective of profanatory acts (Agamben 2007). The holocaust and the negation of the Nakba; the military; the body of the young; the question of land; Jerusalem; the biblical nexus; modern technology; the Jewish intellect – these are the elements of a Zionist subjectivation that has not only crystallised in the well-known hypersensitivity of Israelis in response to any critique of their state and society (criticism that is always perceived as an existential threat), but has also gained a sustained credibility in both the Jewish diaspora and western societies – sources of support vital for the continuation of Israel as a Zionist state.

Again, the deactivation of centres of subjectivation involves a change in the bonds between myths, rites, ideas, events, passions and substances ('things') and their linked social categories such as parenthood, education, citizenship and so forth. Deactivation means rendering ineffective the gravitational forces of centres of subjectivation. A change in these relationships would lay the foundation for disavowing present qualities, faculties and properties, and consequently for rejecting present inequalities and privileges. Indeed, the idea behind the deactivation of present subjectivations is to free 'things' of their existing attachments and uses, thus liberating the subjects from their habitual subjectivising relationship. Freeing 'things' from their role as centres of subjectivation means returning these 'things' to new potential uses (ibid.).

If returning 'things' to their free use involves the deactivation of present uses, how does that deactivation take place? To be sure, profanation is a political task that requires the negation of present uses, present roles and present common sense. But without an accompanying positive process, such negation will clearly get us only halfway at best. In his *Archaeologies of the Future*, Fredric Jameson raises an idea that he leaves under-theorised, namely the notion of *substitution* as a procedure for the disruption of present operations. Substitution, I contend, covers both halves of the profanatory act because it is a manoeuvre by which a present use or relationship may be deactivated as the result of a simultaneous alternative use. Substitution might be materialised through various techniques. Let me illustrate three of these techniques by looking at Israeli civil society.

A voluntary educational alternative has been offered since 1997 by the Centre for Humanistic Education (CHE) within the Ghetto Fighters' House Museum in Israel. CHE works with high school students and teachers from the Arab and Jewish sectors in a structured programme that consists of weekly workshops and a three-day seminar held during the school year. Three themes lie at the heart of these activities: the holocaust as a universal formative crisis; humanist social and political values manifested in the concept of democracy; and Jewish–Arab dialogue as leverage to social and political coexistence (Netzer 2008). In sharp contrast to mainstream education, CHE elicits a connection between the Jewish holocaust and the Palestinian Nakba, aiming to encourage what they call humanistic dialogue:

we cannot accept the idea that the holocaust excuses Zionism for what it has done to Palestinians: far from it. I say exactly the opposite, that by recognizing the holocaust for the genocidal madness that it was, we can then demand from Israelis and Jews the right to link the holocaust to Zionist injustices towards the Palestinians, link and criticize the link for its hypocrisy and flawed moral logic (Said 1998).

But CHE is not alone. Radical Mizrahi educators such as the poet Sami Shalom Chetrit have been unambiguous in their commitment to present the universal lessons of the holocaust (see Oppenheimer 2010: 304–5). Two reasons lie behind the significance of the Mizrahi view on the state use of the holocaust. The Mizrahi perspective on the holocaust is important firstly because the official discourse on the holocaust manufactured a purely European narrative and totally ignored the oriental Jews from Libya, Tunisia, Algeria and Greece, who have suffered a similar fate (ibid.: 305). And secondly, it is important because the sublimation of the holocaust as an exceptional event that happened to Ashkenazi Jews repressed the possibility of enunciating and articulating the Mizrahi cultural massacre and the structuration of their socioeconomic marginalisation for generations to come, executed by the Ashkenazi establishment in Israel since the 1950s. As such, the holocaust became a selective site of belonging in Israeli culture, a mark of distinction entirely unavailable to non-Ashkenazi Jews. This partiality must be corrected, as Oppenheimer explains:

[Mizrahi second-generation writers] such as Amira Hess and Sami

Berdugo clarify that the political perspective of the Holocaust
as solely an Israeli narrative or as a means of cultural control
is inadequate, and demand that an additional, complementary
viewpoint be considered. This complementary stance views the
Holocaust as a necessary basis for understanding the experience
of immigration and displacement of both European and Mizrahi
Jews (ibid.: 303, my emphasis).

A strong and open alternative to the Zionist culture of the holocaust
therefore lies in the Mizrahi deactivation of the European Zionist
lens as the exclusive means of understanding and experiencing the
memory of the holocaust; instead, it offers an engagement 'through
the exilic perspective of one who experienced another holocaust
within the Israeli space and time' (ibid.: 325). Calling the Mizrahi
tragedy in Israel a holocaust is not a provocation but an intervention.
It is needed to reveal the historical fact that the appropriators of
the Jewish holocaust and those who perpetrated and deny both the
cultural massacre of the Mizrahi Jewry in Israel and the Palestinian
Nakba are one and the same. Profaning the name of the holocaust
is therefore the means by which this ghastly intimacy is exposed
and the profits from it are put into question.

However, putting spokes in the wheels gearing the holocaust to
boost militarism is not a relevant operation in Ashkenazi homes.
There, the dissociation of the holocaust from militarism requires
emotional investments at the level of intergenerational relationships.
In the case of CHE's education programme or in the Mizrahi ethnic–
universalistic redefinition of the relationship between Jewishness and
the holocaust, substitution works by *simulation* – as it also does in
the small network of Arab–Jewish bilingual schools[10] where students,
teachers and parents from both communities come together to form
an alternative educational community (Svirsky 2011; 2012a; Svirsky
and Mor-Sommerfeld 2012). These forms of education may appear
to adhere to a standard educational pattern, but this proves illusory
when their internal dynamics and specific agendas are examined.
This is the great advantage of the simulacrum and the way in which
it opens up new spaces: while it bears a resemblance to the model,

its collective operations are turned against that model by exposing its inherent fascist order.

Substitution can also operate effectively when *active refusal* is encouraged, as in the case of the feminist and anti-militarist Israeli organisation New Profile, which aims to weaken the disciplinary role of the army in the life of Jewish-Israelis by encouraging young men and women to consider their imminent conscription in a deeply critical manner and by helping them cope with their refusal.[11] Importantly, New Profile's activities create a space for profaning Abrahamic parenthood – its adult activists, mainly women, withdraw from the social obligation that turns their progeny into soldiers-to-be. Beyond the ideological and symbolic challenge non-Abrahamic parenthood poses to Jewish-Israeli society, its main effort is exerted in avoiding the kind of everyday parental guidance that practically prepares children's bodies as potential offerings on the altar of the nation and the military.

A further form substitution might take is that of *excess*, which functions by targeting assumed knowledge of central social issues. Since 2002, the Israeli non-profit organisation Zochrot ('remembering' in Hebrew)[12] has sought to raise public awareness of the Nakba and of the Palestinian right of return among Jewish-Israelis. Breaking the Silence,[13] another non-profit organisation, run by army veterans, collects and publishes testimonies of soldiers who have served in the West Bank since the Second Intifada, exposing the catastrophic scope of human rights violations perpetrated by the Israeli army. Both organisations surpass official narratives by undermining their reliability, thus weakening the social forces that currently keep Jewish-Israelis bound to one another.

Simulation, active refusal and excess are actualisations of substitution, but there may well be others. These forms of substitution have two features in common. First, as Guattari maintains, the examples illustrate that struggles for the transformation of subjectivity 'are not ordinary forms of opposition to authority' (1996: 176). Rather, they require a sort of micropolitics that brings into question the conspicuousness of the normative individual and hence offers particular responses to specific problems, responses designed to reduce the existential impact of dominant social roles (see ibid.: 176–7). So, as Agamben noted, rather than attempting simply to abolish present uses, micropolitics endeavours to erode them by confronting them with an unconventional use. The second characteristic is negligence, which is expressed in the productive insolence of acts that ignore the separation between normative life and that which is separated from it (Agamben 2007: 75).

§ Relationships between 'things' and specific social fields through which the former become centres of subjectivation are not fragile in any sense. These relationships are at the core of larger textures that function as the organs of society. There are three basic forms of connectivity between the centres of subjectivation weaving those textures. Firstly, profanatory acts must take account of the versatility and multifocal presence of the forces of gravity of each centre of subjectivation animating the various social fields in life. For example, in Israeli society, the militarist appropriation of the holocaust plays out in various social spheres, including the family, education and public discourse; another example is the isolationist actualisation of 'being Jewish' expressed in segregation as the basis of housing, education, the workplace and leisure. Secondly, not only do centres of subjectivation of the same type – inlaid across various social spheres – produce social consistency, but this consistency increases through communication between different centres of subjectivation within each social sphere. Within the family, for example, there is a contiguity and alliance of meanings arising from the mothering roles of women as expected by the nation (Herzog 2003) and the roles generated by the professionalisation of the army industry as a male territory that is seen as a continuation of military service. And thirdly, social consistency is intensified by the general connectivity between different centres of subjectivation across the various social spheres. For example, for most Jewish-Israelis, serving in the army, cultivating a myth of persecution and conducting a segregated life away from Palestinian citizens are all natural sides of the same normative coin. Consequently, social spheres share a resemblance of norms and meanings – they share a common sense.

Resonance is the glue that holds subjectivities together and makes societies. Resonance is the sort of abstract communication across social spheres that bestows a sense of coherence, consistency and stability upon society and its dominant social figures. By communication I mean the reciprocal transference of specific logics, mechanisms and affects that animate processes of subjectivation. Productive conductivity across two or more social spheres causes these spheres to vibrate at the same frequency or, in other words, to resonate together. Resonance enables society to feel that things are related, it infuses a sense of home – or, in other words, it nourishes the fecundity of our subjective territorialities by weaving rationalities, meanings, expectations and interpretations across them. High resonance in a society means a strong and internally hyper-coherent core of meanings, perspectives and dispositions circulating across the social field and regulating processes of subjectivation. High normative communication between the roles of the various centres of subjectivation engenders a sense of indistinctness between ideas and concepts – making them a family of related values that becomes part of ourselves. High degrees of resonance of meanings, perspectives and dispositions clog the social field, leaving little room for dissent, regardless of the democratic façade of official politics. High degrees of resonance necessitate the active and continuous complicity of subjects. Fascism, in other words, depends on the eager participation of society's subjects, rather than being forced upon them.

In itself, this somewhat mechanical picture of how centres of subjectivation work might lead us to assume that all individuals are equally subjectivised, that throughout the process of subjectivation we all depart from and confront the same circumstances and relations of power. To avoid such a fallacy, critical analysis must take into account, in some way, the various ethnicised, racialised, ideological and gendered historical and present-day differentiations intervening in the construction of Jewish-Israeli subjectivities. Otherwise, we are left with a hegemonic and homogeneous image of the subject and preclude learning from 'the subversive possibility of a multiplicity of sectorial centers and ... different, incompatible points of view' (Oppenheimer 2012: 340, note 18). In reality, the mechanics of subjectivation are animated by discursive, material and affective apparatuses that racialise, ethnicise, ideologise, classise and genderise subjectivities – following the logic of power. As Herzog describes:

> Among the more prominent groups for whom the process of building a nation and establishing a state created existential conditions of marginality and exclusion are, first and foremost, the Palestinians. But other groups were also relegated to the margins by the mechanism of Zionist hegemony. This was the fate of Jews originating from Arab countries ... various right-wing groups, and religious Jews, especially the ultra-orthodox. The place of women was also determined by the rules of the dominant discourse (2003: 156).

Nira Yuval-Davis, Orly Lubin and Nitza Berkovitch, among others, demonstrated that 'the Jewish-Israeli woman is constructed first and foremost as mother and wife, and not as individual or citizen' (ibid.: 158).[14] As Abdo explains: 'Herein lies the important contribution of the feminist critique of nationalism. Women in this critique are seen as the keepers, the biological and social reproducers, of the nation state, and as such their domestic, familial or mothering roles are seen to be a priority over all other (public) roles they might play' (2011: 31; see also Sharoni 1995). Whenever this critique assists in the deterritorialisation of Zionist social roles, the text refers back to the critical understanding of 'motherhood as a national mission' (Herzog 2003: 158), through which the role of gender becomes visible.

In regard to the absorption of the oriental Jews in post-1948 Jewish-Israeli society, Yonah and Saporta (2002) offer a Gramscian model that illuminates how the marginalisation of these Jewish communities was produced. In their view, the Zionist hegemonic nation-building process comprises two centres of subject constitution, one homogenisatory and the other differential. The first was universalistic and stressed Jewish union and common fate, while the second placed the oriental Mizrahi culture as the antithesis of the western Zionist project. The tension between the two Zionist arms explains the construction of the marginalisation of the Mizrahim (ibid.: 68–104). Then, as Yonah and Saporta explain:

on the one hand the Mizrahim are perceived as an integral part of the Jewish national public and with the same human value as the other groups in this public; on the other hand, because of their 'backward' oriental culture, they are perceived as having inferior human status compared with European and American Jews (ibid.: 100, my translation).

It is in terms of this racialised inclusion that we should understand both the 'cultural massacre' perpetrated on the oriental Jews by white Zionists (Shohat 1988: 32) and the racial division of labour that originated during the 1950s, thanks to which the strength of the Ashkenazim was constituted at the expense of the Mizrahim (Swirski 1981; Swirski and Bernstein 1993; see also the Adva Center's reports). My intention is to take account of these various, and other, differentiations, to help build *the after*.

However, I do not pretend to expand on or expose a comprehensive review of the multiple differentiations by which Jewish-Israelis' peripheral subjectivities were and are created. That effort must include an analysis of other forms and inputs of Jewish subjectivity, certainly the analysis of Mizrahi women, of the ways in which Jews from the former Soviet Union and Ethiopian Jews are included–excluded, looking at the many subdivisions in these categories, and that effort should certainly address how the 'othering' of Palestinians helps affirm Jewish-Israeliness – a colossal research enterprise in itself. My issue here lies elsewhere. It focuses on the modes of being incarnating what can be called Zionist axiomatics, those practices, attitudes and affects that tie together Jewish-Israelis from various backgrounds – as a further level of subjectivation that coexists with the set of differentiations – forming a strong political settler-colonial and nationalist platform. As I have said, we will look at these ways of being through the features of the normative dominant subjectivities, taking into account the fact that they are embodied by privileged and much less privileged Jewish-Israeli subjects. In no way does this conceptualisation form the basis of an abstract Jewish-Israeli; on the contrary, it highlights the visibility of real and vivid Zionist practitioners. This view does not claim to rise 'above' race, class and gender; rather, it acknowledges the ways in which hegemony infiltrates these categories and animates their actualisations.

Textually, the attack on normative dominant subjectivities can be mounted via different strategies. It can focus on the ways in which dominance and marginality become two sides of the same production and highlight how peripheral subjectivities are constituted, or it can focus on privilege and expose how hegemony reproduces itself. The path we take here is to favour critical voices and practices that assist in freeing us from the historical burden of Zionism, helping to eradicate from the body our Zionist organs – those organs that make us part and parcel of the melting pot of hatred. In more ways than one, this is about deactivating the organisation of the body, weakening the consistency across its extant functions and organs, letting the body become a disorganised platform upon which new organic functions grow and new forms of organisation may take place. The aim of the brief and incomplete discussion of the historical ways in which Zionism interpellates Jewish individuals and collectivities given above is to point in the direction of potential sources that present-day Zionist practitioners may look at in their self-liberatory, though necessarily collective, voyage. The point is, in other words, not to limit the discussion to a critical assessment of how marginalised Jewish subjectivities were constructed in Israeli society but to inform the critical acts of disengagement and reconstruction of subjectivities – at the core of this book – with insights provided by the gendered, racialised, ethnicised, class-based and ideological coordinates of subjectivation that may assist in getting rid of our Zionist modes of being. It should be clear by now that the analyses in this book reject the assumption that it is possible and theoretically beneficial to distinguish and dissociate between 'personal' and 'political' aspects of subjectivity, a division that owes much of its existence to archaic and ideological divisions of labour in the social sciences (Papadopoulos 2008). There is no construction of individuality that is not a collective construction, in the sense of both how we construct it – relationally – and how this construction infuses and is affected by collective practices, beliefs, values and political dispositions.

§ Now we can go back to the idea of affecting subjects in order to induce the re-creation of their subjectivities. Being affected is about being called upon to re-evaluate some aspect of our ways of living, our habits of mind and political dispositions – in other words, our own subjectivities. 'Affect,' explains Shaviro, 'isn't something you have, but something that invests and invades you, that forces itself on you' (2011: 21). One cannot just claim to be affected. Affect is expressed in new acts, in deviations. Activist profanation requires embarking on projects of disorganisation that, as I state elsewhere, 'instigate new series of material, discursive and affective assemblages intersecting actual life, and attempting to swing structures and traditions away from their stability and sedimented identities' (Svirsky 2012a: 14–15). Profanations of subjectivity are experimentations with new elements that oblige the subject to consider – consciously and unconsciously – redefining itself. Processual in character, they create pathways to cultural transformation; therefore, profanation of existing norma-tive identities and the ways of life they animate does not occur in capricious oppositional acts and cannot transpire simply through provocative activism. In addition, it is imperative to contrast profana-tory machines that urge new modes of individuality and collectivity on the one hand with preconceived models of subjectivity on the other. Modelling the former on the latter would in fact force a new referential identity, namely a new form of authoritarian perspective upon life (Guattari and Rolnik 2008: 94–5). As Fredric Jameson once put it: 'If you know already what your longed-for exercise in a not-yet-existent freedom looks like, then the suspicion arises that it may not really express freedom after all but only repetition' (1994: 56). Rather, the profanatory processes reconstructing subjectivities manufacture singular ways of existence that wrest us out of our current attach-ments (identifications and habits) in particular social spaces and at particular times, and hence they are ever changing. Simply put, I am interested in the dynamics of processes of subjectivation, not the authoritative models and identities these processes may produce. Not in ways of being, but in ways of becoming.

As we become exposed to new social contents and new social relationships, more centres of subjectivation are dislocated from

Zionist uses, and existing normative social roles lose their grip on the characterisation of key categories such as parenthood, education and citizenship. They lose their grip on *us*. If the dissolution of Zionist social figures brings Israel into its own *after*, the study of these figures and their disfiguration becomes an activist enterprise in itself. The aim, in fact, is to offer a cultural diagnosis of present-day Israel. However, offering a cultural diagnosis as a transformative horizon challenges the reigning political paradigm that forces us into choosing between political models: two states or one state. But this is a false act of blackmail because there is no choice to be taken: firstly, reaching a two-state condition is a practical impossibility as the only living reality between the Mediterranean Sea and the Jordan River is that of a 'one-state condition' (Azoulay and Ophir 2013).[15] Secondly, many advocates of one state wrongly identify the practical impossibility of two states as equating to the practical possibility of welcoming one democratic state for all. However, the 'one-state condition' that prevents democracy for all is the historical result of a century of Zionist supremacy, diametrically opposed to the egalitarian one-state model. No matter how desired this model might be, it would be false to believe that the actual state of affairs could, as it is, reasonably enable transition into one democratic state.

The confusion of a given reality (the one-state condition) with wishful thinking (one democratic state for all) is exacerbated by the ways in which literature on 'one state' is poisoned by messianic tendencies that mainly vociferate a model without a material strategy for transformation. Affective engagement and well-intentioned proposals, such as in Kovel (2007), or abstract debates over potential constitutional orders, as in Tilley (2005), fail to account for the non-existent cultural infrastructure for such leaps into the future, thus failing to identify the immediate necessities for change. We are faced with a similar disappointment regarding a recent special issue of the Tel Aviv University-based political science journal *The Public Sphere* (*HaMerhav HaTziburi*), issued following a conference held on 17 May 2011 under the heading 'One State from the Mediterranean Sea to the Jordan River – Pipe Dreams or an Emergent Reality?' All the authors in this edited collection start from two axioms – that of perceiving the Israeli-Palestinian condition in terms of conflict and the right to self-determination – they differ only in the ways they think this right should be pursued by both Palestinians and Israelis. All the combinations of land, rights and sovereignty they suggest are deeply anchored in the divisive seas of the right to self-determination. Like the literature I referred to above, the Tel Aviv University collection suffers from that academic disorder, so prevalent among political scientists, of disjointing a given actuality and its already existing ruptures. However, in this collection Grinberg departs from the consensus: he rightly calls for engaging a renewed political imagination of the present and also states that, in order to seriously address the issue of future relations between Israelis and Palestinians, we should reject the two states/one state debate and focus on the construction of new common institutions (2012: 142–54). Sadly, however, Grinberg frames the latter within the walls of his own political model, into which the given reality will appear as if by magic.[16] In recent years, an important exception to this conceptual modelling has been led by activists of Abnaa el-Balad ('The Natives'),[17] aiming their efforts at building alliances on which to base a broad public discourse of 'one state' in Israel–Palestine (see Svirsky 2012a: 115–16). There is also the Jaffa chapter of the global One Democratic State organisation established in 2013.[18] These efforts are an exception to the rule because they invest their activist energies in new forms of collaboration and new partnerships that discuss the idea of the one state, prioritising alliances over the imposition of a model. This is about propelling the idea of the 'one state' as an impulse rather than as a model.

The 'one-state condition' is the historical, still temporary, result of Israeli supremacy, abysmally separated from the noble 'one state' of equal partnership. But if we are to adhere and commit to the idea of the 'one state', strategy should take account of the 'one-state condition' as a historical state of affairs to be dismantled, not as one that is already inviting equal partnership. It is true that, logically, the practical impossibility of two states invites alternative models into the debate, and hence might provide a historical momentum for public discourse to consider the 'one-state' model. But it would be false to turn this practical impossibility into a reasonable passage into the one democratic state: *the conditions for that passage do not exist and must be created.* One cannot squeeze blood out of a turnip. As Behar states, 'as critical, engaging and stimulating as the one-state/ two states exchange is – in practical terms it remains utterly esoteric once juxtaposed with ongoing material politics free from doses of wishful thinking' (2011: 360).

Although most of the 'one-state' literature textually weds an unquestionably necessary critique of Zionism with a moral and legal infrastructure of claims and principles and the final 'one-state' goal, the connection between reality and aspiration is not historicised. Sadly, no magic wand will bring us closer to that goal. As a result, we are left mainly with a new normative debate: two states versus one state. Whereas the idea of a post-national and democratic unified state for Jews and Palestinians is engaging and I personally support it, structural priority must be given to immediate transformative practices, affects and concepts. Therefore, the reduction of the 'Sea to the River' structure (the one-state condition) into a catalyst to change the plausibility of normative models for Palestinians and Jews in the Middle East crystallises a debate that, in more ways than one, hinders the engagement with the pressing question: *how do we actually move away from the one-state condition?* Under no circumstances does moving away from the one-state condition mean working towards a two-state condition. The historical transformation associated with moving away from the one-state condition – and here lies the gist of this move – requires moving away from the ways of life that Zionist supremacy has forced on both Jews and Palestinians. Designing blueprints, devising road maps, relying on noble values and principles, and drawing upon United Nations resolutions – all have little to do with transformative practices. It is surprising, if not literally frustrating, to realise the extent to which existing openings in actual life that point to new directions are dismissed and disregarded in the arrogant and authoritative practice of delivering political blueprints. This is a refusal to hone our senses, look deeply into society and engage with existing radical instigations and demands – practices, affects and thoughts – wounding majoritarian habits of mind and common sense, and, in so doing, opening actual life to new social and cultural rhythms. I cannot agree more with the way in which Guattari understands what transformation entails:

I don't believe in revolutionary transformation, whatever the regime may be, if there is not also a cultural transformation, a kind of mutation among people, without which we lapse into the reproduction of an earlier society. It is the whole range of possibilities of specific practices of change in the way of life, with their creative potential ... which is a condition for any social transformation. And there is nothing utopian or idealistic in this (Guattari and Rolnik 2008: 261).

Blueprint essayists, engulfed by a sense of historical mission and longing to play a role on the stage of international politics, altruistically concede to us a political wisdom whose main function is to draw a line that makes everything else unimportant and irrelevant. The answer lies elsewhere. Life needs to be reinvented. This is not to dismiss the genuine political attempts to establish productive collaboration across the Green Line and with the Palestinian diaspora, aiming to create the foundations of a new post-national discourse. My claim is that there are strong reasons to couple the political paradigm with a cultural-political paradigm that illuminates the still rare and threatened social and cultural activist explorations. In itself, no political solution will save us – only a cultural transformation of present ways of life. Consequently, a necessary step in this repositioning of priorities is to change our perception of the acts of profanation. We need to displace the political paradigm of borders, land and sovereignty from its dominant position, in favour of a cultural paradigm whereby the significance of profanatory exploration can be repositioned. Let me expand on this point: I claim that a certain theoretical and political complicity arises if we look at, in tandem, the prioritisation of the political paradigm on Israel–Palestine on the one hand, and the prioritisation of the narratives of oppression on the other hand. In both, the transformation of subjectivity is perceived by all shades of the mainstream, from right to left, as irrelevant to the foundations of a new society. The effect of this complicity gutters in the oxymoronic assumption that it is the colonial subject who will carry on their shoulders the task of transforming society. *Therefore, the structural role of profanation is to disrupt the resonance between the subject of theory and the perpetuation of the Zionist subject.* In this respect, Israeli scholar Ariella Azoulay could not be clearer:

> it is time to stop misinterpreting the limited presence of such demands – all of which are quite reasonable … It is time to consider the possibility that the limited presence of civil struggle in the public sphere is an expression of a civil malfunction that is a constitutive, structural precept of the regime (2011a: 285).

In this case, however, malfunction should not be construed as a failure to work properly, for no Zionist machine has developed civil functions, nor is there one that for some unknown reason yet to be revealed is not working properly: as there is no such machine, there is no malfunction. Let me, then, take Azoulay's point one step further. The limited presence of civil struggle is a sign not of a civil malfunction but of an extreme scarcity. Israeli-Jewish society originated and was instituted on *the unavailability of civil thought and civic virtues.* Unavailability here does not refer to something that the society lacks and strives to achieve. This unavailability is the result of a historical and collective production of society, the result of encounters, chances and choices that produced civil thought only as an afterthought. By *civil*, I mean the realm of life made unavailable by racism, militarism and segregation. That which is culturally unavailable to be played with is intimately related to the range of dominant subjectivities in Israeli society.

From the early days of European Zionist immigration to Palestine at the beginning of the twentieth century to the present, Zionism has continually evolved by engineering and deploying all sorts of segregation apparatuses; most saliently, these apparatuses structured ethno-national dividing lines between Jews and Palestinians (Shafir 1989; Smith 1993; Svirsky 2012a) and racial–class lines between Ashkenazim and Mizrahim (Dahan and Levy 2000; Khazzoom 2005; Swirski 1999; Tzfadia 2006; Yiftachel 2000). Consequently, the aspiration of life shared by Jews and Palestinians, the prospect of a demilitarised society, the visibility of race and gender within Jewish-Israeli society, the capacity for critical thinking and complex action, the passion for democracy, the readiness to share history, the universal understanding of suffering – all these have been removed as accessible opportunities and possibilities that make for the foundation of a society. They have been removed so that they can no longer enter the domain of the habitual. An act of partition is at work here, between these potentialities and the form of life Zionism has imprinted upon its variegated subjects. It is a historical partition that has placed civil life in a zone of unavailability and has set the conditions for the production of social identities and characters. Simply put, Zionist social identities themselves rest on the exclusion of these potentialities (Agamben 2000: 3–14).

Agamben defines this form of exclusion in terms of an act of consecration, the opening of a caesura, a dividing line by which relations of subjectivation and their effects are placed in an inaccessible zone that then becomes sacred (2007: 73–92). In the historical production of Jewish-Israeli society, civil thought and civic virtues have been placed in such a sacred zone, but a zone sacred not in the sense of being an object of religious devotion or veneration; it is, rather, sacred in the sense that, in Jewish-Israeli society, civil thought is untouchable, unreachable, divinely inaccessible in everyday life. In the best interests of a nationalist and exclusivist society, civil perspectives have been removed from the potentialities of life, and unless significant efforts are made, their scarcity continues to define the subjectivities of Jewish-Israelis. This isolation of civil life in a sacred zone signifies a broken life, a life that can no longer retain the character of a potentiality and for which a specific vocation has been prescribed (Agamben 2000: 3–4). As Agamben says in *Language and Death*, 'that which is excluded from the community is, in reality, that on which the entire life of the community is founded' (1991: 105). Once a caesura is created, society invests in two forms of unavailability: one is the removal of the productive relationship with the realm of civil thought and action; the other is the removal of the possibility of changing that relationship. The first makes Jewish-Israelis into civil cripples, while the second perpetuates that incapacity and secures a Zionist historic bloc.

From the point of view of profanation, however, it is insufficient to define a political community solely on the basis of the oppression it involves: that is to say, in terms of what it excludes from the community. The limited presence of civil struggle should rather be read as a double sign: while it registers the poverty of our civil ways of life, it also stands for what comes *after*, as it calls for the creation of new spaces for civil imagination and civil practice. Hence, a political community must also be defined by the ways in which acts of dissent and difference make visible and scramble the common sense of the sacred. There are not two realms, therefore – one of the norm, the other of its defiance. And there is no dialectical contradiction to expose, since the discursive affection for contradictions only sublimates the model being contested. There is, rather, one plane of life characterised by a struggle for singularity, or, as Guattari has it, for '*a fundamental right to singularity*, an ethics of finitude that is all the more demanding with regard to individuals and social entities the less it can found its imperatives on transcendental principles' (2013: 13). It is in this fashion that the following chapters unfold, each staging situations and moments in which current dominant subjectivities are challenged in different, but interconnected, social fields.

No wrong conclusions should be drawn: the rejection of the false debate over the right political model and this book's aim to point towards a long-term process of cultural transformation of life do not in any sense imply the flagging of spirited and radical targets and objectives, nor the weakening of passions – quite the contrary. Nor are we in favour of adopting deceptive 'small steps of inclusion' à la Zionist-left tradition. Targets and objectives need to be chosen according to the force with which they are capable of maddening the present regime of life and its fervent supporters, regardless of their reasons to do so, by their ability to confuse the regime's logic and weaken its strengths, by their physical, intellectual and emotional investments, short-circuiting its actual segregations and adding to its fatigue – all propelling the present regime of life into transformation. It requires no utopian designs, but rather, in line with Jameson, the kind of utopian impulse invested in 'the detective work of a decipherment and a reading of Utopian clues and traces in the landscape of the real', clues and traces from the *afters* of this present life that express themselves 'in a variety of unexpected and disguised, concealed, distorted ways ... large or small, which may in themselves be far from Utopian in their actuality' (2010: 415).

§ The call for cultural transformation of ways of life is by no means an insignificant demand. It goes beyond political reform in two directions: in the ways we interpret and use history; and in the ways that imagining the future impacts on the present. In fact, this *is* the problem – the lack of political imagination or utopianism involved in imagining and bringing about alternative futures. As Jameson asks, how might we be able to 'revive long-dormant parts of the mind, organs of political and historical and social imagination which have virtually atrophied for lack of use, muscles of praxis we have long since ceased exercising, revolutionary gestures we have lost the habit of performing, even subliminally'? (ibid.: 434).

Just to be precise, renouncing utopian thought and action does not necessarily derive from an acceptance of the 'no alternative' dogma. It can also derive from a disappointing, though honest, sense that 'there is no necessity for an alternative'. So if we give some credit to this position, the forensic question should be how this sense of cheerful conformism and self-satisfaction has been constructed in Israel. One day on Tel Aviv's beaches, in its excellent cafés or nightclubs suffices to breathe that sense of confidence. The reason for this should not be explained in terms of the essentially western life most Israelis lead or aspire to lead, but by the ways in which enjoying this kind of life removes – at the collective level – any ambiguity that might arise from participating in the crimes of a monolithic political culture delineated by the Zionist horizon. So, roughly, utopian thought dissipates as the eyes fill up with addictive rations of national commitment, blinding people from viewing the alternatives, and with postmodern pleasure dazzling them from seeing the necessity for alternatives.

But Israel is not Tel Aviv, far from it. As a capitalist society (Nitzan and Bichler 2002), Israel's social policies have been in decline for decades.[19] Extreme neoliberal policies, such as those Israel's administrations have been adopting for the past twenty years or so, have lethally wounded the sense of satisfaction of many, and people do question their political leadership and their position in society. However, as the wave of social protests that flooded the country in the summer of 2011 and since seem to indicate, Jewish commitment to the Zionist ethos (to maintaining the state of war and segregation) is still sufficiently firm. The spontaneous leadership in these protests refused to link their social demands to any sort of anti-war or radical Arab-Jewish agenda (Filc and Ram 2013). In other words, the commitment to Zionist politics is still resourceful enough not to be put at risk by neoliberal economics or older internal discrimination and segregation of Jewish communities. Hence, while economic hardships do ignite the political imagination, the commitment to monolithic cultural politics in Israel keeps that imagination tethered within the general boundaries of Zionism, away from the terrain of *the civil*. As long as the commitment to Zionism holds sway, the utopian impulse is stifled.

This state of affairs begs the question of *how* the commitment to racist, segregationist and militarist politics is recycled. Azoulay explains it in terms of the civil mobilisation of the Jewish population (2011a). I have used an alternative notion, that of the 'active foundation' (Svirsky 2012b). This is both the collective production of society and that which renders its social consistency and cultural coherence. It is that which animates the body of society and its explicit behaviours and states of mind. If Israel persists in its state of war and exempts itself from civic life and Arab-Jewish ways of existence, it is because an active collective foundation substantiates these preferences in the everyday practices of individuals and groups and in the ways in which they construct themselves as political subjects. These preferences, I argue, cannot be understood merely in terms of leadership, decision making and ideologies. The habitual contribution – conscious as well as unconscious – of ordinary Israelis to the activation of practices of exclusion and segregation, to a war-waging political economy and to the reaffirmation of the cult of militarism explains the workings of society in Israel.

1 | THE HIKER

It's hard to remember exactly when I began to renounce going out on *tiyulim* (hiking trips) in Israel.[1] Probably about twenty years ago. I needed the long trip to South America with my family in 2007 and then our relocation to Wales a year later as a chance to re-encounter nature with joy – even if thousands of miles away Zionist ghosts still haunted my walks. From the Israeli familial point of view, the *tiyul* is the obvious option for all leisure weekend activities. Other activities, such as having a barbecue or visiting places or people, are addenda to the *tiyul*. This is not surprising, as hiking has an almost mythological status in Israeli society (Avishar 2011: 59). People hike individually, or just with their nuclear family, but in Jewish-Israeli society hiking is essentially a collective practice, with a strong gregarious force; it is the way many spend time with friends and relatives. Institutionally, hiking has a strong presence in the school curriculum and youth movement activities as well as in the army – hence, it has a normalising character. Apart from one's own circle of friends with whom to hike, there are myriad hiking societies and as many experts as there are households. 'These hikes,' explains Ben-David, 'are very popular in Israel; they are rooted in Israeli culture and began long before the creation of the state; every year many youngsters and families join in this activity throughout the country' (1997: 143). This outdoors lifestyle is substantiated by an array of civil society-based organisations (most notably the Society for the Protection of Nature in Israel) and state-funded bodies whose area of expertise is hiking and the preservation of nature. A healthy and nature-loving people, one may presume.

But at some point it became no longer healthy for me. Perhaps because the hikes had an overly gregarious appeal, they were excessively organised, and were too predictable. The meticulous preparations for each hike, the sophisticated use of maps, the well-versed talks during the walks, the signposts on the stones along the trail, the well-fitted rucksacks, the obsessive concern with a sufficient supply of water, the intolerable folk songs religiously repeated by the most committed hikers, the planned stops at strategic points – they all flooded me with the uncomfortable sensation that we were not just going out for a saunter in the wildness à la Thoreau, but rather we were part of something sticky, sharing a commitment, even a mission. I could not stand the obsessive deliberations around botanic classification and depictions of every bit of vegetation we encountered; my only escape was to parody their learned conversations by inventing my own, non-existent terms, as I always suspected they did too. Couldn't we enjoy and appreciate nature without cataloguing its sights, or just be immersed in thought as we walked? The more knowledgeable chatterers cited the alleged biblical roots of these names, implying – perhaps compelling – a bond between the distant past and the present. Of the plants' medicinal uses these erudite fellows showed little knowledge. In contrast, my family hikes in the Bolivian Amazon were all about learning what nature offers us and how to respect that gift, rather than how to define it for ideological purposes.

Nor was I ever at ease with the three-strip coloured guiding path marks along the way. Although trail signs are there to provide a sense of orientation and to safely channel the walk, they are also there as active evidence that that very bit of soil has been tracked, appropriated, registered and catalogued – as the signs of an archive. For me, then, they expressed a sort of social contract with those who had been there before us in a bid to affirm yet again a sense of belonging. As Rela Mazali put it: 'Our paces measured and mapped onto the ground our unfolding, forming beliefs' (2011: 187). But it was precisely this exigency to commit ourselves that alarmed and pushed me away from all that. Have we walked this trail before? It seems we have done. Was it with my students, or my family, or perhaps with friends? One more time, and again, and yet again – walking these tracks, repeatedly, certainly felt as if we were singing a monotonous refrain with our own bodies. It took me a while to realise what others were explicitly calling for: 'the land can be conquered not only by settlement but also by treading it repeatedly' (Avishar 2011: 63, my translation).

Once on the trail, the experts cannot resist temptation. A supreme power guides them to intervene, to imbue the hike with sense and reason, without which it would remain meaningless. The experts do not miss any opportunity, particularly if some stranger comes along with the group – and especially if that stranger is a Jewish visitor from overseas. For the experts – and perhaps not just for them – these visitors provide a golden opportunity to make the voice of Israel heard. And then, once on the trail, the expert is eager to exhibit his rich repertoire of gestures and articulations to which we all respond – trained as we are – with respect and admiration. Bless the guide – our sole interpreter of scenes and meanings! Hands on hips, one foot forward and his gaze riveted on the horizon, bearing the burden of historical responsibility. He turns to us eager to convey his knowledge and his confident smile finally engulfs us. So we listen. Not only can the experts not resist the temptation, they seem to feel blessed with a mandate bestowed upon them, anchored in a century-old genealogy. It would have been simply irresponsible of them to miss the chance to portray that landscape properly for us, and particularly for our overseas visitors who could give the message wings in the diaspora. 'On some occasions ... [he] will take upon himself ... the role of the typical youth movement leader and will assume various responsibilities such as looking after the group's cohesion, maintaining its social life, and, at times, even cooking a scout's meal for the group' (Katz 1985: 51). It always starts with navigation skills: he uses his arms to position the piece of mud we are standing on in relation to the four corners of the earth. As far as the eye can see, every hill, road and town is identified and plotted. One already senses that, more than simple geography, this seemingly innocent spatial orientation involves the possession of territory, with 'us' and 'them'. I always wondered, rhetorically, why we needed to be aware of our coordinates just to smell flowers, digest our packed lunch, enjoy our time in nature, and rest from the pressures of urban living. Besides, what is it about their expert education that makes their annoying cartographic skills so easily unravel the natural landscape into discrete units – units to which we intuitively assign value according to ethnic divisions with which we were not necessarily concerned a moment before this cartographic ritual?

Once we are geographically and sentimentally positioned (remember: we just went for a walk), a brief exposition follows that might focus on some sort of modern Israeli achievement to be contextualised there in the open. 'Our' sophisticated irrigation system is frequently a good candidate. Then, if the expert is sure that his flock is submissive enough, he intensifies his speech; clearing his throat, inflecting his voice to adopt that monotone but authoritative rhythm we all recognise at once, he gravely expounds on the strategic significance of that hill over there, not forgetting the battles and the heroes thanks to whom we are now privileged to be standing where we are. That's it; the glue has worked on each and every one present, and eventually one of us exhales, '*Eyin kemo baaretz*' ('No place like Israel'). By the time the group has rested and leaves one spot to advance to the next (we don't walk or hike, we advance!), camaraderie has grown palpably to the point where someone actually shouts: 'Close ranks. We are too dispersed!' (In my days as a high school teacher, I was that idiot myself.) Someone else, consciously or not, conscientiously closes up the column as if we need to watch our fellow hikers' backs (was I that idiot too?) – as if we were performing an ancient indigenous rite and not just projecting military conduct. After all, we are not just having a relaxed stroll on a sunny Saturday. I could not stand any of this. It was suffocating. But it was also intoxicating in its magnetic attraction. More than anything, I could not stand the pleasure my body felt as part of that regimented bunch of hikers.

'No doubt walking practices could be categorized in many different ways,' asserts Edensor in his study of walking techniques in rural Britain (2000: 88). Yet Ori Schwarz's sonic model, which is based on an ethnographic study of Israeli hikers (2013), may prove helpful in giving a preliminary framing of our Zionist hiker. In his model, Schwarz identifies four modes of engagement of walkers or hikers with nature. The first category corresponds to nature 'absorbers', formed by those attentive, noise-hostile, silent and spiritual hikers who absorb nature in order to let it transform their interiority (ibid.:

388–91). Another type of hiker comprises those who use nature as a mediator, not to transform but to explore their given interiority through reflective self-expression (ibid.: 391). In the third category nature is used as an active locus for talkative social interaction (ibid.: 391–3), while the 'fourth way to engage with nature is through its physical properties, the challenges it poses to the user's body' (ibid.: 393). In this last category, hikers 'employ masculinised consumption techniques, which in Israel are strongly associated with hegemonic masculinity' and militarism (ibid.: 393). As we shall see, the Zionist hiker who is the focus of this chapter synthesises Schwarz's third and fourth type. In his use of nature, he takes advantage of nature to forge a nation, often by applying militarist techniques. Therefore, it is more exact to see our Zionist hiker not as a 'nature user', as in Schwarz's model, but as an *appropriator* of nature.

Schwarz adds a further level of analysis that unveils 'the contribution of sonic preferences to the reproduction of social hierarchies' between Ashkenazim and Mizrahim as consumers of nature (ibid.: 398); at first sight, this analysis appears to have the potential to contribute to a more nuanced characterisation of the Zionist hiker. Unsurprisingly, Schwarz found that his middle-class Ashkenazi interviewees showed an aversion to 'loud' hiking modes, shouting and having barbecues in nature – behaviours stereotypically attributed in Jewish-Israeli society to lower-class Mizrahim (ibid.: 395–9). But despite Schwarz's critical efforts to lean on his working-class interviewees to transvalue Ashkenazi hierarchisation of modes of hiking, the stereotypical dichotomy associated with the correlation between race/class and sonic preferences remains in place, but with inverted polarity (a standard consequence of identitarian analyses). So loudness, for instance, obtains a positive value in Schwarz's transvaluation but remains stereotypically attributed to Mizrahim.

In addition, when looking into both the genealogy and the current educational practices of Zionist hiking, the stereotypical racial dichotomy of sonic preferences seems to have no explanatory role. As the following sections show, this genealogy is rooted in a primarily white Ashkenazi history, one that largely evolved through an engagement with nature as a site of intensive socialisation and militant nation building rather than through ascetic or self-reflecting modes. Official educational practices of hiking in Jewish-Israeli schools continue to maintain these patterns, whether in middle-class or lower-class neighbourhoods. This does not mean that the distinction between silent and loud modes of engagement with nature does not exist in Jewish-Israeli hiking; rather, this distinction may yield stronger critical outcomes if operationalised not in terms of signifiers of ascribed racial identities and social positionings that serve only to reassert social differentiations, but instead conceived as a multiplicity that lacks the authority of a single referent. Traditional Zionist hiking, for instance, in the family circle or otherwise, requires normalising moments through lecturing and active participation as well as silent passages of military simulation. In this respect, 'out of place' acts of loudness or quietness may be disruptive or positively profanatory. Schwarz's ideal sonic types omit the profanatory potential of these combinations. In other words, rather than simply being conceived as signs of identity, sonic preferences in hiking can also be interpreted and activated as productive mechanisms of withdrawal or disengagement. Unconsciously or not, having a noisy barbecue gathering where my hegemonic adversaries prefer to saunter or abstaining from the joy of their all too expected conversations and spatial preaching can both be seen as expressions of counter-hegemonic disengagement. Therefore, the study of sonic preferences in hiking may have more to offer than just moulding a continuum stretched between antithetical poles.

§ One cannot comprehend the nature-appropriator mode of hiking – which might appear bizarre outside the Jewish-Israeli milieu – and its role in everyday culture in Israel without analysing the presence and significance of hiking in the history of white hegemonic Zionism. Studies have established that since the early days of Zionist Eastern European immigration to Palestine in the beginning of the twentieth century, theoretical knowledge of the geography of Eretz Yisrael and hiking throughout that geography evolved as inseparable core elements in the ideological indoctrination and the physical preparation of the Jewish immigrant-settler (see, for example, Almog

2000; Avishar 2011; Benvenisti 2002; Stein 2009). Familiarising oneself
with the landscapes of Palestine through one's feet helped the former
diasporic Jews of Europe to recapture the land, Judaising it anew.
In other words, a particular practice of hiking became part of the
nation-building process.

The historical fabrication of a nation should be sought in the
changing and intricate material, discursive and emotional ways by
which encounters and events turn into opportunities and choices.
Chief among these nation-building processes are 'existential territories', which, according to Félix Guattari (1996), are spaces of life
that become defined, stable and habitable through the cultivation
of subjectivities – our identities, habits, traits, gestures and dispositions. The political mobilisation of the *tiyul*, I argue, involved the
constitution of two types of interconnected existential territories,
one being the body of the Zionist Ashkenazi pioneer and the other
the land itself. Zionist national ideology that called on people to
re-encounter the ancestral homeland and reclaim it in order to build
a Jewish national home cannot in itself explain the hiking narrative
in the Zionist annals of Palestine, or how the hiking narrative helped
European pioneers sprout and take root in their desired old-new land.
Unlike the native Palestinians and the Sephardi[2] families who lived in
the country, the Eastern European pioneers did not know the land,
so practical goals such as acquiring knowledge of the land's physical
and human geographies were a significant inspiration for these Jewish settlers to go out into the open, to explore, study and physically
experience the terrain. As Neumann explains, 'the *halutzim* [pioneers]
thirsted for knowledge of the land ... one way they slaked this thirst
was by travelling and hiking its length and breadth' (2011: 98).

Education in the growing Zionist enclave played a decisive role in
promoting the practices and ideologies associated with hiking and
landscape. As Avishar describes:

this educational approach aspired to implant the meaning of
being connected to the land of Israel as it was settled anew after
2,000 years of diaspora. The hike was recruited to this end as
treading the paths, taking in the views and finding shards of the

distant past while Judaising the landscape; all deepened the bond of the hikers to their homeland (2011: 62, my translation).

This sense of historical remoteness was not shared by Sephardi Jews who lived in Muslim countries and up until the 1930s practised 'religious pilgrimages or business trips to Palestine' (Shohat 1988: 10). But it was precisely that sense of 'remoteness' and the desire to end the diaspora – exogenous to Sephardi Jews (ibid.: 10) – that formed the background from which European Zionism articulated an ideology of reconnection, rebirth and Jewish regeneration.

In 1905, the first Hebrew school, founded in Rishon LeZion in 1886, led the way. Its headmaster inaugurated what was to become a tradition, that of the annual school field trip (Almog 2000: 166–8; Avishar 2011: 61). 'According to its practitioners, knowledge of the (home)land was to be transmitted to the Jewish pupil through both intellectual and sensory means ... [and] the *tiyul* was considered among the most important of such sensory means' (Stein 2009: 337). As Mayer explains: 'These hikes were the climactic events of each year both in school and in the youth movement, gradually increasing in difficulty as each youth moved up the movement hierarchy. Eventually they would also become an important rite of passage in the Israeli Defence Forces' (2000: 290). At first, historical sites were the obvious choices, helping to weave a reconnection with the land of the Bible (Stein 2009: 339), but as the Zionist project developed, the repertoire widened to include sites that allowed 'for a witnessing of the Zionist enterprise and its accomplishments on the ground' (Katriel 1995: 8).

The desire for knowledge of the old-new land eventually resulted in an educational discipline of its own known as *Yediat ha-Aretz* (knowledge of the land), which in Israeli universities is studied in liberal arts departments under the heading *Limudei Eretz Yisrael* (Eretz Yisrael Studies). According to Stein, '[b]y the 1930s, *Yediat ha-Aretz* had been established as one of the dominant sites of Zionist pedagogy within Jewish Palestine and had spawned a field of both popular and educational literature including teachers' manuals and textbooks' (2009: 337; see also Almog 2000; Katz 1985). The point is that 'knowing the land', as Kadman notes, never included any know-ledge of Palestinian existence in its past and present landscapes, this existence having been conceived of as something that a Jewish-Israeli does not need to know about (2008: 48). However, this is only true at the societal cultural level. Objectified in strategic terms, knowledge of Palestinian life became a priority for the leadership of the Yishuv (the pre-state Jewish community in Palestine) and for their plans to eventually execute a massive expulsion of the Palestinians. In this vein, the Jewish National Fund (JNF), the main Zionist settler-colonial institution in the pre-state period, was commissioned to prepare a detailed inventory of all Arab villages, 'the villages files' (Pappe 2006: 17–22). The villages were extensively surveyed and mapped; academics and other professionals participated in the production of such knowledge. By the late 1930s, the archive was almost complete and it was updated for the last time in 1947. These archives and maps, narrates Ilan Pappe, were all that remained of the villages after 1948 (ibid.: 18).

The field of *Yediat ha-Aretz* developed on the shoulders of geo-graphy education (Bar-Gal 1993; Bar-Gal and Bar-Gal 2008)[3] and of an emergent Judaising cartography (Benvenisti 2002). The Zionist re-mapping and symbolic appropriation of the land – which also comprised the signposting of places and trails and the Hebraising of the ancient Arab names of those places (Avishar 2011; Benvenisti 2002; Kadman 2008) – were driven by a craving to reconnect and revive Jewish existence by means of uncovering and exposing the landscape of the ancient homeland upon which renewed Jewish existence could find a further layer of self-justification for the settler-colonial project, in a sort of historical short-circuiting of times (Benvenisti 2002: 249). As Stein explains:

> By bringing the Jewish hiker into intimate contact with the home-land, such travelling practices were thought to foster a powerfully tactile sense of national awakening, affording the Jewish walker with first-hand knowledge of both land and homeland. In terms of the broader Zionist pedagogy in which they played an important role, *tiyulim* were deemed a crucial means of linking nature to

nation, of connecting Jewish history in Eretz Yisrael to a set of
Zionist political claims in the present, therein fortifying the latter
(2009: 335).

Pedagogical and symbolic technologies never work alone but
intertwine with somatic functions. As Neumann warns: 'The claim
that the pioneer experience of rebirth is but a linguistic trope, a
poetic expression, a literary metaphor, a subjective experience, a
symbolic re-enactment of biological birth or some similar phenomenon, stamps the *halutzim* [pioneers] with precisely the tags from
which they sought to liberate themselves' (2011: 44). Indeed, one of
the main tenets in early white European Zionism was the rejection
of the 'exile paradigm' and of the spiritual life Jewish communities
had led in the diaspora, to favour instead the constitution of a new
Jewish subjectivity, a 'new Jew', incarnated in a masculine 'muscular
settler Jew' to be shaped by physical training and hard labour (Mayer
2000; Neumann 2011: 17, 126). For the early Zionists in Europe, this
was necessary because the diaspora 'had given Jews many feminine
characteristics and made them, as a result, easy targets for anti-
Semitism' (Mayer 2000: 284). In 1895, Theodor Herzl, the father of
modern Zionism, wrote:

> I must train the youth to be soldiers. But only a professional
> army. Strength: one tenth of the male population; less would not
> suffice internally. However, I educate one and all to be free and
> strong men, ready to serve as volunteers if necessary. Education
> by means of patriotic songs, the Maccabean tradition, religion,
> heroic stage-plays, honour, etc. (1956: 37, cited in Mayer 2000: 285).

For the new Jewish settlers, Palestine furnished the open space
and wildness that provided them with the means to remake Jewish
masculinity (Gluzman 2007; Mayer 2000). 'Long, exhausting hikes
in the rugged terrain of Palestine became an important tool for
merging the Zionist message of love of the land and the building of
physical strength' (Mayer 2000: 290). So, if Palestinian nature offered
a smooth space in which to build a new collective self-perception of
the Jew – this Jew being the white Jew – the *tiyul* was a significant

practice that materialised the constitution of that racial subjectivity. As Neumann describes, the pioneers 'prepared their bodies through physical education, hikes and camping' (2011: 127; see also Mayer 2000: 287–8). The practice of hiking was seized as an opportunity to constitute aspects of the 'new Jew': '*Tiyulim* characterised by struggle and danger were thought integral to the production of these New Hebrew bodies and subjects, both through the physicality of the hiking practice and through an overcoming of its associated challenges' (Stein 2009: 340).[4]

As security became an emerging priority for the Jewish settlers, particularly in view of the Arab revolt of 1936–39, the *tiyul* allowed the constitution of an additional somatic component through the constantly evolving edifice of the Zionist Jewish body. Hiking turned into a means of partaking in proto-military training as preparation for future acts of self-defence, attack and land conquest (Almog 2000: 173–4; Stein 2009: 338). Beyond instruction in the use of firearms and in small-group soldierly manoeuvres, this training relied on hiking as its experimental field of action. Unsurprisingly, the physical education curriculum played an equally important role in the Yishuv in the making of a 'physical culture' for the new Jewish body, which, as Ben-Israel explains, was materialised through a close association with paramilitary training (2007). Hiking gives a suitable and relatively safe outdoors context in which to undertake long treks, survey the scenery, carry weights, and practise food rationing and survival techniques, among other practicalities, all essential components of military training (Avishar 2011: 63). Schools and youth movements were paramount in this respect: they provided the growing paramilitary Jewish organisations on the ground with well-prepared and enthusiastic youth. As Mayer explains, 'in the late 1930s and early 1940s, as a result of both an ideological program for a strong *New Jew* and increasing Arab attacks on Jewish settlements, paramilitary training became an integral part of the curriculum of both high schools and youth movements in Jewish Palestine' (2000: 292). In summary, the military function of hiking – together with the practices of knowledge and rediscovery and the new Jewish body – completed a bundle of technologies that became vital in the production of Zionist subjectivity.

Conquering the land – the basic axiom of any form of colonialism, settler-based or not – found an ally in hiking, a sort of living territory that helped root the Jewish pioneer and expand the range of spaces, social spheres and political goals through which the nation was being built, to the point that Avishar can safely claim that 'the youth conquered the land with their feet; they learned to know her first hand. Both the military conquest and the conquest by means of hiking share a physical element that bonds the body with the land, by walking, sweating and even sleeping on the ground' (2011: 76, my translation). Conquest is more than a simple act of satiating domination: it has the energies of a conceptual role in Zionism, an event-concept. In early Zionism, this idea not only blurred the boundaries between military applications and the relation to nature as embodied in hiking, but, as several studies have shown, it ravaged labour, housing and the economy with its separatist impetus to eventually found a *corpus separatum* in relation to both the British occupying administration and Palestinian life (Bernstein 2000; Shafir 1989; Smith 1993). As a nation-building technology, hiking not only helped rewrite Arab Palestine as a Jewish geography (Benvenisti 2002; Kadman 2008; Stein 2009), *but it substantially became a living space for the actual possession of the land*, and, as a consequence, its practices became a significant arena of subjectivation.

§ A professor of history from Bayit VeGan[5] took his family out for a picnic at a quiet pine grove near Giva't Shaul, formerly Deir Yassin. It was not too cold to stay in the shade, nor too hot to light a campfire, so the professor taught his son camp skills he had acquired in the army. They arranged three squared stones in a 'U' shape to block the wind, and left the fourth flank open. They piled up broken branches on top of twigs, on top of dry pine needles. He let his son ignite the pile. When they listened carefully, they could hear a weak and soft murmur coming from the curves in the road. The trees hid it; the professor did not speak of the village, the provenance of the stones. He did not speak of the village school, now a psychiatric hospital on the other side of the hill. He imagined himself and his family having a picnic, irrespective of the village; enjoying its land outside of history (Shelach 2005, my translation).

Deir Yassin was a Palestinian village of about 750 inhabitants, 120 of whom were massacred at 4 a.m. on 9 April 1948 by members of Jewish gangs, in spite of the fact that the village had previously reached a non-aggression pact with the local Jewish leadership. Later that afternoon, the survivors were loaded onto trucks and deported, and their houses destroyed to prevent their return (ATG 2008: 151; Pappe 2006: 90–1). In 1946, the village 'had two schools, many shops, a club, a savings and loan committee, and a bus company that connected Deir Yassin and Lifta to Jerusalem' (ATG 2008: 150). One year after the massacre, Giva't Shaul expanded over Deir Yassin's lands. 'Houses which had not been destroyed were given to Orthodox Jews, mostly from Poland, Czechoslovakia and Romania' (ibid.: 150).

The *tiyul* as a re-enactment of conquest is indeed better understood today by noting the disdain most Jewish-Israelis show – while hiking – towards the ethnic cleansing of Palestine in 1948–49. According to Khalidi (2006), most villages were totally destroyed, although, while hiking through the length and breadth of Israel, you will probably encounter physical remains of any of the 678 Palestinian cities, towns, villages and neighbourhoods that the Jewish forces destroyed during and immediately after the 1948 war, as the land was ethnically cleansed of over 700,000 Palestinians, forced to become refugees (Khalidi 2006, Morris 2004; Pappe 2006). Parts of the Palestinian villages were completely destroyed so that new towns and rural settlements for Jews could be erected. Palestinian urban neighbourhoods were pillaged and appropriated by Jewish families (Benvenisti 2002; Kadman 2008; Khalidi 2006). However, most sites that were Palestinian villages prior to 1948 lie within unbuilt open spaces where, since 1948, 'groves were planted, parks were created, national parks and natural reserves were declared, and pathways for hiking were opened' (Kadman 2008: 68). As Noga Kadman describes in her groundbreaking book, the point is that:

> Travelling in Israel, it is nearly impossible to avoid piles of stones, ruins, remnants of walls and structures overgrown with almond

and fig trees, rolling terraces crumbling with disuse, and long hedges of prickly pear. These integral parts of the Israeli landscape are all that remains of Arab communities that existed before the war of 1948 (ibid.: 11).

According to Kadman, the built-up areas of 182 of the destroyed Palestinian villages lie within more than 100 tourist sites built by Israel since 1948 (national parks, trails, forests, groves and picnic spots), most of them maintained by the JNF and the Israel Nature and Parks Authority (NPA),[6] while the visible remains of 108 other Palestinian villages can be seen in present Jewish-Israeli communities – some of these are not mere remains at all, but houses that are still standing and were given to Jewish families (ibid.: 68–9). The fact that so many remains are situated within national parks and nature reserves is no coincidence. As Kadman explains, after 1948 'the JNF afforestation project served to cover up the remains of the Palestinian villages, to cause their being forgotten' (ibid.: 42; see also Slyomovics 1998: 234). This was the JNF's way of 'contextualising' anew the prehistory of the State of Israel and particularly its ethnic cleansing: not remains that are a live testimony of a catastrophe, but landmarks of a greater Jewish picturesque landscape consisting of biblical ties, tales of heroism and breath-taking views.

Chances are high that, as you head out to your *tiyul*, you will be driving on roads that were originally built at the time by the authorities of the newly founded Jewish state, using the stones and rubble of destroyed Palestinian houses crushed into gravel to become the bedding layers under the asphalt (Gardi 2011: 25–8). After all, as Israeli Foreign Minister Moshe Sharett stated in the Knesset on 2 May 1949, just a few months after the fighting ended: 'We tend to see all abandoned property as the property of the State of Israel, and to do with it as we please' (quoted from Kadman 2008: 21). One year later, the Knesset enacted the Absentee Property Law (1950), which officially legalised the appropriation of property pillaged by the state. Chances are high, as well, that as you walk the length of Israel's terrain you will be treading the same dirt roads trodden by Palestinian families on their forced way to exile. And even though you drive on roads made out of destroyed Palestinian villages, and walk through the remains of Palestinian houses, and pass the typical plants that have endured as witnesses of a life violently put to an end, even when your soles tread the same soil that scathed Palestinian feet in that summer of 1948 as Jewish forces showed them the routes out of their homes and their land – chances are absurdly high that most Jewish-Israelis will not see these as remains or evidence of a disaster that in any way concerns them: a continuous non-encounter of sorts keeps taking place.

Growing up in Jerusalem, I was taken on many a tour with my school or youth movement to Lifta, the partly ruined depopulated Arab village near the entrance to the city; a spring still bubbles among the ruined homes, pushing water into a small pool. The visits left me with the vague impression that Lifta is ancient, a ruin that has always been like this – desolate, slightly mysterious, beautiful and in some way intimidating with its silence and the narrow paths winding among the heavy-set houses and walls (ibid.: 11).

Among its many other significant activities, since 2002 the Israeli non-governmental organisation Zochrot ('remembering' in Hebrew, in the feminine plural) conducts guided tours to destroyed Palestinian villages as acts of commemoration. Eitan Bronstein, one of the organisation's founders and central activist, tells me that an average of fifty to seventy people participate in each of these tours, generally guided by Zochrot's personnel and, importantly, reinforced by Palestinian survivors and witnesses, former residents of the villages visited (interview 27 May 2013). Palestinian citizens of Israel and Jewish-Israelis, as well as international visitors, attend the tours, which take place about seven times a year. Zochrot's rationale has two complementary aspects: raising awareness of the Nakba, primarily among Jewish-Israelis; and helping support the case in favour of the Palestinian right of return, which the organisation sees as the necessary historical remedy of the Nakba and crucial for the establishment of a new society with a shared foundation.

Ronit Lentin defines Nakba commemoration by Israeli Jews as

co-memory, 'the memory story of Palestine indelibly and dialectically woven into the story of Israeli Jewish dissent – co-memoration of victor and vanquished, united ... in grieving the loss of Palestine' (2010: 186). For Lentin, Zochrot practises a performance of co-memory, 'because without the Palestinian witnesses and survivors these acts of postmemory remain abstract' (ibid.: 198). However, Lentin raises a few questions with regard to Zochrot's practices that are worth looking into. One of them is the issue of perpetrators using victim testimonies. As Lentin explains: 'Refracting Palestinian refugee testimonies through the voices of members of the colonising collectivity, often in mediated or attenuated format so as to make them palatable to a hostile Israeli Jewish public, runs the risk of perpetuating their victimhood, and separating the Nakba past from present Palestinian reality' (ibid.: 202). Moreover, the use of Palestinian testimonies by members of the colonising collectivity runs the risk of turning into a classical orientalist situation in which the victim is incapable of representing itself, Lentin rightly adds. I cannot but fully agree with Ronit Lentin's fears and anxieties. However, my response is not that Zochrot should consider withdrawing from the project of accessing Jewish-Israeli society with the sort of content Zochrot has been trying to convey for more than a decade or so, but that it must take these arguments and sensibilities into account. Another issue Lentin raises is Zochrot's practice of signposting to commemorate Palestinian sites. As she argues: 'Though these signposts have a huge impact on tour participants, my question is whether this signposting is enabled by the ultimate Israeli control of the geo-political landscape and its re-memorialising' (ibid.: 206). On this point I disagree with Lentin regarding the way in which Zochrot's members are represented. Portraying them as 'Israelis' who continue to control the geopolitical landscape is somehow misleading. Zochrot's activists can barely be identified as Israelis. They do not share with most Israelis the most fundamental assumptions about the history of the country, nor their vision of its desired future. Identifying them as Israelis is, in a way, re-territorialising their subjectivities. Hence, we should be looking at their activities as being performed by people struggling to de-subjectivise themselves from Zionism's existential territories.

'Some questions remain unanswered,' as Lentin appropriately says (ibid.: 208) – particularly striking is Zochrot's lack of work to connect its actions and research to present-day oppression and continuing ethnic cleansing, but I prefer rather to ponder on them from the perspective that sees in organisations such as Zochrot potentialities to profane.

§ Although Zochrot tours are not designed as traditional hikes, they do make visible and intelligible that which for most Jewish-Israelis – on their hikes – are no more than old mouldy stones and enigmatic ruins. This point should be stressed further: as an official policy accompanying the ethnic cleansing of Palestine, Israel has made every effort not only to prevent the return of the expelled Palestinians after 1948 (Piterberg 2001), but also to erase any residue of active memory of that ethnic cleansing, to prevent its rising from the ashes (Kadman 2008; Slyomovics 1998). In Amal Eqeiq's words, '*Nakba* is not a one-time event that occurred more than half a century ago. *Nakba*, I came to learn, is an ongoing event of erasure, occupation and dispossession' (2012: 502). Nowhere is there any official sign attesting to the location of Palestinian cities, villages, towns and neighbourhoods that existed prior to the expulsion. As Kadman explains, in the JNF and NPA sites, signposts welcoming the hiker or tourist disregard the Palestinian villages whose remains lie within. In cases where these signs do refer to villages, it is in a careless and partial manner, occulting their Palestinian origin and their history. What these texts stress, indeed, is the Zionist narrative of those sites, either by entirely bypassing modern Palestinian existence, shortcutting across pre-modern times and Zionist times, or by referring to Palestinian villages in terms of the danger they posed to the Zionist project (Kadman 2008: 69–71). When references are made to them, Palestinian villages' remains appear in the tourist information provided by both the JNF and NPA merely as part of nature, as 'a-historical sites in the landscape, as creeks or watercourses, or as a landmark on a hike trail' (ibid.: 71). Student hikers from both primary and secondary schools, the teachers hiking with them, the family member hiker, the youth movement hiker, the soldier hiker and tourist hiker from overseas – all are equipped with this ideological text that totally marginalises Palestinian existence before 1948 when they go to the national parks, nature reserves and hiking trails. Remains of Palestinian habitation and abandoned orchards are not understood as evidence of a life that existed not so long ago, unless something or someone drives us to ask.

Not once in their years of state education will Jewish-Israelis encounter the history of the Nakba and Palestinian society that existed prior to 1948, nor will they get to know of the various social spheres in which Jews and Palestinians forged and shared a life together that competed with the segregating mechanisms of Zionism (Azoulay 2012; Campos 2011; Lockman 1996). Except for the knowledge available to Palestinian descendants or efforts by civil society organisations such as ADRID (Palestinian Association for the Defence of the Rights of the Internally Displaced) or Zochrot to re-designate landscapes, Jewish-Israelis might quite well pass their whole lives in total ignorance. Obscure to them is the destruction of an entire life and landscape upon which sovereign Jewish existence was built.

For Bronstein, the Nakba is a common tragedy of both Palestinians and Israelis, albeit with entirely different consequences, and hence the correct political action Zochrot has chosen to follow is to bring Jewish-Israeli society to recognise the ethnic cleansing of Palestine, to actively embody its memory, and to envisage ways to repair that tragedy. As he persuasively states:

Zochrot wants primarily to change the discourse in the Jewish-Israeli society, both regarding the recognition of the Nakba and the need to discuss and accept the Palestinian right of return ... and when one decides to change public discourse the question of who is your audience becomes crucial ... the Jewish-Israeli public is the one who must go through an enormous self-transformation ... and even when this public is ready to listen they need to make true efforts as nothing is easily available in their ordinary ways of life (interview 4 November 2012).

Recently, Zochrot published a colossal work, a Hebrew-Arabic bilingual tour guide entitled *Once Upon the Land* (Gardi et al. 2012). The guide offers eighteen routes through destroyed Palestinian neighbour-hoods and villages. This unique text is the result of collaborative work by Jewish-Israelis and Palestinians who volunteered to prepare a study of the tracks and write them as tours, each in their own style. However, as Tomer Gardi explains in the foreword, the guide is formatted more in the vein of Jewish recognition of the Nakba and the Arabic text is mostly a translation from the Hebrew (ibid.: 8–18). Importantly, the guide does not follow the dictates of the genre. Rather, Zochrot's guide is an activist text that – by using the walking body – explicitly invites the reader to challenge the Zionist ways of appropriating nature and its landscapes. As Amal Eqeiq says in her 'Not an epilogue' to the guide (ibid.: 500–8), apart from statistical information about the Palestinian neighbourhoods and villages that the book provides, the text assembles spatial and temporal cartographies in an attempt to lead the reader-hiker to have not just a cognitive experience but also, and primarily, an affective one. Some of the tours invite us to greatly extend our senses and try to imagine life in the villages before the Nakba as a way to open our hearts and engage with a past that has been institutionally erased. Hence, as Eqeiq explains, 'the tours ... show that from a Jewish-Israeli perspective, taking a tour following the guidelines of *Once Upon the Land* can be an intense emotional experience' (ibid.: 506). Niva Grunzweig wrote tour number 17, 'Returning to the South: A tour across Simsim, Huj and Burayr'. In the mid-1940s, Burayr had a population of about 3,000. Its main institutions were located at the village centre – two primary schools, a market, a clinic, a mosque and a grain mill (Khalidi 2006: 92). The village was conquered by Jewish forces during the night of 12–13 May 1948. According to several testimonies, including those given by the forces' soldiers, fifty-five men and women were massacred in the attack (Morris 2004: 258); all the rest fled to Gaza. Here is Niva's own experience while sauntering through Burayr's remains:

> While walking along the paths and among the trees, it was hard
> not to think of the people who were slaughtered there in 1948.
> The wind blowing across the eucalyptus trees sounds like people
> whispering. Perhaps they, the eternal dwellers of the village, are

trying to tell their story and the story of their place to me and to other visitors who come to rest in the grove. The heaps of rock and the strong sense of absenteeism that envelops the place drove me to shudder and reflect. In every Palestinian village I have visited one can feel this absenteeism – after all, they have all been destroyed and not a soul lives in them anymore. But in Burayr – perhaps because of its size, perhaps because of the violent history, or perhaps because of the ancient paths that remain even sixty years later, and mainly because of the fact that an attempt has been made to erase the place and its history by planting a nice shady grove – in Burayr, absenteeism is present with greater strength (Gardi et al. 2012: 451, my translation).

Other texts in the guide are similarly emotional. What is most salient about Zochrot tours is that they require a change in perception and in political disposition regarding the history of Israel-Palestine through an intimate somatic experience of its historical landscape. This is a change that requires one to forgo the split between points of view and to extinguish any legitimacy that has been conferred upon the perception that ethnic cleansing is a catastrophe only 'from their point of view – "their", of course, referring to the Palestinians' (Azoulay 2013: 564). It is the hidden past that is summoned to impact the present and, hence, the future. A desire is ignited to have the original owners of the land back. Hiking with *Once Upon the Land* reveals a country that differs entirely from the one that Jewish-Israelis know and are prepared to die for. It is the country that was 'once upon the land' and upon its destruction a new country was built. Hiking along these trails affords a strong material understanding of what a settler-colonial project entails. As Edna Shemesh describes in her review of the guide in *Haaretz*: 'The editors aim at overturning the genre. They intentionally use a known textual form with the intention to decolonise the very idea of the tour, while hiking into destroyed Palestinian neighbourhoods and villages' (2013). Indeed, from the point of view of Jewish-Israelis, Zochrot's hikes are a serious exercise in political re-education, in more ways than one, or should we say that they are about driving the hiker into a unique personal catastrophe – one that seems crucial for cracking one's own codifications – as the only way to confront and embrace one's part in the Nakba launched sixty years ago against an entire nation.

The paths do not lead the hikers back into their childhood provinces or to the landscapes of good old Eretz Yisrael; they will neither walk in the Hasmoneans' footsteps nor follow the plight of the thirty-five (Palmah) heroes along Netiv Halamed-Heh. This text is in fact an invitation to reveal what lies under the Israeli settlements built after 1948 (ibid., my translation).

The fact that many of Zochrot's hiking routes lie within Israeli national parks or natural recreation areas enhances their significance. Now, imagine two groups of hikers, both intending to explore the Burayr area. One group seeks the eucalyptus grove enveloping Burayr's ruins to build a small campfire and have a picnic, as described in the short narrative about the professor of history quoted earlier. The other group wanders about and around Burayr's ruins and reflects on the scene, and as they discuss what they see and feel, they stop for a break. Both groups of people have been through the same school system and have walked the country more than once; very probably most of them – if not all of them – will also have served in the Israeli army. How do these two groups relate to each other? How do their respective visits relate to nature? While the latter dares to explore thresholds, the former gives itself to mere repetition, to duplication. The most significant challenge is to bring the emotional investments of these two groups to affect each other. Once we dare to explore that threshold, new political imaginations manifest themselves in one's own. The militarist gestures with which we were so entangled on our hikes are now thrown at us, causing nothing but shame and disgust. A natural estrangement from old habits follows these new affects, and therefore a fundamental re-creation is called for in our customary relation to nature.

With reference to the French semiotician Emile Benveniste, Agamben explains that in order to profane a sacred technology, such as Zionist hiking, the myth or the narrative needs to be separated from the practice that stages the story (2007: 75–6). In this vein, there are two basic options: one is to drop the myth and preserve the rite; while the other is to destroy the rite and preserve the myth. In a sense, Zochrot's *Once Upon the Land* does both. It clearly rejects the Zionist myth that was imposed on hiking, but it also rejects the physical aspect of Zionist hiking. But nature has much more to offer beyond this kind of political sauntering.

A warning is required at this point. We should avoid analysing practices as if there were just two opposite options. There is much more in between. It is more exact to keep in mind the fact that revolutionary standpoints are generally betrayed by fascistic and paranoiac drives in revolutionaries, just as we can always find escapes and liberating spillovers in tight-knit racial or totalitarian commitments. The encounter with the Nakba in nature might happen before a transformative moment or it can catalyse it. At first, guilt, remorse or nostalgia might overwhelm the known positions of the subject. The question, then, is whether these emotions are a passageway into new emotional states that might relocate the subject in productive affective territories. In itself, internalising the past can be a very short-sighted transformation. For instance, guilt and remorse cannot be a source of further transformation; they are moralising, obsolete, static and restraining. Nostalgia might be another hindrance. Zochrot tours and acts of re-signposting the destroyed Palestinian villages might easily engrain nostalgic territories. The past that preceded ethnic cleansing was surely safer than the present that followed it, for both Palestinians and Jews. But beyond the affirmative longing for a past deprived of its potential, yielding to that past can seriously shrink the potential of the encounter with the past today. Nostalgia does not suffice for looking forward. The encounter with that past is surely necessary and inescapable, and yet the affects it produces need to be oriented to nourish the construction of new presents – specifically, the construction of new relationships with nature and history. For instance, as Azoulay suggests, new forms of civil partnership can emerge from a 'shared awareness of catastrophe' (2011b: 233). In recent years, Zochrot has been promoting practical thinking about Palestinian return by means of written texts, talks, exhibitions and conferences. This policy extends the ground on which new collaborations might be built, as it reaches a step beyond remembrance into co-memory (Lentin 2010), through the idea of reparation. If we aim to keep the encounter with the destroyed Palestinian villages in motion – namely to rescue it from degeneration, from becoming just a ritual that for some redeems their tormented souls, while for others it offers a sentimental refuge – connecting it with return is one significant route to take.

§ We need the knowledge of the country even more for the sake of our existence and security. Both our security and safety cannot be established without knowing every single path of our country. (David Ben-Gurion, First Prime Minister of Israel)

For about ten years during the 2000s I accompanied many excursions in my capacity as a high school teacher in Israel. Ideological hiking starred on these trips. We either had our own guides among school staff, or else the school hired the services of private firms for this purpose – there was no difference between the two, as they both provided the same ideological seasoning. My students had no chance to acknowledge the Nakba on these hikes. Like the professor of history from Bayit VeGan, our guides were blind to Palestinian ruins from 1948, as was everyone else, on school hikes and in the youth movement alike:

> The choice to hike through, self-sufficient, implied the zones
> around our routes to be unspoilt nature. And we actively un-saw
> the stone houses of Arab communities that we never linked at
> the time with the term Palestinian, a term which I had yet to even
> hear. Or, at most, we saw them as quaintly picturesque, tribal,
> exotic, part of nature ... Our youth movement marched out a con-
> cretization of the Zionist delusion of virgin land to be possessed
> and fertilized in gorgeous glory (Mazali 2011: 187).

As far as the curriculum is concerned, the guide book *Once Upon the Land* has no chance at all of ending up in the hands of a Jewish-Israeli student, either at school or in one of the Zionist youth movements. In fact, any teacher daring to use their capacity as such to suggest or lead one of the book's tours risks losing their job. This is because of the so-called 'Nakba Law', enacted by the Knesset in March 2011: 'Amendment no. 40 to the *Budgets Foundations Law (1985) – Reducing Budget or Support for Activity Contrary to the Principles of the State*' (new Section 3b). The law authorises the Minister of Finance to reduce state funding or support to an institution if it engages in an 'activity that is contrary to the principles of the state'. One of these activities is defined in the law as 'commemorating Independence Day or the day of the establishment of the state as a day of mourning' (Clause B4). Therefore, planning, preparing or taking a class out into nature on a visit to Palestinian remains from 1948 will compromise the school's status in the eyes of its ministry inspectors, and will probably lead to severe measures being taken against the rebel teachers. So what do teachers have as normative guidelines for touring and hiking?

Although there have been changes in Israeli education with regard to hiking activities and pedagogies since the pre-state days – ecological and environmental approaches, for instance, have been adopted particularly in the last twenty years or so (Avishar 2011: 70–2) – the same indoctrinatory core has remained.[7] As Stein put it, 'what does merit note is the endurance of the particular discursive and ideological coordinates that have been associated with the *tiyul* since the early decades of state formation' (2009: 348). According to Ben-Israel (1999), a comparison between the Jewish Teachers Union's curriculum that incorporated hiking in the official programme of study in 1907 and the one issued by the State of Israel in 1997 shows that the two programmes are very similar regarding the nationalist educational goals (cited in Dror 2011: 24). Even if the peak of normalisatory hiking – the annual school hike – has been shaken by certain criticisms in the recent past, '[o]ver the years, school trips and hiking have become an essential ingredient of growing up Israeli; a ritual gesture of "belonging" that is rarely reflected upon or questioned' (Katriel 1995: 6).

Today, hiking pedagogy in schools is managed by a special department in the Ministry of Education called Shelah veYediat ha-Aretz ('*Shelah*' is an acronym for 'field, nation and society', and '*Yediat ha-*

Aretz' literally means 'knowledge of the country'), which functions as an arm of the Society and Youth Administration within the Ministry. In essence, *Shelah* studies at school combine pedagogies applied in the classroom and in the field, covering hikes and excursion activities from kindergarten through high school. The *Shelah* syllabus for high schools, for example, is saturated with Zionist themes and topics (Ben-Yosef and Shaish 2006: 49–63). Biblical narratives, the Zionist transformation of the landscape, war heritage, Jerusalem, demography, and the Arabs within and outside the country – all are summoned to be spotted and plotted on the maps. To a lesser extent, nature-oriented content, such as conservation, fauna and flora, water, soils and climates, is included. As an illustration of what happens in class in terms of the preparatory teaching for field trips (one hour a week), in the student handbook for the *Shelah* programme (for junior high schools) we find an exercise called 'Zionism Now!' (Ben-Yosef and Shaish 2005a: 93). This textual exercise requires the student to choose the most Zionist image in their opinion from various images representing Israeli types in contemporary life (a soldier, a national park inspector, a singer, an Orthodox Jew, a kibbutznik and so forth) and to explain their choice. The exercise then requires the student to identify any non-Zionist image and again to explain the choice. It delves deeper and deeper into this nationalist abyss. In another section, we find the lyrics of the national anthem, *Hatikva*, and the students are called upon to interpret it, using notions and ideas taught in class (Ben-Yosef and Shaish 2005b: 77).

Most *Shelah* teachers hold an academic degree in Eretz Yisrael studies or geography and a two-year teaching certificate, having specialised in the area of *Shelah*. The *Shelah* department has four 'major' formal areas of operation within schools – the core programme, the '*Shelah* Star', 'Ascending to Jerusalem' and the 'Israeli Travel' – and one main structural function, which is the crystallisation of all aspects of Zionist school teaching and preaching through walking the land. As the editors of the official textbook explain, the programme relies upon an extensive *fabric of links and associations* between activities on the ground and what they perceive as the system of values of the school. This is created by connecting the hikes and journeys with the subjects of study – history, civic education, bible studies, homeland studies, geography and so on – according to age (Ministry of Education 2008: 9). These links give *Shelah* a gravitational force that gleans Zionist meanings from various teachings at school. Importantly, however, it is the physical experience that helps this agglomeration, pouring and regimenting these meanings into young bodies. This is shown, for example, in the inaugural words of former secretary general of the Ministry of Education Shmuel Abuab in his preface to the official curriculum in 2006: 'This programme is one of the most important foundations in the teaching of values in school, and the discipline of *Shelah* constitutes an integrative and cohesive nucleus in this endeavour' (Ben-Yosef and Shaish 2006, my translation).

The '*Shelah* Star', 'Ascending to Jerusalem' and the 'Israeli Travel' are three educational components that reinforce the core programme, which I shall discuss below. The first focuses on expanding knowledge and field experience in one chosen region of the country (for high school students), while the second promotes the touring and knowledge of Jerusalem (primary and junior high school). The Israeli Travel – for sixteen- and seventeen-year-old students – entails the preparation and performance of a six-day hike in the field, with about 15,000 students participating in this special programme every year. It is defined by the Ministry of Education as the pinnacle of the educational value-oriented process at school, aimed at 'strengthening the student's personal, Jewish and Zionist identity so as to connect that identity to himself and to other circles in society and the community, as well as to his nation, his land and to the State of Israel' (my translation).[8] Let us have a closer look at how the *Shelah* programme explains the role of nationalism, referred to here as the 'national circle':

> The establishment of the State of Israel as the state of the Jewish people in the land of Israel renewed the historical bond of biblical times between the people and its land. The national circle is comprised of three layers: the Land of Israel, the People of Israel and the State of Israel ... Underlying this orientation is the view that

the People of Israel, its historical legacy and its culture are connected to the *landscape* of Eretz Yisrael, and that the State of Israel
was established precisely because of that essential, historical
and cultural bond of the people to its land. In order to materially
manifest the bond between land–people–state, the *field journey*
travels throughout Eretz Yisrael and introduces central events in
the history of the people – from biblical times to the Zionist project – and by means of connecting the past with the present of the
State of Israel ... This connection to the national circle enables the
student to reflect on his sense of belonging to the Jewish people
and on his Jewish identity as inalienable parts of the historical
sequence of generations (my translation, my emphasis).[9]

The authors of this text, its practitioners in schools and the inspectors of its practice, as well as the parents of its students and the
students themselves, will not see anything problematic in this text.
The immoderate nationalist educational recipe lying at the heart of
this text escapes their notice, their passions and their cognition. It is
invisible to them, as invisible as the Palestinian ruins on their hikes,
where 'a cyclic, self-perpetuating process, the sensual experience
then powerfully reaffirmed our active unseeing' (Mazali 2011: 188).
The fact that they do not see the immoderate nationalist educational
recipe at the heart of the *Shelah* programme can be partly explained
by institutional efforts to wrap it in a sound pedagogical discourse
centred on notions such as 'society and community', 'democratic
citizenship' and 'environment'. But let us not be misled. In fact, these
notions are secondary and subsumed into the national ideology.
In other words, by 'society' or 'community', the *Shelah* programme
means the Jewish-Israeli society; by 'democratic citizenship', it has
in mind the sort of democracy that only Jewish-Israelis enjoy – at
the expense of the non-democratic life of non-Jews; and lastly, the
idea of 'environment' is disentangled from any of its segregated
actualisations in the Israeli public space. Everywhere in the curriculum, as well as on the lips of its instructors and educators – as
anyone who has spent enough time in the Israeli school system can
confirm – we find and hear these notions uttered with full faith and

passion. But these concepts are empty vessels serving to ornament a pedagogy that breathes nationalism, body and soul, and they attest to the Zionist democratic spectacle, displaying linguistic pirouettes and gestures that are used to explain and justify policies of privilege and national ideologies. Thus, the fact that the *Shelah* discourse is seasoned with a *bouquet garni* of pseudo-democratic terms needs to be understood exactly as that, and not as an indication of spirit. However, the main problem with this sort of pedagogical language lies in the cognitive and emotional harm it causes, instilling an equivalence of nationalism and democratic life. I will expand this point in the next chapter, where I discuss the high school citizenship education curriculum. For now, let me just say that this damage explains not only certain aspects of how civil thought is actually made unavailable, but also the falsely constructed belief that one possesses such thought.

Physicality and challenge are further aspects of the core programme. 'Going out into the open, exposure to irregular and unknown circumstances, and confrontation with the physical and mental challenges involved in the hikes and journeys, all create a wide scope of opportunities to express the students' qualities and engender social interaction as well ...' (Ministry of Education 2008: 14, my translation; see also p. 27). These goals are achieved by experimenting on the hikes with an array of scout techniques such as intensive and long walks, educated observation of scenery, use of maps, practising the timing of rest periods, sleeping out in the open, field cooking and so forth (ibid.: 27–8). Exactly the same sorts of hiking techniques are used in the youth movements, which since their emergence in the 1920s have been a phenomenal cradle of subjectivation (Naor 1989) and are still regarded as having a 'long-term effect upon the national attitudes and cultural assumptions of youth movement alumni' (Katz 1985: 68). According to the Research and Information Centre of the Knesset (2010), in 2006 about 170,000 youngsters were members of Zionist youth movements in Israel (half of them in primary schools), which represents roughly 17 per cent of Jewish students in the Israeli school system that year (Ministry of Education website). In her autobiographic essay *Home Archaeology*

(2011: 187), Rela Mazali shares with the reader her memories of her hikes in the youth movement days of the early 1960s:

> From age fifteen to eighteen, we hiked the land for days and weeks on school vacations, carrying backpacks with all our food and water and sleeping bags and towels and toilet paper and extra socks and underpants and shirts and pants. Out of all proportion with practical constraints, we moved through the landscape as a self-sufficient unit – a tight-knit bickering intense group. We could have been met en route by pick-up trucks with food and equipment, like the non-socialist 'scouts' we completely scorned. We could have detoured into villages to buy fresh-baked bread and cheese and humus. But we carried with us even cartons of eggs that we bought in an excited flock at the neighbourhood grocery store (of pre-supermarket days) at home and then wrapped individually in newsprint and reinserted into the carton to minimize breaks along the way, working together on the floor of the youth movement meeting pre-fab. And we lugged with us kerosene stoves and big tin jerry-cans of kerosene that banged against my shins as I hauled it up a steep path in front of me. Most of us never complained and silently struggled with the oppressive weight, with assaulted shins, with inevitable falls, with breathlessness and vertigo and heat and cold and thorny overgrowth as we emulated, at least emulated, elite units of the pre-state paramilitary, the *Palmach*, a decade and a half after it had been dismantled, seeing as we'd missed out on the real thing. And it was this – our abiding sense of excitement missed and the resultant effort-to-simulate – that made us vaguely, almost aware of the role we were playing; a quasi-military bivouac, marking out proprietary.

The expectation that the hike needs to be difficult and challenging enough to 'form' or 'shape' the students physically and mentally is not a paramilitary element in itself; it becomes so in conjunction with other elements in the programme. Looking into the *Shelah* high school curriculum (*Derech Eretz veDarkei Haaretz*; Ben-Yosef and Shaish 2006), we find two such elements. One is the 'young guide' service and the other is the use of the 'sortie' technique.

The young guides (*mashatz* in Hebrew, an acronym for '*Shelah* young guides') are junior and senior high school students who volunteer to be active in school, helping to prepare the hikes and assist the teacher guides in the field, both with their own age group and with younger classes. Generally, they have acquired some such experience in their activities in one of the youth movements, but they are still required to pass a field training course that lasts nine days and is organised by the *Shelah* regional departments in the summer. The curriculum defines the '*Shelah* Team' as comprising the teacher guides and the young guides, and so it grants the young guides a kind of official status. This system trickles down from the aura of the teacher guide, the complete field person, careful not to dispel his mystique as students whisper about what his military service might have entailed. As the young guides practise their role and skills in the field with students younger than themselves, the kind of admiration is spawned that shapes a pyramid structure of discipline, a game of rank and hierarchy: student – young guide – teacher guide. Young guide graduates who have been active for a year in school are permitted to take part in two specialist courses (for ages sixteen to eighteen). The first focuses on scouting and navigation skills, and in the past was held in cooperation with the Israel Defense Forces (IDF). The second is a survival course. These courses and activities might sound attractive for the young, and rightly so, but that is not their point: the aim of 'young guide' practice, as the official programme states, is to engender a young leadership capable of:

> developing self-confidence and the belief in their power and capability to act and to succeed on their own, by means of self-fulfilment and a sense of satisfaction for their contribution that confers meaning and value to their actions, for the sake of promoting participation and commitment in the school community, in the process of consolidating the future Israeli citizen (ibid.: 32, my translation).

We should take a good look at these notions of defining the young guide: *self-confidence, capability to act, self-fulfilment, sense of satisfaction for their contribution, meaning and value, process of consolidation as a citizen, contribution to society* and so forth. Is this really about assisting the *Shelah* teachers in the practice of hiking? What do these notions of self-constitution have to do with hiking in the school curriculum? The text imposes upon the students a technology of the self, an exploration of self-constitution – but one that is tabulated along one axis with a sense of debt to society (individual satisfaction arises from contribution to society), and along another axis with preconceived collectivist goals (to consolidate Israeli citizenship, conceived as Jewish exclusivist citizenship). Bearing in mind the genealogy of hiking in the Zionist settler-colonial project, this text externalises the wisdom of generations that, through hiking, formal education should and can guarantee the production of certain subjectivities, of particular forms of being. In a straightforward, conscious and unmediated manner, this text illustrates the obsessive pursuit of subjectivising practices.

The 'sortie' technique (in Hebrew, *giha*) is no less appalling. To begin with, in Hebrew, *giha* means a sort of charge or assault performed by a besieged military force against its attackers, or a surprise attack of troops. Now, compared with other field trips, hikes and class teaching in the *Shelah* programme for high schools (ibid.: 6), the sortie is unique in many ways. It is an intensive and demanding two-day journey with overnight camping during which the young guides practise significant leadership roles. The curriculum defines very clearly the order of operations and activities to take place during the sortie, from the moment the class arrives at the campsite until the encampment is folded up. Although individual teachers implement these instructions very differently in the field, it is important to examine these guidelines or instructions as a window into the 'soul of the sortie'. The first day must begin with an opening ceremony that includes raising the Israeli flag and singing the national anthem, followed by the teacher guides holding an opening talk with their respective students in which discipline and camp routine are elaborated. They also pass on their know-how in the theory and practice of erecting the encampment, lighting a camp fire and cooking. There is then a joint ceremony for all classes present and, lastly, an hour of nocturnal reconnaissance of the field around the camp.

On the second day, the groups set out on a long four-hour hike (to a specific site, with specific content), learn observation skills with topographic maps (including the identification of at least three or four items in the landscape), take part in various social activities, and attend a concluding talk facilitated by the teacher guides and a final ceremony that includes awarding certificates to outstanding students and lowering the flag while singing the national anthem. Then, at last, the camp is folded up (Avidan et al. 2007: 25–7; Ben-Yosef and Shaish 2006: 23–7). Line-ups are performed prior to every exit from the camp (Avidan et al. 2007: 24). In summary, exaggerated use is made of national symbols, field skills, physical and mental challenges and outdoor discipline; above all, a sense is instilled in participants that they must closely survey the place day and night and familiarise themselves with it. Although it maintains the same core elements we have already seen in other manifestations of Zionist hiking, the sortie exacerbates those aspects that make it more acutely resemble the arduous military trek or march (*masa* in Hebrew; for a comparative typology of the hike and the march, see Almog 2000: 173–4).

A hike of epic grandeur in high school is the trip to Masada in the Judaean desert. On the summit of an isolated plateau, Masada was built as a fortress by Herod the Great (30s BC). In the year AD 73, faced with a prolonged siege by Roman forces, Hebrew rebels who took over the fortress decided to commit collective suicide to avoid being captured by the invaders. About 1,000 people perished. On the site are remains of the fortress, which with time has become a very popular tourist attraction. Zionism seized the story and turned it into a powerful myth. This tale favours the courage required to kill oneself over the peril of life in slavery, representing the kind of proactive Jew that Zionism dedicated itself to promoting. In the early twentieth century, Masada became a pilgrimage site for Zionist immigrant-settlers. During this period, school children were taught to look to Masada as a story of strength (Ziv 1998). At some point on their trips, youth movements adopted the motto 'Masada shall not fall again'. This slogan accompanies the swearing-in ceremony of various IDF combatant units who end their basic training by climbing the Masada. Because of its grandeur, as Gratch suggests,

'Masada can be a place to find artistic inspiration, a place to discuss environmental issues, or just a place to feel alone in the world for a moment' (2013: 157) – but for the students and teachers hiking up the Masada, the associations that come to mind connect and synthesise with other elements: the biblical story, the idea of courage, the siege mentality underlying the story, the physical effort involved in climbing the steep mound, and its association with the military. As a mother of a seventh grader, feminist activist Ruth Hiller decided to do something about this link between hiking and the military. A few years ago, when she received her son's school syllabus, she realised that the programme in geography included seven field trips, and each of those trips was to a different battlefield.

> I called one of the geography teachers on the phone. I tried to explain my point of view and how I felt that the children would be learning more about battle heritage than geography with this program. I repeatedly explained that I felt the emphasis in any lesson should be about the positive nature of the subject. Should the children learn about the battlefields, they should also learn about the different options of making peace, of conflict resolution and preventing future wars. I emphasized that I was quite willing that they also learn something about the Palestinian history of the places they were to visit and what was their eventual fate.[10]

As she reports in her article, Hiller's attempts to establish a dialogue with the geography teacher were doomed to fail. The head of the geography unit at school, a former high-ranking army officer – who on retiring from the military at the age of forty received free state training to become an educator – showed no more empathy than the teacher. Eventually, Hiller's pressure bore fruit, as a few months later the school principal informed her that the programme had been changed to include learning about the water resources in Israel.

Eventually, most Israeli youngsters will enlist in the army. There, they will experience two types of hike. One is the hike they are familiar with from school – an activity managed by the IDF Education Corps that takes place mainly during their basic training. The other is the military trek or *masa* that these youngsters have been preparing for since childhood and practise many times during military service. One is tempted to claim that, as regards the roles and practices of hiking in Israel, education is the link – explaining a sequence that ranges from family all the way into the army. However, it would be wrong to understand the operation of hiking as an upward-surging spiral of pedagogy. Subjectivation processes are far more complicated, not linear. We will not only fall short of understanding important aspects of these processes if we reduce them to a chain – from family, to school, youth movement, army, and family again – but, no less importantly, such an interpretation reinforces the normative logic of that chain of subjectivation, one that, in fact, we aim to disrupt. This is why we cannot simply attack processes of subjectivation at a certain point, as if it were possible to cut a line and expect the entire system to crumble. These processes operate throughout the body from various focuses and planes – corners of life – as networks of forces. On the one hand there are Zionist discourses and narratives that are not necessarily expressed through the hike, spanning different nuances and tones in distinct social spheres – family, school, youth movements and the army. On the other hand, there are the hiking moves of the body in nature, maintaining a certain form across the distinct social spheres of Israeli society. The intersections of the two forms – the discursive and the material – bring about operations of power that subjectivise, that generate subjects with recognisable identities and dispositions (Deleuze and Guattari 1987: 66–7). We need to look at this, then, not from the point of view of the individual going through successive 'circles' of subjectivation, with the success of one circle resulting from that of a preceding one; rather, in order to grasp the power of hiking in Israel, we need to adopt the point of view of the abstract map of hiking or the network of subjectivation that is crystallised through hiking. The individual as such, and in his gregarious state, is made subject through minute operations. On the one hand, each of these operations, in a slightly different manner at distinct social sites, conditions his body through tales and narratives; on the other, they arrest potentialities by imposing on the body particular movements and gestures while displaying the body in nature. This double capture welcomes meanings and interpretations to sculpt the body, as it were, regimenting it to become organised and arranged. In a regimented body, stories and motions are now its integral organs. Other passions and productive relationships with nature, its landscapes and secrets are silenced, stifled before they emerge.

§ 'You were placed to be in the Galilee. You must not leave.'
'What? Why are all the Yemenis on the frontiers and all the Ashkenazim in Tel Aviv? Do you want us to be your Arabs?'
(Cited in Kemp 2002: 65, my translation)

Every year a few of my students were reluctant to participate in the school's hikes. They just refused. Intentionally, they used to come to the hikes in inappropriate footwear or they would 'forget' to bring their water bottles or other compulsory equipment. Back then, it seems now, I did not have what it takes to think in a profound anti-hegemonic way. I never saw those attitudes as a sign of resistance, as an attempt not to succumb to an activity that has all the aspects of hegemony. I saw their acts of disengagement as acts of youthful disobedience, interpreting the motives of my students as a regimented teacher. In the Mizrahi history of protest in Israel I found the proper spectacles that helped me to see those minute acts of resistance clearly. There, we find a rich résumé of practices of disengagement from Zionist territories from which to draw profanatory motivations (see Chetrit 2010). Let me refer to just one of these cases.[11]

As noted in the introductory chapter, the massive waves of Jewish immigration from the Arab countries during the 1950s and early 1960s were absorbed into the country in ways that structurally devastated their chances of building a decent life in Israel. It is during this period that we find the roots of what is called 'the second Israel' – the Israeli social classes that Sisypheanly lag behind the hegemony. Among other discriminatory policies, thousands of the Jewish Mizrahi families who arrived in that period were sent by the government to populate remote agricultural towns, recently established primarily to fortify demographically the frontiers attained in 1948, and also in order to cultivate the lands robbed from the ethnically cleansed Palestinians (see Swirski 1999: 114–16).[12] These families were, as Adriana Kemp put it, 'reluctant pioneers' (2002: 39). They had no agricultural experience and they were not willing to become farmers. The new villages lacked basic infrastructure for agricultural work and proper housing, not to mention the precarious security situation these immigrants had to face (ibid.: 47). As Shohat explains: 'Sephardi [Mizrahi] border settlements lacked, furthermore, the strong infrastructure of military protection provided to Ashkenazi settlements, thus leading to Sephardi loss of life' (1988: 18). But they were assigned a role in the Zionist nation-building process; they were compelled to cultivate an existential territory they did not want to be part of.

Many Mizrahi families opted to find employment outside the farms, even if that employment was temporary or seasonal. They neglected the land and did not put to work the basic agricultural equipment they were provided with. Not as an organised protest movement but as strong-minded individual *acts of disengagement*, as Kemp defines them, more and more families left their farms to look for better horizons near urban centres. Between 1951 and 1956, almost 2,000 families left their farms (Kemp 2002: 60). They literally refused the role they were assigned in the national project (ibid.: 42); they refused to commit to the territory – land, frontiers and agriculture – they were supposed to conquer. The state reacted violently. A law was enacted to compel the Mizrahi families to re-main on their farms (the Candidates for Agricultural Settlement Law of 1953; ibid.: 52) and severe penalties were enforced such as denying food coupons to those who left the farms. The government involved the police to enforce its policies on the Mizrahim, who were required to pay fines for leaving; they were also blacklisted in national employment services and were refused alternative state housing (ibid.: 61–4).

What these struggles show is that by refusing to turn land into productive national territory, many Mizrahim rejected their racialised incorporation into the white Zionist project – however minor and non-organised these acts of citizenship were. Their withdrawal or disengagement from these territories-to-be is a lesson that sheds new light on other withdrawals from landed territory, including hiking. The application of the lessons learned from these episodes in the Mizrahi struggle to the practice of hiking is not a far-fetched fabrication considering the experience of space as represented in Mizrahi fiction. According to Yochai Oppenheimer, contact with the landscapes of Israel on hikes 'does not create a sense of home or of belonging to the homeland' for the protagonists in Mizrahi novels who 'are unable to detach themselves from the periphery – that is, from the consciousness of being shut up within an ethnic enclave' (2012: 360). In other words, for its victims, marginalisation has an ideological toll that hegemony is not able to amend, rendering space 'divested from its ideological signs' (ibid.: 360), devoid of the magnetism early European Zionists invented. When viewed from the margins, the centre lacks the uniformity Zionism claims to be responsible for: between the universalistic hand that homogenises into Jewish wholeness and the hand that differentiates by racialising and marginalising (Yonah and Saporta 2002: 68–104), a body of life arises, a body that is inaccessible to full ideological pervasiveness. Mizrahi writers, as Oppenheimer explains, offer an alternative view of space detached from its nationalistic investments, one informed by the experience of class and race, that of the periphery (2012: 364).[13] In these novels, 'the "land" always remains unfamiliar and nameless', and 'for the Mizrahim ... the Israeli space was not an object to be conquered actively' (ibid.: 358–9). Detachment from hegemonic existential territories – whether as a result of racial marginalisation, as with the protagonists of Mizrahi fiction, or ideological, as in my own case – may function to propel alternative subjectivities. They convey a perception of the nationalised landscapes as hostile. In essence, the refusal in their midst disarms the possibility of *making the hike productive for Zionist purposes*.

§ In recent years, Jewish-Israelis have taken up a new trend in hiking that, at first sight, seems not to insist on the myth while preserving the corporeal measure of Zionist hiking. This is the Israel National Trail (INT, in Hebrew *Shvil Yisrael*), a long hiking route of about 1,000 kilometres that crosses Israel longitudinally from Dan in the north all the way to Eilat in the south. The National Geographic Society voted the INT one of the best epic trails in the world, and since its official inauguration in 1995 the INT has been walked by hundreds of Israelis every year. The entire walk requires one to two months, although hikers also do it in segments. It is interesting to take a look at the questionnaires that tertiary education students in Israel use to research the INT experience. I have found many items in common in two of these questionnaires.[14] In both, ideology and love of country are optional answers to the question 'What are your motives for undertaking the hike?', alongside nature, curiosity, satisfaction, fun, health and social motives. Respondents are asked to sort different statements by degrees of agreement and disagreement. Six out of the thirteen statements deal with the themes that make up Zionist hiking: physical and mental challenge, identification and love for the land of Israel, expression of ownership of the land of Israel, and opportunity to know the land of Israel. Such questions and statements indicate the presence of a certain ethos relating to hiking, something that is part of the investigators' (and hence of their tutors') evident logic as well as of their respondents' logic. But one can hardly say that these questions and statements have a universal character.

Recently, more and more parents have been hiking the INT with their sons and daughters in what seems to be an environmentalist alternative to more traditional ways of celebrating the *Bath* or *Bar Mitzvah* (girls at the age of twelve, boys at thirteen). Some agencies are already exploiting the business niche of what can be called '*Mitzvah* journeys' and offer organised trips with guides and various social activities. Hiking the INT maintains the same physical relationship to the hike as in traditional Zionist hiking: numerous family stories can be found on websites as well as in blogs about the INT, all stressing this long and interesting hike as a challenging opportunity to test your body and mind, and rightfully so. However, on these websites the hike itself is not grounded, at least not strongly, in nationalist narratives. They focus on the experience itself, and on enjoying nature. The point, however, lies elsewhere. I sense that the *Mitzvah* journey along the INT is limited in its intent – pursued consciously or not – to rise beyond Zionist traditional hiking. One needs to remember that the trip is performed as part of a celebration that is essentially understood in Jewish tradition and culture as a rite of passage. But the message of the passage, the promise to become a full member of the tribe, is actualised by means of mental and physical challenges. These 'means' are in fact a familiar space of practice for most Jewish-Israelis, as we know it from school, the youth movement and in the army. The end result is that the text of the *Mitzvah* passage – materialised through our familiar embodiment in nature – easily falls captive as being strongly reminiscent of and evoking the one paradigmatic passage in Jewish-Israeli society: conscription. Ultimately, even if unconsciously, the *Mitzvah* hike on the INT turns into one more field experience that prepares participants for the army, inhibiting the possibility of other potentialities to play out in this particular hike.

§ The 'Law of Return' (number 5710), which was enacted by the Knesset in 1950, grants every Jew the world over the right to immigrate to Israel and become a citizen of the state. In Zionist discourse, a Jew immigrating to Israel actually 'ascends', performing *aliyah* (Hebrew for 'ascent'). In contrast with other citizenships, the kind Israel grants a Jewish immigrant entails many economic benefits to help the new immigrant settle in. Demographics was the name of the game at the time the law was passed, and for several decades afterwards, but in our neoliberal times, *aliyah* is seen more as an ideological idea that continues to illuminate the way rather than as a practical policy. More than immigrants, nowadays Israel needs political and financial support, as the Zionist epoch has never known such attacks as are launched against it at present. A politically well-connected Jewish community in the United States, comprising about 75 per cent of the diaspora – and in other strategic places such as Canada, the United Kingdom, France and certain places in Latin America – is far more important to Israel than having them literally in the country as problematic immigrants. As Veracini recently noted, this change in perspective has permeated the priorities of the Jewish Agency, having 'shifted its focus from supporting immigration to promoting the links between Israel and Diaspora via the sponsor-ship of temporary visits' (2013: 36). In this vein, last year the Jewish Agency considered discontinuing its funding of higher education for new Jewish immigrants and focusing instead on 'Jewish identity-building' programmes for Jewish communities overseas. The reason, explains Jewish Agency Director-General Alan Hoffmann in his letter to *Haaretz*, is that 'while a robust absorption basket is crucial for the success of those who have already chosen to make the move to Israel, it is not raising the numbers of those making that choice' (2012). Consequently, the Jewish Agency has been working to focus on a new mission: 'bringing ever-larger circles of young Jews to visit and experience Israel' (ibid.). Although Hoffmann claims that the new policy 'will encourage *aliyah* in ways that are far more relevant and effective for today's generation', I would like to claim that this new policy does not reflect a new solution to an old problem – namely encouraging *aliyah*. More than anything it expresses Israel's pressing political necessities.

Let me explain. Although the official Palestinian leadership (representing the Palestinian Authority) has recently achieved some success in the international arena, notably the acceptance of Palestine as a UNESCO member in November 2010 and the United Nations 'non-member observer state' status in November 2012, Israel is no less preoccupied with the slowly but steadily increasing support for the growing boycott movement (Boycott, Divestment and Sanctions or BDS) around the world. Renowned physicist Professor Stephen Hawking's decision to pull out of an Israeli conference hosted by Israel President Shimon Peres in June 2013 has granted BDS un-precedented prestige and a strong cultural imprint. BDS is openly regarded by Israeli politicians as a threat to the state, and a special law was enacted in 2011 that criminalised public calls to support the boycott. The point is that, in order to persevere as the kind of state and society Israel is, it cannot afford to trust American administra-tions without helping to fuel ongoing Zionist political pressure on Washington by the Jewish leadership through the Jewish lobby and AIPAC (American Israel Public Affairs Committee). In this context, as pathetic as it may sound, closing ranks within the American Jewish community has become a matter of national security for Israel. This is rapidly becoming an urgent mission as the impact of BDS grows in the United States as well as in other countries, particularly on the academic and cultural front. Of great significance is the fact that, in December 2013, the American Studies Association courageously voted to support an academic boycott of Israel. Naturally, Jews in the United States are exposed to this growing debate more than others, so for the Zionist leadership in Jerusalem the question is how can Israel help them cope, for Israel's own sake.

This is where the changing agenda of the Jewish Agency makes sense, a change that has been defined by Claudio Manaker, the Jewish Agency representative for Latin America, as a paradigmatic change of policy (Iton Gadol 2011). From its own perspective, Israel needs a strong emergent Jewish leadership in the diaspora, certainly in the United States, with which to oppose the BDS epidemic. In his study of young American Jewish leadership, Wertheimer found that '[i]n the aggregate, the overwhelming majority of leaders in all age groups claimed to care about and feel attached to Israel, with over 90 percent of older and younger establishment leaders affirming their emotional attachment and nearly 85 percent of non-establishment leaders claiming such an attachment' (2010: 15). His team also found that '[a]bout 56 percent of younger Jewish leaders of all types have participated in ... long-term programs. In contrast, just about half as many (30 percent) of older establishment leaders have spent as much time in Israel on a single visit' (ibid.: 26). The wide range of visiting programmes sponsored by the Jewish Agency aims, as Director-General Hoffmann states, to make sure that '[t]omorrow's Jewish leaders will be even more connected and knowledgeable about both Israel and their Jewish heritage as a result' (2012). These programmes are officially defined in terms of establishing meaningful Judaism and strengthening the link to Israel by means of a 'significant Israeli experience'.

As Shapiro indicates: 'It was recently estimated that there are over 200 Israel programs, which include kibbutz work, archaeological digs, art trips, and Jewish studies programs' (2006: 6). Under the general management of the Jewish Agency subsidiary the Israel

Experience (founded in 1958), these programmes, tailored mainly for Western Jews, offer a week-long visit to Israel as well as longer ones – up to a year – with names such as 'Livnot U'Lehibanot' ('To Build and Be Built'), 'Taglit-Birthright Israel', 'Masa', 'Sar-El' and 'Gadna'. Most programmes are tailored to young people in their twenties and early thirties. From the United States alone about '16,000 young American Jews travel to Israel each year' (ibid.), while about 500 Jewish youngsters a year come from Latin America (Karlik 2012). These programmes concentrate mainly on Judaism and Zionism, but, importantly, a major component in all these visiting packages is hiking. In her rich ethnographic account of the programme Livnot U'Lehibanot, Shapiro recounts:

> Although these hikes often appear to begin in the middle of nowhere, they are actually routed along parts of the extensive system of marked trails that criss-cross Israel. Participants carry a day's supply of water on their backs – usually three or four litres, depending on the season – and ingredients for a picnic lunch. The point, according to *Livnot* staff, is to 'hike Jewishly', that is, not necessarily to hike quickly or cover lots of ground, but to be aware of and appreciate one's surroundings, both in nature and history. The hiking itself is physically challenging, but the group breaks often to enjoy the environment and its significance: sitting on a windy slope over an ancient city to learn of its first-century hero- ism, relaxing in the shade of a large tree to understand the Jewish significance of the carob, or stopping near abandoned mills to learn about the sixteenth-century textile industry ... While some participants have hiked and camped in the wild before, most have not 'roughed it' to this degree, and must adjust to experiences like urinating in the woods and, on longer hikes, sleeping outdoors without tents. One of the highlights of the program is a three-day hike, which represents an extraordinary test of determination and commitment ... Later in the program, the two-day Desert Hike offers ... a different sort of physical, emotional, and spiritual chal- lenge (2006: 26–7).

We have found these characteristics in the domestic forms of

Zionist hiking. As Shapiro explains: '*Livnot* places a high value on the hiking process and presents itself as a program that uniquely combines work, study, and hiking. These *tiyulim* come to form some of the most potent and cherished memories that participants take home from *Livnot*' (ibid.: 27). Everyday life poses obvious limits to ideological education as regards its own domestic clients, but these are circumvented when the clients are foreign. In other words, in more than one sense it is easier to indoctrinate a Jew visiting Israel, particularly if they come with a preconceived mission. In their case, taking their Jewish bodies on hikes is not about training them for the army but about experiencing Jewish and Zionist myths in a contemporary manner. My contention is that by means of these programmes, and particularly through the hiking component, Israel goes to great lengths to expand the circle of Jewish consumers and practitioners of the motto 'One needs to conquer the land with one's feet.' As Shapiro goes on to say:

> Through participants' extensive hiking of Israel, the land becomes perceived as 'theirs'. No longer simply an abstract concept, nor just another location far from home, Israel is transformed into a place that belongs to participants by virtue of their Jewishness and the presence of their footsteps. Israel is also presented as a country that has been marked with the presence of Jews through-out history, and is ready to be similarly marked by the presence of *Livnot* participants (ibid.: 58–9).

Elements from the past are operationalised to constitute new magnetic axes of subjectivation for these young non-Israeli Jews. As O'Sullivan explains, drawing on Deleuze and Guattari, these objects 'are then mobilised in the present and in order to move beyond that present' (2006: 316). 'Beyond the present' here are the political dispositions these youngsters will deploy as future leaders of their communities in America and elsewhere. Everything resonates here: Jewish Agency Director-General Alan Hoffmann is aware that 'Western, largely English-speaking Jews are not moving to Israel in significant numbers' (2012), and thus the funds and energies invested in these Jews under the new Jewish Agency paradigm have a different goal than that of *aliyah*. Building their Jewish identity and roots to combat assimilation are the explicit aims of the new policy and are perhaps being achieved, but I contend that the main goal is to develop a long-term cadre of future leaders who are able and willing to fight for the continuation of a Zionist Israel. Hiking is perhaps no more than a small cog in this subjectivation machine conjointly operated by Israeli and global Zionist forces, but it is certainly an important one as it leaves a strong imprint on the body and can always be summoned to substantiate a political stance: 'I have been there, I have seen it with my eyes and walked it with my feet.' The ideological and somatic features of Zionist hiking instil something that cannot possibly be provided by the traditional ties between Jews in the diaspora and their families and friends in Israel; it ignites affect in ways that enable people to feel the strongest connection to the land, bodily maintaining a continuous emotional flow that persists as somatic memory, intentionally constructed.

In a sense, sharing Zionist hiking practices with diaspora Jews gives away something that for about a century was nurtured as the image of the new Jew in Israel – the '*Sabra*' (native-born Jewish-Israeli) – in fact, the image Ashkenazi Jews built of themselves as the 'proper' Israelis (Almog 2000). If we like, this sharing expands the right of return granted to every Jew into the actual right to the land. At the very least, this process spreads a strong sense among the diaspora Jews that 'the land becomes perceived as "theirs"', as Shapiro put it (2006: 58). And in a way, this can be seen as part of what Veracini has recently defined as 'recolonisation', a process 'in which the entire settler colonial project of Israel depends, once again, on external support' (2013: 35). As Veracini explains: 'Recurring emphasis on Israel as the country of *all* Jews rather than the country of Zionists inevitably produces a recolonisation effect, subjecting Jewish Israelis to the political determination of others' (ibid.: 35). The point here is to look at the ways in which Israel willingly participates not only in the production of its own Jewish subjectivities but also in the fabrication of subjectivities of potential Jewish leadership overseas. As they visit the country, these future Jewish leaders learn that the command is not merely 'walk the length and the breadth of the land', but rather it becomes 'walk the length and the breadth of the land, and return to the diaspora to defend us'.

§ That hiking has a strong presence in Israeli social life has now become clear. 'By now, trips and hiking have become a cultural idiom that extends far beyond the pedagogical domains of school and youth movement; bookstores abound with texts that lay out the rich possibilities for hiking trips that are open to the public' (Katriel 1995: 11). The website of the Israeli Ministry of Foreign Affairs states that 'the Israeli passion for hiking has biblical roots – just as the Israelites conquered this land, so too can modern Israelis stake their claim by walking every trail and nature path'. And they certainly do. True, '[i]n the act of hiking both the individual and the group mark out a territory, claiming possession by use of the body – that is, by the act of walking' (Ben-David 1997: 140), but Israelis already possess the land and they control it 'with a mighty hand and outstretched arm', so why does Zionist hiking continue to play this formative role? What sorts of territorialisation does hiking involve nowadays? And what do they express? The siege mentality inculcated by Zionism in generations is looped in an infinite quest to ground itself. One channel is to continuously confer indigeneity upon Jewish existence in Israel as a process by which Palestinians are de-indigenised. As Veracini put it (2010: 21–2): 'Indigenisation is driven by the crucial need to transform an historical tie ("we came here") into a natural one ("the land made us").' Hiking might be seen as a corporeal means of indigenisation; 'Our bodies,' explains Janz, 'do not stop at our skin, they stop somewhere beyond, where our space becomes identified as ours' (2001: 397). That identification is gained through a process of discursive mediation, in which *a* past is summoned to bear on the body of the hiker; the biblical past and that of the proverbial early Zionism pioneer – both somehow interlaced in a productive relationship – are summoned in a quest to reincarnate them in the hiking body organising itself to become a soldier. This cannot be done in one fell swoop; in fact, this should be done continuously, in a series of endless repetitions, calling for a national home with hiking bodies, marking territories, as when birds sing their refrains. If the nuclear family or the closest group of friends 'fails' in its duty to indoctrinate through hiking (either because not all Jewish-Israeli families are fond of hiking or due to a more nature-oriented style of hiking), the school will take care of it. Some young people, approximately one in six, will have this reinforced through high doses of hiking in one of the youth movements. And just to make sure, the army will generously offer hiking practice that gives individuals the chance to finally put everything together: 'Oh, so this is what hiking was meant to be!' It is no coincidence that pre-military preparatory frameworks in the private sector offering expensive courses to eleventh and twelfth graders include hiking in their repertoires. They acknowledge the value of the relationship between hiking and military training. But these are not really mere repetitions. As Rela Mazali put it, this is about 'a cyclical, self-perpetuating process' that relies on the sensual experience that powerfully reaffirms capacities and incapacities (Mazali 2011: 188). This is a process that construes the range of our gaze and the sorts of objects our sensors and radars are able to detect. Every repetition is different in the sense that it adds a certain amount and modality of accumulation to the process of producing identities and dispositions towards life. And time and again, from one walk to the next, a rhythm arises: 'My subjectivity lies in the set of rhythms and repetitions I have found to be useful' (Janz 2001: 396). Some hiking rhythms for diaspora Jews and others for domestic Jews; while the former express the promise of future political and financial support, the latter express the forces that defend the fortress here and now.

Thus, the question is how to supplant the *tiyul* as the ritualised practice that it is in Israeli culture (Katriel 1995) by enabling the body to express new potentialities in its relation to nature – perhaps by engaging in a sort of political saunter as suggested by Zochrot, by means of sonic or bodily disquiet, by refusing the productivity of Zionist hiking like the Mizrahi agricultural refusal, or in a more ecology-oriented alternative, as in ecofeminism. Zionist hiking, as we saw, is profoundly gendered. It evolved as a space of nationalistic and military training. In schools it is introduced to students predominantly by male teachers (in the *Shelah* classes), despite the fact that most school teachers are women. The deterritorialisation of Zionist hiking must take into account the gendered division of labour at work. Ecofeminism aims precisely at that intersection: 'The philosophy of ecofeminism is based on an examination of the interconnections between the domination of women, the domination of nature, and the need for transformation of traditional ways of thinking' (Henderson 1992: 50; see also Andrew et al. 2005; Gaard and Murphy 1998). Re-creating hiking in Israel should therefore be about abolishing the macho-military appropriation of nature, among other things, to give way to forms of non-gendered collaboration with nature. This is not only about transforming our own subjectivities but is simultaneously about changing the earth's subjectivity, by freeing the constraints and captures that made land into territory.

2 | THE TEACHER

A mass of green uniforms hid the school administration offices where I was headed. As I approached, the former Israel Defense Forces (IDF) Chief of Staff, Lieutenant General Shaul Mofaz, stepped away from his entourage and with no preliminaries I suddenly found myself facing him. I answered his greeting with a 'good morning' and walked on elsewhere, disturbed, confused. It was the 2001–02 school year, and I was a high school teacher at the Leo Baeck Education Centre in Haifa. I needed a few moments to reflect. I was not unaware of how education in Israel relies on the teachers' body to convey and implant a militarist disposition, but I was disconcerted by physically bumping into the highest military figure in my own school hallway. I can't remember whether I knew of his visit in advance, nor why he visited this particular school. Even if I knew that military men visited schools in Israel on a regular basis, the sight of that uniformed entourage startled me.

To avoid such an encounter I would have had to teach at a Palestinian school. Perhaps this is the simple and straightforward solution for the race traitor: migrate to adjacent political territories. Why was I actually so surprised by Mofaz's visit? In hindsight, his presence seems to have embarrassed more than enraged me. *His presence made mine more evident than ever.* His physical presence in my very workplace and the reverence my colleagues showed him were the affirmation of my co-optation, of my surrendering to a system where it is perfectly normal to host – with ovations – the Commander-in-Chief of one of the world's most warmongering and human rights-abusing armies of our times. As long as I was *there* but hidden behind my own little acts of resistance, as a sort of rebel teacher, I could shoulder the burden; however, there were moments when being in the wrong place was unbearable, and Mofaz's visit provided one of those moments. As if in his morning greeting to me he was saying, 'You are one of us, son. Thank you for your contribution.' I dare say this is what shook me, that bonding affirmation and the sudden visibility of my own captivity, which I was taking such pains to conceal. Only one organisation dares raise its voice against the hideous phenomenon of IDF officers coming into schools as if into their own backyard – New Profile, the Movement for the Demilitarisation of Israeli Society. On 23 December 2004, New Profile activists demonstrated in the city of Netanya against the Ministry of Education's new programme called 'The Next Generation' ('HaDor Haba' in Hebrew). The programme was a joint enterprise from the Ministry's 'Society and Youth Administration' (Minhal Hevra veNo'ar) and the Israeli army, designed to boost the motivation of youth to serve in combat units. As part of the programme, high-ranking IDF officers meet with students in schools and share with them their personal and battle stories, and generally help them choose which units to join when they enlist. On 25 March 2008, New Profile activists demonstrated again, this time in front of Tel Aviv's Aleph High School of Arts. The reason for this demonstration was the launch of an IDF programme geared at strengthening relations between the IDF and high schools in order to 'fight' draft avoidance. As part of this programme, about 8,000 soldiers were sent to 450 high schools throughout the country to reinforce teenagers' desire to enlist (Mandel 2008). This was not a one-off initiative. 'In 2009,' as Rela Mazali reports, 'the Ministry of Education invited 600 school principals to hear a lecture by General Gabi Ashkenazi, the Chief of Staff, about the social significance of the draft.'[1] And there is more. In November 2012, the Israeli Ministry of Education launched a new package of financial incentives for high schools: differential bonuses will be paid to teachers based on the percentage of students who perform military or civilian national service. The principle of differential bonuses is part of a reform signed with the Association of Secondary School Teachers in August 2011 (Nesher 2012).

There are those who think that these efforts to boost the motivation of the young to enlist are a sign of desperation on the part of a system that has had to adapt drastically to a changing society in which the military ethos and national identity have been relegated (see, for example, Gur-Ze'ev 2009; Harel and Lomsky-Feder 2011; Levy et al. 2007). Unsurprisingly, in these discourses the sorts of values that neoliberalism and globalisation advance are to blame. There are two problems with these approaches: first, they draw the wrong conclusions from correct descriptions; and second, they implicitly convey anti-activism. These approaches rightly depict the emergence of new mentalities and dispositions in Jewish-Israeli society – such as individualism, instrumentalism and competitiveness – that depart from the sort of Zionist collectivism that monopolised the shaping of Jewish subjectivities from the early twentieth century, and, according to those approaches, until about two decades ago. But the conclusion that these new trends obliterate the centrality of the common commitment to Zionist national projects – and more specifically to the military – is simply wrong and does not pass the final test of reality, evident in the vigorous continuation of these projects. As David Harvey argues, neoliberalism 'mobilizes nationalism in its effort to succeed' (2005), and, in fact, other scholars have also shown that the values and policies of neoliberalism and nationalism may be interdependent (for example, Davidson 2008; Harmes 2012) and do not replace each other. Neoliberalism and globalisation are forms of reorganisation of capitalism (Davidson 2008), not forms of social cohesion to replace the nation state and its affective loyalties. Bearing this in mind, diversification of identity by individualist, instrumentalist fragmentation still needs collective forms of 'psychological compensation', which nationalism and militarism continue to provide: 'as neoliberal capitalism fragments social experience, nationalism becomes ever more important in gluing' (ibid.). Although I truly identify with the wish to get rid of military influence on society once and for all, and especially in education, it seems to me that right now the premature announcement of the 'death of the army' in Israeli society, more than anything else, works in favour of letting the army go about its business – in other words, this premature announcement seeks to discourage anti-militarist activism and reform. But the pervasiveness of military influence in education is still firm and abiding.

I cannot possibly give a full portrayal of how this pervasiveness is woven and maintained. I cannot even aspire to encompass the entire list of official syllabuses and extracurricular activities carried out at Israeli schools that unmistakably shape our little personal forms of fascism, in both teachers and students. These would fill libraries. My feeling is that the idea of the 'hidden curriculum' is somehow redundant in Israeli education. No Jewish-Israeli educators or education officials admit that the major side effect of Israeli education is the building of aggressive subjectivities, but this lack of admission is merely a matter of interpretation. We do agree about the facts. There is no dispute that the 'major educational goals' are deeply entrenched in Jewish militarist ethno-nationalism. Educators and officials, however, would not see this as having any negative educational impact on the constitution of our subjectivity, even if they were to admit that these goals nurture Israel's exclusivist political culture and the militarisation of society. What could possibly remain 'hidden' with an education that consciously and visibly organises moral training through an array of formal administrative units and departments in the Ministry of Education directly linked to the army, the Ministry of Defence, local and regional councils? A system that employs professional personnel enjoying well-resourced budgets – all to promote what is dubbed 'social and values education'? The main official body designing moral education in the Ministry of Education is the Society and Youth Administration mentioned earlier, but this is just the tip of the iceberg. The point is that Zionist moral training is embedded through infinite connections between the Ministry of Education's morality special forces, schools, other official bodies such as the army, and civil society organisations. They all have their share, infusing this moral training across the formal teaching of subjects, extracurricular programmes, and relations between teachers, students and parents. Make no mistake: there is no conspiracy, no secret plan. The tighter this moral training web is spun by adding more connections and resonances, the more explicit and applicable it becomes – and the more Zionist educators can rest assured that they are fulfilling their mission. This is not to say that Israeli education is monolithic. Israel's official state school system is formally and physically segregated into four streams: the Jewish secular, the

Jewish national-religious, the Jewish Orthodox, and the Arab – on top of which we must add race, class and geography as determinants of further lines of segregation (Swirski 1999).

However, the point I am trying to make is that changing educational fashions – such as multiculturalism, individualism and environmentalism – have blurred to some extent the pervasive centrality of Zionist education but have not replaced its core values, practices and content. In her *Citizenship Under Fire: Democratic education in times of conflict* (2006), Sigal Ben-Porath defines Israeli education as 'belligerent civic education', pointing to the educational dimension of Zionism's belligerent citizenship. In his caustic review of the book, Ilan Gur-Ze'ev claims that Ben-Porath's narrative could have possibly described Jewish society many decades ago, but '[s]ince 1973 this situation has changed dramatically in many respects ... [and] Ben-Porath in her implicit-consistent manner insists on telling us that this is still the situation today in Israeli education' (2009: 173). In essence, Gur-Ze'ev argues that Israel has changed: that Jewish-Israeli society has become far more individualistic than collectivistic, no longer driven by militarism as it was in the past, that the number of draft-dodgers is steadily increasing, that people's lives are driven by neoliberal and creative values, and so on. He explains:

> Military service and self-sacrifice in the army was traditionally central to the Israeli ethos and offered the Ashkenazi elite rewards in social status and political strength. But for two generations now, this dynamic has eroded and been deconstructed by the local manifestations of global capitalism and its culture industry, introducing new, supposedly individualistic, instrumentalist-oriented ideals, strivings, yardsticks and dreams; offering an alternative, informal, normalising education that is far from humanistic yet is no longer 'republican' or militaristically-oriented and sometimes is even pragmatic and anti-militaristic, as in the case of the Israeli secular middle and upper-middle class elite (ibid.: 179).

Gur-Ze'ev is quite right in his description but wrong in his conclusions. Education in the Jewish-Israeli streams has endured as nationalist and militarist-oriented, a phenomenon still recorded and analysed by scholars from different disciplines (for example, Bar-Gal 1993; Gor 2005; Hiller 2001; Peled-Elhanan 2008; 2010; 2012; Podeh 2002; Swirski 1999). True, the number of army avoiders seems to have slightly increased during recent years, and, as I argued at the opening of this chapter, Jewish-Israeli society, like Jewish-Israeli education, has inevitably diversified as a result of Israel's intense contact with the world, and particularly with the forces of empire. But this diversification of life has had no transformative impact on Israel's official education, nor, more broadly, on its settler-colonial, exclusionary and militarist projects. If Gur-Ze'ev were alive now, I would have liked to ask him whether the tens of thousands of Israeli soldiers occupying the West Bank, those who violently repress and kill unarmed Palestinian demonstrators and incarcerate children while protecting Jewish settlers, are driven by individualistic values alone. Do instrumentalist standards or neoliberal professionalism explain the actions of the tens of thousands of Israeli government clerks implementing the discrimination of Palestinian citizens? It is in terms of anti-nationalist impulses that we should understand the actions of my former neighbours in the Galilee who ardently invested time, money and energy to set up and maintain 'admission committees' in our all too white Jewish townships so that Palestinian families could be prevented from building their homes on the very land robbed from them several decades earlier. I would have asked Gur-Ze'ev, if only I could, whether globalised mentalities and prag-matic values substantiate the personalities of those many hundreds of thousands of parents who still mindlessly shove their sons and daughters into becoming war criminals. If only I could, I would have asked Gur-Ze'ev if any of his 'alternative' yardsticks can explain the betrayal of many hundreds of thousands of teachers who faithfully fascicise the lives of their students, from kindergarten through school and all the way until the very seconds before recruitment, with obsessive and paranoid narrativism. Thus, in terms of abolishing the national Zionist projects, what is the perceptible significance of such 'individualistic' and other social and cultural changes? On the one hand, these changes have helped destroy our belief in social welfare, and on the other they have forced the Zionist apparatuses to readjust themselves without losing the tenacity of their historical core values. But, fundamentally, the cultural conditions that determine the production of Jewish-Israeli subjectivities continue to revolve around centres of subjectivation and logics that induce ethnocentric and militarist dispositions, even while pirouetting to the beat of neoliberal and globalised rhythms. These are, indeed, subjectivities enriched with, among other things, instrumentalist-individualism, and yet rather belligerent.

I will have to withdraw my argument if the amalgamation of practices listed below outgrows the umbilical role of militarism and nationalism in the education of Jewish-Israelis: the subordination of nature and hikes to nation-building goals; the monochromatic character of subjects of study in the social and human sciences; the use of 'education' or 'values' hours by tutors to provoke students into adopting the right values through debates on 'actuality'; frequent and recurrent memorial and national days ceremonies that imbue the school community with feelings of grief, anger and vengeance; the manipulation of the Jewish holocaust, exploited to replace the Nazi with the Arab; and a special programme that prepares youth for

---

My teacher's cuisine: preparing a fascist – the recipe*

- many servings of national ceremonies
- ample use of symbols
- abundant doses of hiking the homeland
- at least one portion of military training
- a yearly sparkle of holocaustic images
- encouraging one monthly act of volunteerism
- two to three doses of soldiers' visits
- one anti-democratic syllabus of civic education
- assuming ethnic segregation
- use the Bible at discretion

* Mash meanings thoroughly, but for the exact mixture please attend official workshops.

their military conscription and that includes visits to army bases, a week of paramilitary training in the eleventh grade (the Gadna), and hosting army officers for lectures and various induction seminars at school. Personally, what worries me most and above all is the naturalisation of segregation between Jews and Palestinians and the indifference of all towards the necessity to change this state of affairs. The historicity of segregation as the cause of the conflict and not its result is deeply buried and hidden. Can we really claim that, collectively, the formative forces behind these practices do not continue to reproduce generations of committed Zionists?

I believe I might be able to catch more than a glimpse of our self-inflicted everyday captivity as high school teachers and students by looking into just two items. One is the citizenship education syllabus for high schools (*Ezrachut*) and the other is the Gadna (the Hebrew acronym for *gdudei no'ar* – youth regiments), a compulsory paramilitary training that serves as part of the preparatory programme for mandatory military service in Israel. Let me begin with the Gadna.

§ To put things in context, imagine teenagers who, for years, have had to undergo intense indoctrination, the kind that inspires hate and enmity. Imagine their textbooks intentionally erasing any trace of the narratives of their mythological other. Imagine them now, as they are periodically seen on TV, with firearms and national symbols, standing there ready to serve their homeland. Imagine their parents proudly expressing their satisfaction, as if they could afford to give away the lives of their children. *This is the image of a Palestinian pupil in the Gaza Strip that Israel asks us to have.* However, this is not an image but the very reality of life of most Jewish-Israeli youngsters.

The Gadna is a paramilitary educational framework established in 1940. With military conscription just a year or so away, the Gadna prepares eleventh graders for army life by means of a five-day training programme at one of three specialist military bases (Tzalmon, Joara or Sde-Boker). This activity is obligatory. As Harel and Lomsly-Feder explain:

during the week, an attempt is made to simulate basic training, so the pupils encounter the meaning of the military experience. This includes being cut off from home and civilian life; military discipline; a structured daily routine and time pressure; wearing uniforms; military activities such as field subsistence, treks, and shooting practice; and educational activities such as learning about Israel's wars (2011: 192).

Importantly, as Ruth Hiller from New Profile expands:

they are commanded by female soldiers who drill them in a very amicable way. This gives a feeling that the army is something very soft and [a] friendly place to be. It makes it less foreboding and more user-friendly. Even the drills at the rifle range and the face-to-face combat are presented in such a way that they really seem like fun and not hard work.[2]

In the main, beyond the drills and the ideologies the students are bothered with, the point of the Gadna is 'to get used to it' – to get used to the army, its language, its logic, its madness.

Cold water has recently been poured over the anti-militarist critiques of the role of the Gadna. Those who celebrate neoliberalism and globalism never rest. In an attempt to minimise its significance, Gur-Ze'ev, for instance, points out that only one sector of Jewish-Israeli education still undergoes Gadna training, namely secular Jewish students (2009: 174), but Gur-Ze'ev missed the fact that the Jewish national-religious stream does the Gadna as well, together comprising about 60 per cent to 65 per cent of all students in high schools in Israel (the rest are Jewish Orthodox and Palestinian students). Harel and Lomsly-Feder go even further in their critique, and by basing their account on an ethnographic study of a small group of middle- and upper middle-class secular Jewish students, they claim that:

contrary to the goal of bringing the pupils closer to the military experience and substantiating their attachment to military duty as a civil contribution to the state, the *Gadna* week became an arena where they practice their distancing from the republican perception of citizenship and demonstrate their withdrawal from the military ethos (2011: 194).

Harel and Lomsly-Feder explain their findings in terms of neoliberal and globalising values such as individualism, instrumentalism and professionalism displacing collectivist attachment, and hence weakening national identity. This new set of values, they argue, is developed by the young hegemons in alternative paramilitary private courses that offer the sort of individualist and professional preparation for army service that sculpt these young fellows so that they can gain privileged positions in the army and, therefore, reproduce themselves as the ruling class.

As I explained earlier, critiques such as those of Harel and Lomsly-Feder and Gur-Ze'ev confuse what they see as the dislocation of nationalism and militarism in the social field with their actual relocation, now ventriloquising themselves through neoliberalism. Harel and Lomsly-Feder even stress that private paramilitary frameworks have become attractive for those groups interested in maintaining their 'power in the military arena' (ibid.: 195). They also point out that the privatisation of paramilitary training offers a sort of continuing 'support group' that can be seen in terms of social capital (ibid.: 194). If the interest in keeping power in the military as a sounding board for hegemonic positioning in society at large still holds sway, and if collectivist relationships are born within the private paramilitary frameworks, then I have difficulty understanding their claim about a weakening military ethos, and agree even less with their claim that the younger generation attempts to establish a sort of 'contractual' and conditional relationship with its military duty. If anything, I see here a functional adaptation of old needs and aspirations that privatisation and neoliberal instrumentalism are fit to provide. More clearly, from Harel and Lomsly-Feder's study we cannot deduce that militarism has gone with the wind. In fact, we can only deduce that the national heart of Israeli soldiers has made some room for neoliberal standards.

Perhaps some aspects of the Gadna seem archaic, overly retro and dated for the privileged among the 'Generation Z', but the basic aims of this programme of indoctrination – gluing together those fragmented souls who cannot gather the inner forces necessary to serve their country – are still very vivid: the more privileged of its entrepreneurial clients do not refuse these aims, they just want to make sure that they are achieved more professionally. A look at those less privileged in Jewish society might help at this point. In January 2012, the IDF announced that it intended to cancel all Gadna training due to budget cuts by the government. Within a few days, demonstrations were organised against the IDF plans by high school students who, in contrast to Harel and Lomsly-Feder's interviewees, do prioritise the Gadna as an instrument for belonging and to gain some social leverage that may counterbalance their low socioeconomic positioning (Landau 2012). Beyond the fact that the IDF was using the students' enthusiasm for the Gadna to milk the Ministry of Finance, what is important here is the reaction of the high school students who felt betrayed by the same army they go out of their way to serve. In the 'only democracy in the Middle East', democracy-related oxymorons are the common sense: headmasters were telling whoever would listen how proud they were of their students who were willing to practise their democratic rights to show their national commitment. As linguist Idan Landau laments of this story, little can be more depressing than a model of civil protest whereby one demonstrates in favour of the ruling power and its norms (ibid.). In other words, contrary to the critiques, it seems that the Gadna has not entirely lost its relevance, neither for its pushers nor for its junkies.

Neoliberal discourses on the Gadna are erroneous first and foremost because they isolate the Gadna from: 1) the specific educational apparatus that 'prepares' youth for conscription; and 2) the nationalist-militarist indoctrination taking place in schools through a myriad practices and teachings. I shall refer to the second shortly by analysing the citizenship education curriculum. As for the first, it is not my aim to survey this entire field (see Gor 2005). The point, however, is that the Gadna is part and parcel of the IDF Preparatory Programme (Tochnit Hachana leTzahal). This programme has been carried out in high schools for thirty years now, but in recent years it has been formalised in an official document, the *Activity Agreement*

משרד החינוך והתרבות
מינהל חברה ונוער

משרד הביטחון
אגף בטחוני חברתי

הסכם פעילות
הבנה לצה"ל

**[Activity Agreement
IDF Preparatory Programme]**

2.1 Copy of the original front page of the Agreement in Hebrew, and its English translation

IDF Preparatory Programme, which sets out the cooperation between the Ministry of Education, the IDF and the Ministry of Defence (see Figure 2.1). The implementation of this programme in schools was made obligatory by the Ministry of Education through the General-Manager Ordinance 2007-8/3c, which in turn is detailed in a 300-page dossier called *Readiness and Preparedness for the IDF Service*. The 'Agreement' between the three state institutions is attached in the dossier as an appendix (Activity Agreement 2007: 265–78). Importantly, both legally and normatively the Ordinance and the Agreement are anchored in the Defence Service Law 1986 (ibid.: 267), which defines and regulates the obligation to serve in the IDF. No less importantly, Agreement and Ordinance activities are financed and accounted for in the annual state budget approved by the Knesset.

Practices can hardly be made official without corresponding forms of everyday social production. Nonetheless, this pair of formal and obliging documents (the Ordinance and the Agreement) are solid evidence that militarisation in Jewish-Israeli schools is not a passing fashion or the lunacy of some old-fashioned Zionists. Under the Ordinance, activities of military indoctrination are targeted at the three upper high school grades but the bulk of these activities takes place in the eleventh grade, since this is when students begin to receive their official summons from the IDF. Generally speaking, the aim of the IDF Preparatory Programme is to gear up youth for mandatory military service, and, more practically speaking, the goal is to 'raise the percentages of conscription', namely to reduce the numbers of those who manage to avoid the obligatory service (ibid.: 268). The Agreement regulates the roles of the parties in the contract and conveys the principal educational policies that class activities should follow, comprised of three basic dimensions: the value-oriented, the informative and the experience-oriented (ibid.: 270). Everything in the Agreement and the Ordinance is crafted down to the last minute detail: every school is profiled with a 'conscription index' that identifies the history of the school in terms of its conscription percentages, including the units to which its graduates were recruited; every school is assigned a high-ranking IDF officer who coordinates the programme in consultation with the school and

THE TEACHER | 103

officials of the Ministry of Education (mainly the Society and Youth Administration) and the Ministry of Defence (Society Department); and specific activities are allocated according to the school's profile and age grouping. The psychological counselling service at the Ministry of Education (SHEFI) is also harnessed for this effort to stop up 'leaks' in students, teachers or parents, and even the Gender Equality Unit in the Ministry of Education plays its role. Biopolitics at its best!

The Ministry of Education dossier is incredibly rich.[3] All aspects of life are covered by establishing their logical and natural connection with conscription. Nothing has escaped the minds of its authors, a fact that more than anything else best defines Zionist attempts to generate social gluing – mental, discursive and corporeal. Adapting the contents of this dossier is one of the main roles of eleventh grade staff in high schools. I have been there. It can get nasty. The space for negotiation is practically nil. Suggestions to discuss alternative paths of civil life rather than conscription are immediately rejected. Every year, each school issues its own IDF Preparatory Programme booklet of activities even though they are all very similar. For several weeks, homeroom sessions (educator hours) are devoted to this objectionable indoctrination with the aim of *helping students to feel more confident about their imminent recruitment.* The class discusses decision-making strategies (to help students make good decisions as to which military unit they should join); the class ventilates feelings (to help students cleanse negative emotions about the army); the class learns how to leave behind civil life (to help students understand once and for all that there is no escape); the class plunges into identity games (just to make sure that all have the proper Zionist identity); the class collaborates with parents for joint events (bonding age-wise, both laterally and vertically); CLASS, ATTEN-TION! – CLASS, AT EASE! Little resistance is offered by the students. The teacher is placed as the executor of the Agreement and Ordinance – or teachers as executioners ...

Within this monstrous matrix of military indoctrination, the Gadna fills the experience slot. But it is not alone. Since 2004, 'A Day in Combatants' Footsteps' has become a very popular activity for twelfth graders. Every year, about 80,000 students participate in an outstanding military spectacle in the Golan Heights, watching tanks, jets and ground forces display themselves on the robbed lands of the Golan. The list goes on and on. Please keep in mind that the discussion here focuses on highschools, but the military and nationalist indoctrination starts at kindergarten and does not slacken off in primary schools.[4] Thus, it is wrong to judge the significance and relevance of the Gadna or of any of the other militarising activities separately from the whole. At the most wide-ranging level, this is why the neoliberal critiques of the Gadna are deeply erroneous.

When cracks and escapes are not feasible within, we must look for adjacent territories or endeavour to create new ones. Escaping the pervasiveness of military indoctrination or struggling to suffocate its malignant propagation is possibly the most significant yet hardest task we might face. Travelling across parallel universes, as in the British-American film *Sliding Doors* (Howitt 1998), is one option. But, in fact, we do not necessarily need to speculate about the paths our life could take depending on whether or not we catch a train. Changing one's place of residence sometimes does the job. I was fortunate enough to have that possibility back in the late 1990s in Israel. Had I been born a Palestinian in Israel, I probably could not afford to move as I please. Regardless of its socioeconomic positioning, a Palestinian family cannot afford to move wherever it desires because the vast majority of Jewish home-owners in Israeli cities and towns will not rent or sell their property to non-Jews. As simple as that; no need for strict apartheid laws, as people always do the racist job better of their own accord. But born as a male, white Ashkenazi Jew in Argentina and having migrated to Israel, almost everything was on my side. So just about the time *Sliding Doors* was screened at the cinemas, we slid our doors and left Haifa for the Galilee. In the joint Arab-Jewish bilingual school Galilee, my son did not have to bear the weight of militarism. Had we moved to Jerusalem and had our children attended the Arab-Jewish high school there, we could have avoided the Gadna too. Balancing my own criticisms (Svirsky 2011; 2012a; Svirsky and Mor-Sommerfeld 2012) regarding these joint schools – and eager as I am to have more shared and less separate practices – I could not agree more with my friend and colleague

Aura Mor-Sommerfeld that these bilingual schools are the best thing we have. They challenge reality in the most deliberate way possible.

§ Bearing in mind the discussion set out above about the Gadna and its associates, I cannot possibly claim that the formal study of citizenship in schools plays a primary role in forming Jewish-Israelis' political subjectivities. In fact, this entire book is about the ramified and interconnected nature of this complex process. Nevertheless, the politics of official knowledge (Apple 1993) always lead to interesting findings. In this case, the official text of citizenship education for high schools in Israel helps the reader to comprehend what the official definition of Israel as 'Jewish and democratic' actually means for Jewish-Israelis simply because the curriculum underpinning the text was shaped as a national curriculum (ibid.). This curriculum for citizenship education in high schools was designed in the late 1990s, which – from the point of view of today's explicit ultra-nationalist state of mind in Israel – was a short-lived period of mild, good-intentioned liberalism. In spite of the fact that Jewish exclusivism took over this supple break in the years that followed, Michael Apple is right in his claim that the politics of official knowledge are nevertheless the politics of accords or compromises (ibid.). As he firmly states, these compromises have contradictory outcomes, so 'there is a space for a more democratic cultural politics in education and elsewhere' (ibid.: 10), even in monocultural political settings such as Israeli education. And yet a word of warning is in order here: I read Apple's idea of 'contradictory outcomes' not in the sense that official knowledge necessarily accommodates anti-democratic and democratic content and expressions side by side, thus giving rise allegedly to a balanced inconsistency. Contradiction here is to be understood in a Deleuzian–Guattarian sense that looks at how alternative knowledge cuts loose territories captured by royal science (Deleuze and Guattari 1987: 367). The differences are remarkable: the former view gives prominence to pseudo-emancipators since it assures 'some' representation of their democratic visions; whereas the latter view acknowledges both the strength of majoritarian forces and the role of difference in profaning the constructions of these forces.

In the early 1990s, Orit Ichilov defined three distinct periods of citizenship education in the life of the Jewish settlement in Palestine (1993). The first is the pre-state period (1882–1948) in which citizenship education evolved as a form of explicit and self-righteous Zionist indoctrination. In schools, Jewish nationalism was taught as a project that realised rather than contradicted universal values, and the Jewish settling of Palestine was seen as a modernising blessing to the backward Palestinian natives and unrelated to Palestinian opposition to the Zionist project itself. A tradition of banning controversial issues in class was inaugurated under the umbrella of national unity. The second period (1948 to the 1970s) was characterised by the formal adoption of the official Western model of citizenship education. The first state curriculum on citizenship education was issued in 1953 but implemented only in the Jewish secular sector (ibid.: 87–90; Lemish 2003: 62). It included the teaching of the formal aspects of government and democracy alongside the continuation of Zionist socialisation. In this period, in response to massive Jewish immigration from the Arab countries, Israel's infamous 'melting pot' theory came into being. Notwithstanding the fact that no legislation was in place, the tradition of prohibiting political opinions in class became axiomatic. The third period extends from the 1970s to the late 1990s and, according to Ichilov, is noted for a certain measure of relaxation. In contrast to the two previous periods in which the content of citizenship education was taught via other subjects, in 1976 the Ministry of Education introduced citizenship education in the Jewish school system as a separate subject of study (Pinson 2007: 358). It was introduced a few years later in the Arab sector, yet each educational stream had to use different texts and study the subject under different guidelines (Barak 2005). Political debates with which society was grappling began to be reflected in the teaching of citizenship education. Chief among them were the rising polemic on the character of the state and the 'situation' vis-à-vis the Arab world. In this period, the 'Arab minority' in Israel was introduced as a topic of study for the first time, albeit in an orientalist fashion that racialised this community. The study of democracy and democratic values, particularly human and civil rights, was finally getting a boost.

In the late 1990s, the teaching of citizenship education entered a phase of reorganisation and change. In 1994, a curriculum committee within the Ministry of Education, which had begun its work in 1989, recommended 'to create, for the first time, one unified curriculum for all state high schools' (Pinson 2007: 360). This was extended by another committee, the Kremnitzer Committee (headed by professor of political science Mordechai Kremnitzer), commissioned to re-evaluate the teaching of citizenship in Israel. Its recommendations were adopted by the Ministry of Education in 1996. The Kremnitzer report defined the aims of citizenship education ambitiously in terms 'of promoting skills to understand and analyse social and political questions, encouraging the commitment to the democratic regime as well as the will to become active citizens' (Kremnitzer 1996: 10). Alongside these goals, the report also supported the 'internalisation of the values of the state'. A task force was set up by the Ministry of Education and a new state textbook was produced, *To Be Citizens in Israel: A Jewish and democratic state* (Adan et al. 2001), and made obligatory as the only textbook approved for use. This curriculum was gradually implemented nationwide and today it is imparted by all educational streams – Jewish secular, Jewish national-religious and Arab – while an alternative version of this curriculum is taught in only about a half of the Jewish Orthodox schools (Visblay 2012: 16). It is worth mentioning that in this last phase in the development of citizenship education the discipline was institutionalised. Until then, there were no specialist teachers' training programmes in universities for this subject, so most high school citizenship education teachers were in fact history teachers. It was assumed, rightly, that the most committed educators should undertake the job of teaching the practical meanings of citizenship in the Jewish state. Today, there are five universities and one academic college offering a citizenship education programme (Barak and Ofarim 2009: 18), including the BEd Teaching Certificate in Civic Education and Political Science at Haifa University, which I wrote and developed and which was officially launched in 2003.[5] In addition, bringing all practising teachers of citizenship education into the same fold, the Ministry homogenised the disciplinary practice using various means, such as the 'Teaching

Licence', which is now a formal requirement, state-funded teacher training courses that take place on a regular basis, new programmes connecting citizenship education with other subjects, publications and many other activities.

To Be Citizens is based on a liberal approach of sorts, which at least at the declaratory level aims to tip citizenship education towards a more democracy-oriented approach. However, two major features characterise the text of *To Be Citizens*: the hegemonic and homogeneous image of the Jewish citizen that stands at its core; and the Jewish kind of democracy it promotes. From the very beginning the text drew fire from nationalist and religious forces who found that the programme weakened the idea and the legitimacy of the Jewish state. Right-wingers and left-wingers soon found themselves struggling over the textbook to the point where some truly believed that the citizenship education curriculum is intoxicated with paradoxes (see, for example, Pedhazur 2001; Pedhazur and Perliger 2004). Just one year after the implementation of *To Be Citizens*, Daniel Polisar, the chief editor of the Zionist journal *Azure*, was already complaining about the new textbook, claiming that:

> This is a troubling development, to say the least. If the current trends are left unchecked, the next generation of Israelis may well enter adulthood without any clear understanding of why their state should be a Jewish one, and burdened with the belief that the Jewish state in which they live cannot be truly democratic (2001: 68).

Well, in the face of what in the future will surely be termed the peak of Israel's Racist Age, Polisar should not fear as much, as his own criticism has more democratising impact because of the polemics it stirs than the text in itself. In his article, Polisar meticulously analyses the textbook to conclude that:

> The new text eviscerates the compelling ideas that have long been at the heart of the Jewish state by transforming them into a collection of squabbles among rival camps, deprives the Jewish state established in 1948 of purpose and meaning by disconnecting the

historical motives from the results, and turns most of the actual policies that have reflected the country's national character into the object of so much discord...' (ibid.: 96; see also Hazony 2000).

And in the other corner, ladies and gentlemen ...
Halleli Pinson is a Ben-Gurion University scholar who has published critical accounts of *To Be Citizens* from a liberal-democratic standpoint. As she states:

> Wittingly or unwittingly, civic education in Israel still perpetuates the differential structure of Israeli citizenship and the tensions emerging from it. True, in some moments the textbook adopts a critical perspective designed to highlight the complexities inherent in the notion of Israeli citizenship and the definition of Israel as Jewish and democratic ... However, like its predecessors, the textbook, as contemporary official discourses of civic education, still reinforces the hegemonic Zionist account which defines membership in the civil collective in terms of ethno-national belonging (Pinson 2007: 373).

I cannot help but ask how could you, Halleli, expect anything else? Can a society wholly immersed in a settler-colonial project for over a century, one that draws its self-accredited legitimacy from an ethnic cleansing it has never recognised as its own product, a society that has coiled itself around ethnicity, race and militarism in every possible realm of life, and, stunningly, still manages to recruit its citizenry into a restless army, a society that overwhelmingly approves the marginalisation of the Palestinian minority really produce and maintain a democracy-oriented education for its citizens? No need to rely on sophisticated philosophy for an answer: Aristotle already stated long ago that education, virtues and the character of the polity are the corners of an equilateral triangle. The question that emerges, then, is definitely not 'what might be a successful formulation of civic education in a conflict-ridden and highly divided society such as Israel' (ibid.: 374). That question is answered by the very factuality of power relations that makes official knowledge a reality. To promote democratic education or just a practical critical perspective in an Israeli classroom, we do not need the permission or guidance of the state. Devising new alternative curricula with which to demand that the Israeli Ministry of Education undertakes the proper reforms that democracy-lovers desire seems to me a mere waste of intellectual and activist time. Nor can we expect the Israeli Ministry of Education – particularly at this intensely racist moment in history – to involve 'different stakeholders representing various groups in Israeli society' (ibid.: 375). Is it really productive to demand ethnocratic Israel to include representatives of the Palestinian and other marginalised communities on educational committees and decision-making forums in the Ministry of Education? If this ever does happen, it would not be because we have found the right curriculum for Israel that can be successfully marketed to the authorities. The point is that a transition into a different kind of time needs *profanations within the current curriculum*, enacted here and now. The entire discussion should not be about perfect blueprints for societies that do not yet exist, but about how to eviscerate the present majoritarian formation. But let us slow down for a moment and first give the reader a clue about what the citizenship education teacher actually teaches, armed with *To Be Citizens*.

To Be Citizens is a massive 600-page textbook. Until recently, the Ministry of Education allocated one credit towards matriculation, namely three weekly hours to teach its contents during a single school year (in the eleventh or twelfth grade). Every year a Ministry directive was issued to specify a 'focus' of study (*mikud*) and of examination. Five years ago the Ministry upgraded citizenship education to two credits and it is now taught in the last two years of high school. As part of the two units, students are required to turn in a written assignment in which some aspect of social or political life in Israel is addressed. Only in a few schools can students choose to study five units of citizenship education (Orly Picker, interview, 11 November 2012). As a result of intense pressure from right-wing civil society organisations, academics and politicians, in 2011 Gideon Sa'ar, Minister of Education in the second Netanyahu government, decided to refocus some parts of the curriculum in order to expand the study of Israel as a Jewish state. He also approved two additional textbooks by authors known to be associated with the political right and with older, more conservative versions of the curriculum in citizenship education (Diskin 2011; Shachar 2013). However, the vast majority of teachers continue to use *To Be Citizens*, as they were trained and have gained many years of experience in doing so. Hence, in what follows I will focus on *To Be Citizens*.

The textbook *To Be Citizens* has four parts:

- a short 'Introduction' on the meaning of the Israeli Declaration of Independence as the founding document and spirit of the nation state;
- 'What is a Jewish State?', which mainly surveys the different approaches to the definition of the state, the issue of national identity, and Israel as the state of the Jewish people;
- 'What Is a Democracy?', which introduces basic concepts of democracy, democratic principles and their limitations and boundaries; and
- 'Regime and Politics in the State of Israel', which is dedicated to a conceptual and practical synthesis of the previous parts applied to the particularities of the Israeli regime and society.

Every chapter in the book includes exercises on the topics just learned. These exercises engage a variety of examples from Israeli as well as other societies, with historical case studies. The exercises in the textbook as well as the respective matriculation exams are oriented towards text analysis. I shall come back to these textual exercises later. Following Diana Keller's model of educational text analysis (1997), it is plausible to contend that the plot in *To Be Citizens* is the construction of belief in the idea of cohabitation of Jewishness and democracy in the State of Israel. The coherence of this plot is constructed through various textual and discursive devices. First, the didactic structure of the text creates a sense of natural connection between the Jewish and the democratic elements by dramatising a narration that flows as follows: starting with the Declaration of Independence, which alludes to both foundations (Jewish and democratic), the textbook then moves towards a non-negative dialectic summation in two parts, one about the Jewish foundation and the other about the democratic foundation, to finally synthesise both in the image of the Israeli regime in the book's last and longest part. The naturalisation of the text is also strengthened by filtering out 'uncomfortable' events and topics. Among these, most salient in their absence are the Nakba and the Palestinian right of return, the impact of the ongoing Israeli military occupation of the West Bank, Gaza and East Jerusalem on the 'democratic foundation' of the state, and a serious debate about the group rights of the state's Palestinian citizenry. Lastly, the text bluntly ignores the significant life-shaping fact that in Israel Jews and Arabs live segregated from each other. Undoubtedly, these missing topics help the textbook make sense: alongside what the text actually states, the staging of the 'other' is another way of learning about the text's ideological agenda. In a recent book, Nurit Peled-Elhanan studied the 'discursive and visual means that legitimate the exclusion, the discrimination and even the killing of Palestinian citizens and non-citizens' (2012: 223). Peled-Elhanan explains that despite the fact that *To Be Citizens* 'devotes substantial paper time to Palestinian views and events' (ibid.: 55), the civics text is also impregnated with techniques that disqualify Palestinians as the legitimate native people of Palestine and as potential and equal political partners, as are geography and history textbooks. For instance, the text fragments Palestinian existence in Palestine by using names such as 'Mandatory Israel' to denote the period before the Israeli state (ibid.: 55). More importantly, the text uses legitimisation techniques (ibid.: 226–7) to represent events through the filtering light of Zionist interpretation. Such is the case with the Nakba and the refugee problem:

> In the course of the war 700,000 Arabs who lived in the land of Israel during the British mandate fled or were expelled. They moved to Arab countries and to Judea, Samaria and Gaza. This is how the Palestinian refugee problem was created in the Arab countries and added a facet to the Israeli-Arab conflict (Eden et al. 2001: 289, quoted in Peled-Elhanan 2012: 87).

First move (de-legitimisation): the 700,000 Arabs lived not in their land but in 'the land of Israel'; in other words, if they left or were expelled, this was not from *their own* country but from *ours*. Second move (concealment): the 700,000 Arabs 'fled or were expelled', but why and how were they expelled, if they were? And who expelled them? Third move (detachment): 'This is how the Palestinian refugee problem was created *in the Arab countries*'; namely this did not happen in *our* country and therefore it is neither our problem nor our responsibility but that of the Arab countries to which the 700,000 Arabs fled. Fourth move (repositioning): the refugee problem, says the text, 'added a facet to the Israeli-Arab conflict'; that is to say, neither the colonisation of Palestine nor the ethnic cleansing carried out by Jewish forces was the cause or the main issue of the conflict. In the textbook, one of the main consequences of these two major events, if not the most tragic – the refugee problem – is just one more aspect of the conflict. Thus, at once and without further ado, Palestinians are textually robbed of their indigeneity, the causes of their expulsion are concealed, any Israeli responsibility or relation to the event is denied, and then the 'issue' is repositioned and stripped of its major significance. What this short text legitimises is not an institution or a narrative but a political attitude, namely the refugee problem as a non-event in the lives of Jewish-Israelis.

Let me now give an illustration that I believe fits the 'seen one, seen them all' attitude. Chapter Six, in the third part of the textbook, deals with the 'boundaries of democracy'. There, the book analyses the ninth amendment to The Knesset: Basic Law (1958) enacted in 1985 (Article 7a) as the Knesset's response to the election of the extremist, racist political party Kach in 1984. This amendment introduced the practice of what is termed 'defensive democracy'. The textbook presents this amendment to the law that stipulates who – political parties and individual candidates – may be elected to the Knesset on the basis of three conditions: a political party or a candidate will be banned from running for the Knesset if they support: 1) the negation of the existence of the State of Israel as a Jewish and democratic state; 2) racism; and 3) armed struggle against Israel. What I find interesting is not the fact that the 'Jewish reason' for disqualification is aligned with the others in the law – this was the result of political compromises in the Knesset. It is the fact that the textbook conveys the idea that defending democracy can be about defending the Jewishness of the state. The text holds no discussion whatsoever of this strange symbiosis of reasons for defending democracy (see Adan et al. 2001: 229–30). As a result, what the text transmits is that, in the name of defending democracy, the struggle against anti-democratic practices (Jewish exclusivism) is presented and taught as a good reason for disqualifying those leading that struggle. This makes sense only if that which one defends is not really democracy.

One more example illustrates how this curriculum invokes this kind of symbiotic strangeness: since the imposition of *To Be Citizens* as the only official textbook for these studies in high schools, the textbook market has had to accommodate this by changing its preferences. The publishing of citizenship education textbooks has been replaced by the publishing of citizenship education workbooks to prepare for the matriculation exam based on *To Be Citizens*. The kind of exercises we find there tell us quite a lot about what students should take into account in their preparation. Moreover, many of the exercises in these workbooks reprint questions that appeared in previous matriculation exams. Naturally, exercises are based on conceptual, educational and political assumptions that give the curriculum a certain sense. Last year, in one of these workbooks, I found the following exercise:

> As a result of the publication of internal documents of the human rights organisation Yesh Din (which works in the Occupied Territories), some MKs [Members of the Knesset] are looking for ways to outlaw the organisation and even to demand a police investigation of their actions. From the documents we learn that the goals of the organisation are: gathering and dissemination of information about systematic violations of human rights, raising awareness of these human rights violations and disseminating that the IDF commit war crimes against Palestinians in the West-Bank. According to one of the MKs, the IDF is a moral army that investigates itself with diligence and hence the attempt of allegedly humanist organisations to present the IDF as a body that commits war crimes distorts reality.

a) Indicate in the name of which human right Yesh Din acts. Explain your answer according to the text above.

b) Indicate what is the human right of the IDF soldiers the MK tries to defend. Explain your answer according to the text above.

At first sight, what this question tries to exercise is the practice of balancing rights in specific conflict situations. It then asks the student to place the right to freedom of expression alongside the right to security. But this malevolent equalisation pales in the face of the deeper manipulation at work here. To begin with, the text portrays Yesh Din as a traitor body inflicting unjust harm on the good name of the national military. In so doing, the narrative on the violation of human rights is relegated as defamatory. Consequently, the practice of human rights protection carried out by Yesh Din disappears as morally insignificant. So, the presentation of the issue of human rights violations by the IDF serves to buttress its image and commitment to its causes. The fact that in the text MKs attempt to silence organisations that whistle-blow army violations of human rights is not an issue that begs reflection. Two major wrongs are presented in the exercise – the IDF human rights violations and the MKs' silencing of Yesh Din – while the space for the student to engage in any sort of critical reading is crushed. The exercise pushes in another direction altogether: whitewashing the military occupation of the West Bank and the human rights violations committed by IDF soldiers who have 'the right to security'.

And there is more: in the only (failed) attempt to de-homogenise the content of the civic education curriculum – and strongly inspired by University of Haifa sociologist Sammy Smooha – in its third section, *To Be Citizens* depicts Israeli society as comprising multiple social divisions. According to the book, the concept of 'multiple divisions or cleavages' encapsulates both the de facto pluralism that characterises Israel and the tensions between ethnic, racial, national, religious, class-based and ideological groups. A look at the sub-chapter on the split between Ashkenazim and Mizrahim – in addition to the illustrations regarding the attitudes towards Palestinians – provides another chance to grasp how an official text helps racist attitudes emerge and attain students' hearts. In line with Smooha (1993) and the Israeli academic consensus, the book defines the Ashkenazi–Mizrahi split as a 'communal' split (*e'dati* in Hebrew, from *e'da* which means community or congregation), a split seen as internal to the Jewish nation, which is essentially conceived as an organic whole. Distorted information is given in the text with regard to the segregative and hierarchical practices adopted by the white establishment towards the oriental Jews during the 1950s and the 1960s (Shohat 1988, 1999; Swirski 1999); it is as if nothing has been researched or written about this. According to the book, during the 1950s the Ashkenazi government faced overwhelming challenges while establishing the foundations of the new state, and did the best they could to absorb the waves of Jewish immigration coming into the country from Arab societies and those who survived the holocaust coming from Europe. 'The government built for the Mizrahim development towns ... and established factories so the Mizrahim could work ...' (Adan et al. 2001: 319). In an act of textual lip service, the book also states that these towns were located far away from urban centres and that their factories required unskilled labour and paid low wages. Eventually, 'development towns with low levels of education and high levels of unemployment ... were formed' (ibid.: 319). 'Were' formed. Not formed by particular policies designed and implemented by specific white people with a sophisticated white taste. They 'were' formed. The passive form, without agency. The general impression the text gives is of people who were unable to excel in the face of the difficult economic conditions the country was experiencing (as the ethnic cleansing of the Palestinians had just been completed, the state was organising its new institutions to exploit the fruits of the pillage). So something was inherently wrong with the competences of these people, one may start to assume. 'Couldn't they find jobs? Couldn't they give their children a proper education?' *To Be Citizens* is not alone; in fact, it mirrors the general content of Israeli textbooks, in which 'Ashkenazi Jews are thought to be descendants of European, Western and modern culture, thus having acquired modern educational, human and cultural capital, [and] Arab or Mizrahi Jews are perceived as backward and traditional, with women imagined as being concerned only with the domestic sphere' (Abdo 2011: 155).

Listening to the teacher who speaks the language of *To Be Citizens*, one can certainly come to believe that the social, economic and educational inequalities between Mizrahim and Ashkenazim have little to do with the racialised inclusion of the Mizrahim (ibid.: 40–3; Swirski 1999: 165–98), namely with their inclusive exclusion. The language of *To Be Citizens*, which is the language of official education, continues the white epistemology that for so long has been erasing the racist reasons for what turned into a structural inequality between Mizrahim and Ashkenazim. 'The starting point of the Mizrahim was lower than that of the Ashkenazim' (Adan et al. 2001: 320), as the text educates us – but on the real conditions that caused that existential difference, and on Mizrahi resistance, the text is violently silent. 'Culturalism' is another strategy used in the text to justify the unbridgeable split (Mamdani 2007; Motzafi-Haller 2001): Mizrahim brought with them tradition (read: backwardness) at the time when the 'whitefellas' were trying to move ahead with a modern (read: developed) society (Adan et al. 2001: 320). The text is also silent with regard to the rich scholarship at hand on the racist roots of Mizrahi discrimination and marginalisation. The recognised and internationally acclaimed works of Ella Shohat, Smadar Lavie, Sami Shalom Chetrit, Henriette Dahan-Kalev, Avi Shlaim, Yossi Yonah and Yehuda Shenav – just to give a few names – do not exist in the language of *To Be Citizens*. The situation Shlomo Swirski identified in 1999 that the historical and cultural heritage of the Mizrahi Jewish communities has an 'extremely marginal position in the Israeli curriculum and in Israeli schoolbooks' has not been disrupted by the contemporary civic education text:

> The historical and cultural world represented in the Israeli curriculum was, and still is, almost exclusively the world of European Jewry. Furthermore, it is a history and culture that valorises the aims and achievements of the Zionist movement – in which ... the Jews of Arab lands played only a marginal role (1999: 166–7).

From the mouth of the teacher who speaks the language of *To*

Be Citizens, the racist attitude finds its way into our minds – where other racist attitudes await there already to absorb and enmesh new arrivals. So we come to believe that 'these people' are responsible for their own marginalisation, that something deeply retarded in their culture holds them back from becoming 'modern', and that Ashkenazim – who bear the responsibility of reason – should be more benevolent. Students are evaluated, given marks, and have their matriculation based on this kind of 'knowledge'. It is the pedagogical use of this language that makes teachers into Zionist teachers, whatever the colour of their skin, whatever their ascribed identity.

And in spite of this evidence, since the official adoption of *To Be Citizens*, elements in the Jewish-Israeli school system and in civil society have not been happy about what they see as a too liberal-democratic approach to civic education.[6] One of the main organisations that agitates public opinion regarding the curriculum of citizenship education is the Institute for Zionist Strategies (IZS), which functions as a follow-up think tank that 'measures' and lobbies for Zionist legislation and policies. In 2009, one of its members, Isaac Geiger, published a lengthy report on *To Be Citizens*, mostly complaining that the textbook is considerably inspired by post-Zionist positions. Geiger (2009) suggested various corrections not only at the level of the syllabus itself but also at other levels, such as changing both the selection criteria for members of pedagogical committees at the Ministry of Education and the contents of teacher-training programmes and textbooks. Geiger's arguments are framed in terms of civic republicanism, interpreted as Jewish collectivism, and oppose liberal democracy, while the general aim of his criticism has been to divert the curriculum from its dangerous democratising potential in order to suit a more national approach. In 2011, *To Be Citizens* was indeed corrected, but not to the extent that Geiger and the IZS expected. Most of the additions are to the study of the Jewishness of the state, including relations with the Jewish diaspora, as well as to the historic events that preceded the Declaration of Independence; in particular, they introduced the study of a series of legal and historical documents that are supposed to offer students better grounds for forming a proper consciousness to legitimise the establishment of the State of Israel. Needless to say, the Nakba is not included in these additions, although it is *the* major event that begot the State of Israel as a nearly ethnically pure Jewish state. The Ministry of Education did not bother to translate the new text into Arabic for the 2012–13 academic year for about 100,000 students in Arab high schools. Teachers had to teach the material from the Hebrew text and were told by the Ministry that 'they should translate the text by themselves if they like to have it in Arabic' (Nesher 2013). It is unclear what the best option is. The Arabic translation of the sociological textbook used in Arab schools, as Abdo explains, 'is extremely poor and replete with mistakes and incomprehensible phrases. In the whole of the book there is no reference to Palestinians, to the Nakba, to Arab or Palestinian history, while the terms "Jewish", "Israel", "Zionist", and "Jewish history", are well covered' (2011: 152).

In December 2012, the IZS issued a further report, checking the changes introduced by the Ministry. In that report, it stated:

> Fortunately, the awakening of the public debate helped to stimu-
> late the will of various factors in right-wing and religious ambits
> of Israeli society to contribute and influence the teaching of
> citizenship education. If this trend will persist, it is possible that
> in the future Israeli democracy and civic education will no longer
> belong to a certain section in the Israeli society but will become
> the property of all (IZS 2012: 5).

Importantly, by 'all', the IZS does not mean the Palestinian citizenry. I still owe an answer to the question about what kind of Jewish and democratic cohabitation *To Be Citizens* conveys. The common answer critical scholars have provided so far has been the dominance of the Jewish foundation (and all its associated values and principles, for instance 'security', as we saw in the last illustration), though regulated by a certain tension that arises from the definition of the State of Israel that the citizenship education textbook respects and replicates (see, for example, Lemish 2003; Pedhazur 2001; Pedhazur and Perliger 2004; Pinson 2007). Let me suggest another interpretation: the only tension that actually exists is in the academic discourse raised by these critiques. That is to say, this academic discourse voices Zionist hopes that wish Israel to be perceived as a political regime at pains to accommodate democratic desires and principles. Even worse, this political discourse conveys a false message according to which the kind of democracy Israel offers can be extended and upgraded. But there is no tension in reality. After a decade of teaching *To Be Citizens* in various high schools in Israel, participating in numerous official workshops, discussing teaching with colleagues and officials in the discipline, publishing articles in newspapers and professional journals (Svirsky 2000; 2001; 2002), presenting findings at conferences and teaching undergraduate students to become *To Be Citizens'* teachers, my conclusion regarding the citizenship education curriculum is that it is an honest educational enterprise that tries to do no more than reflect Jewish-Israeli understanding of what Israel is and should continue to be – a Jewish democracy. Israel is an exclusivist ethnic state that manages its goals by democratic procedures. This is how these two elements cohabit. Democracy in Israel is just administration, and citizenship derives from this combination. Hence, no deep, fundamental engagement with human rights, equality or justice should be expected to fill the pages of the citizenship education textbook. But this is in no way the important point. The important aspect of *To Be Citizens* is its pretence, because in its pretence we find our chance to challenge it.

Commentators agree that *To Be Citizens* is different from previous citizenship education textbooks (and the curricula underpinning them) in several respects. One of them is the fact that *To Be Citizens* favours coping with conflict as it is conceived within the consensus, to the point that Pinson argues that 'the current Israeli civic education curriculum attempts to echo the various political and social conflicts in Israel' (2007: 374). This does not make *To Be Citizens* a liberal democratic or multicultural curriculum, but stages its pretence to be so. Precisely because it pretends to be so, however, it creates a discursive arena in which all actors and actresses can play liberal, democratic, multicultural and critical roles. In other words, the citizenship education curriculum can be turned against itself. In particular, the exercises the textbook uses to illustrate the different topics are a comfortable space in which to act, but there are other spaces as well. Teachers may, should and can disturb the common sense of the textbook.

Zochrot stubbornly insists on opening some doors in Jewish high schools. And it certainly offers something to help teachers profane curricula such as the one underpinning *To Be Citizens*. This is the case with its *Study Guide: How do we say Nakba in Hebrew?* The guide is comprised of thirteen units, each of which includes lesson plans and activities tailored for students aged fifteen and over. 'Methodologically, the guide is multifaceted, using primary and secondary historical sources, films, photographs, artwork, demonstrations, and computer presentations, as well as unique original materials prepared especially for this project' (Zochrot website). The guide is modular in structure, so teachers can choose to focus on the units of their choice without having to follow a linear sequence.[7] In essence, the guide targets Jewish teachers in Jewish schools, but teachers in the bilingual shared Arabic–Hebrew schools as well as Palestinian teachers and students also recur to this valuable source in their studies and teaching. In the brochure advertising the guide, Zochrot explains:

> Learning about the Nakba raises questions and presents challenges: How can we learn and teach about the Nakba in the Israeli educational system? How can we deal with the fears and uncertainties that arise when we learn about the Nakba? How are we to present historical accounts that are so different from the ones we grew up on? How can we develop tools to critically analyse these new accounts? And how can we bridge the gaps between the familiar historical and current stories and the new ones we just start to know?[8]

Ayelet Kestler is Zochrot's new coordinator for the educational programmes. I spoke with her in August 2013. Last July, Ayelet coordinated a two-day training seminar based on the guide. This event is offered annually, and about fifteen teachers from the official education sector, educators and dialogue-oriented coordinators take part. In this seminar, participants are familiarised with the basics of the guide's units, they listen to testimonies (written and videotaped) of survivors of the Nakba, and are also offered a guided visit to the remains of one of the hundreds of destroyed Palestinian villages (typically from Zochrot's *Once Upon the Land*). At present, about 450 teachers and educators maintain continuous contact with Zochrot – some of them having participated in past training seminars or workshops, or in one of Zochrot's other activities – and receive counselling and guidance regarding the guide's contents. Ayelet tells me that in the last seminar the group discussed the role of national ceremonies in school, militarism in education, the refugee problem, and the theme of the Palestinian return (interview 5 August 2013). Not every participant in the seminar will necessarily teach the Nakba in their school – and not only because of the 'chilling effect' of the Nakba Law (2011) that threatens state-funded institutions with financial sanctions for marking Israeli Independence Day in terms of mourning (Schoken 2012). 'The main challenge,' says Ayelet, 'is to try to find the breaches and loopholes in the system in order to see how we can insert our intervention' (interview 5 August 2013), keeping in mind that the idea is to enable a certain exposure to content and interactions that may eventually affect the students. As regards the Nakba Law, for instance, it specifies clearly that state-funded institutions must not mark Israeli Independence Day in Nakba terms. However, the law is silent regarding activities during the rest of the year. 'Another important issue is to help these teachers to build some safe space for themselves, by finding allies, people with whom they can talk and receive support in case of necessity,' explains Ayelet. 'They should avoid isolating themselves, retreating into their own classroom. Once you raise the Nakba subject in class, it is not possible to "keep it quiet", so we suggest they build alliances' (interview 5 August 2013).

Since 2009, the Hebrew press has been reporting that right 'under the nose of the Ministry of Education' (Kashti 2009), Zochrot distributes material on the Nakba for use by teachers in Jewish schools, material – as put by the *Haaretz* journalist Or Kashti – 'that was not approved by the Ministry of Education'. In 2011, another article was published, also in *Haaretz* (Shtul-Trauring 2011). In the article, the author reminds the readers that in 2009 Minister of Education Gideon Sa'ar prohibited the use of any pedagogical material about

the Nakba, and that in the same year the Ministry ruled to revise *To Be Citizens* – to 'clean' it of anything that might be perceived as harsh criticism of the state. Interestingly, this article includes snapshots from interviews with high school teachers of history and citizenship education, who report their positive experiences in using Zochrot's educational materials.
Of what is this controversial study guide comprised?

The study guide is grounded in the principles of critical pedagogy. It seeks to provide students with tools for interpreting the reality in which they live, coping with it emotionally and intellectually, and exercising critical thought ... Learning about the Nakba challenges the foundations on which many Jewish Israelis were raised. But it also has the potential to create a future based on reconciliation and to establish a new set of relationships between Israelis and Palestinians ... (Zochrot website)

When I taught citizenship education, this particular activity of Zochrot was not yet available so I had to develop some profanatory strategies of my own. Two of them were particularly helpful. Although it involved quite a lot of preparation, I used to teach two syllabuses: one was official – students had to be tested on it for their matriculation; the other was a potpourri of theories, examples and debates that I brought to every citizenship education class. I carefully managed two notebooks, and always insisted in my teaching that it is imperative to distinguish between 'this is what you should answer in your exam' and 'this is what is significant to think about when we discuss this topic'. For instance, instead of starting the teaching of *To Be Citizens* with Israel's Declaration of Independence as a sort of messianic event in itself, I used to open the year with the development of late nineteenth-century Jewish immigration to Palestine, in order to set the conceptual framework for understanding the settler-colonial conditions that eventually led to the ethnic cleansing of Palestine in 1948. Ultimately, the aim was to see/read the Declaration of Independence in light of the Nakba – as the two events occurred simultaneously. Bringing one's own activist experience into class may prove beneficial as well. Thus, while studying the chapters on human rights, the debates were generally about real cases through which we questioned the 'naturalness' of Jewish privilege in Israel. Students respected my commitment to their need to get good grades in their matriculation exam. Perhaps that was why most of them were willing to listen to the more critical teaching, which, generally, was no music to their ears. Students were thus faced with the challenge of building contiguous cognitive and emotional territories in which to locate the new sounds. In other words, the critical movement here is made possible not by the alternative content in itself, but rather by the sort of communicative bridges arising from the need to manage that content. With this kind of Freirean practice, I meant not only to expose my students to the assumptions and structures that bear Israeli oppression, as well as to the profanatory readings and debates in which we engaged, but also to pose questions about the reasons that drive the state to educate them in ways that normalise Israel's systems of oppression. These practices might put teachers at occupational danger. I was myself fired from work a couple of times, but I was not alone. On 22 January 2014, Haaretz reported on the ORT Tiv'on high school intentions to dismiss Adam Verete, a philosophy teacher who engages his students in political debates.[9] Some of the students were particularly uncomfortable with his radical teaching and decided to send a letter to the Ministry of Education. Others did not shy away from expressing their support for Verete. Where there are fascist informants, there are potential insurgents.

The second strategy I used took me a while to establish as a viable option. In the year 2000 I submitted to the Leo Baeck Education Centre in Haifa, where I was teaching, a proposal to establish a new educational framework as part of the citizenship education studies in the eleventh grade. I called the project 'Active Citizenship' (*Ezrahut Pe'ila*). At the broader level, the programme's aims were aligned with the Kremnitzer report, so I hoped to gain approval by using official discourse. Abiding by the obligatory requirements to have their subject approved and be allowed to matriculate, students in this programme would have to participate in a weekly two-hour workshop for the duration of the school year, on topics that all related to the citizenship education curriculum. In 2001, the school approved the programme and it has been compulsory ever since. It is still assessed alongside conventional internal exams and tasks. The workshop themes changed over time, but the core centred on human rights, Arab–Jewish coexistence, critical media, humanist learning of the holocaust and environmentalism. All workshops were run by civil society organisations with which I established contact; these organisations all used professional mentors. The idea was to create opportunities for students to gain knowledge of and practice in civil society organisations by focusing on specific issues that were socially and politically significant. I intended the main aim of the programme to be the promotion of critical thinking. As Ayelet Kestler rightly put it, in essence, the hardest challenge is to find where and how to inject these interventions in the midst of the official curriculum, potentially to help others to create their own critical assessments of Israeli society beyond the limited and all too nationalist boundaries of Israeli education.

Opposition to national curricula may also arise from families who, by their own marginal acts of citizenship (Isin and Nielsen 2008), launch new viewpoints on educational alternatives. Let me recount two persuasive stories. The first is the story of Mizrahi families during the late 1950s who opposed the Ministry of Education's policy to force downgraded education onto their children. The second focuses on Palestinian educational initiatives from the last few years. The first is the story Yonah and Saporta (2002) tell of the relationship between the institution of pre-vocational education and the creation of the working class in Israel during the 1950s (see also Swirski 1999: 180–2). Pre-vocational education was intended to funnel junior high school students into a sort of basic professional training in manual labour areas chosen by the state. However, this course of study had no universal foundations, as the Ashkenazi educational establishment believed that it would serve better Mizrahi children who 'are not capable of abstract thinking, and are unable to benefit from any sort of teaching which has no practical ends' (Yonah and Saporta 2002: 78). In other words, pre-vocational education trapped in it Mizrahi children, while preserving the academic gymnasium for Ashkenazi children. This story is worth reading fully to better grasp the already rooted racist assumptions the Jewish 'whitefellas' had about Mizrahim in the early days of the state and to understand the historical mechanisms of social selection that explain persistent present-day inequalities. However, the point I would like to engage with is the reaction of the parents. Aware of the meaning of routing their children into pre-vocational education for their future educational and employment opportunities, parents refused to accept the role their children were assigned to fulfil in the grand Zionist project. They protested, organised demonstrations, and published articles in the press (ibid.: 86). Their social struggle, part of the more comprehensive Mizrahi struggle since the early 1950s, as Yonah and Saporta state, highlights not only the authoritarian history of Zionist education but, more importantly, the struggle shows the possibilities of challenging that education from a familial perspective. This story incites our political imagination. Imagine families opposing the Gadna, or demanding to change the citizenship education curriculum. Imagine them refusing the roles their children are meant to play as Zionist practitioners-to-be. Mizrahi opposition erupted again, in a much more organised fashion, during the late 1980s and early 1990s at the time when the Israeli educational system started to immerse itself in a process of neoliberalisation (Dahan and Levy 2000). From this period onwards, 'grey education' (self-financed additional teaching) was pushed by middle-class and affluent parents, and hence, as a result of 'the subjection of education to the rules of the market', the educational gap between Ashkenazim and Mizrahim was deepened (ibid.: 429). As Dahan and Levy explain, 'in this context ... two [Mizrahi] responses emerged: *Kedma* [literally 'Eastward'], an alternative academic high school, and the educational network of *Shas*, an ultra-orthodox *Sephardic* political party' (ibid.: 430). While the first initiative – commenced by parents and radical educators – was aimed at offering a high-level academic alternative to Mizrahi students in underprivileged neighbourhoods and development towns, the latter sought to use its ultra-religious educational network to base its political power by way of broadening its constituencies.[10]

Since 1994, Kedma has become the only fully academic high school serving disadvantaged youth in Israel. The school is located in Jerusalem in the Katamonim neighbourhood, and there have been attempts at establishing more branches in other cities. Its operational principles are commitment to the full matriculation certificate to offer an alternative to vocational studies and integrated education (in which Mizrahi students typically rank low), equality of opportunity through a policy of open admission, and multicultural education that includes fostering the legitimisation of Mizrahi history and culture. As is stated on the school's website:

> Whereas the curriculum of the Ministry of Education is based on materials that are drawn from a narrow area of the globe – mostly the West – at Kedma we aspire to expose students to the rich encounter between East and West, including examination of the complex relationships between Jews and Arabs in the Middle East. The Kedma curriculum aims to foster students' sense of belonging both to the nearby community and to their cultural backgrounds, the broader Israeli society, and the world.[11]

As Dahan and Levy describe, at Kedma students have the chance to become acquainted with the works of Mizrahi writers and poets, and equally to rearticulate the place of the Mizrahi Jewry in Jewish history and to understand the Mizrahi exilic experience in Israel since the early 1950s (ibid.: 431). To celebrate this educational intervention just as a particular type of multiculturalism is an injustice that downgrades its significance and even awards the state with honours it does not deserve. Its force resides elsewhere, in the ways in which it punches through the sticky and poisonous web of Zionist meanings and practices.

Levy and Massalha bring us the second story (2012). The forces required to initiate an educational escape from the corridors of Zionist hegemony are no less gigantic for Palestinian parents and teachers than those recruited by Mizrahim. Since 1948, the education of Palestinian children in Israel has been managed and closely controlled by the Ministry of Education through the department for Arab education (see Abdo 2011; Abu-Saad 2006; Jabareen 2006; Swirski 1999). In addition, as Abdo explains, 'almost all subjects taught in Arab schools, including children's stories, depict Arabs in racist ways

– as inferior beings lacking culture or values' (2011: 151). Central to the textbooks used for Arab schools 'is the Zionist message of the "Jewish" nature and character of the country and the total denial of Palestinian national identity and actual lived experience in the country' (ibid.: 152). However, Levy and Massalha documented the acts of citizenship involved in three significant parental and communal educational initiatives in the Arab society, spanning across the period from 1997 to 2009. These three initiatives are: Yaffa, the Arab Democratic School; the Kufur Qari elementary democratic community school; and Deritna, a junior high school also located in Kufur Qari, which was established in 2009 by Arab parents whose children were about to graduate from the bilingual Arab-Jewish elementary school 'Bridge Over the Wadi' and refused to send their children back to state-funded (Arab) schools (Levy and Massalha 2012: 912). As Levy and Massalha claim, what is remarkable about these three schools is that they go beyond 'the script that is imposed on Arab citizens by the state', and hence 'seek to make a change where the state seeks to retain its hegemony, namely in the educational arena' (ibid.: 911, 915). Yaffa's and Deritna's salience resides in the determination of the parents to support a curriculum and pedagogy that strengthen the sense of Arabness and a national Arab-Palestinian identity, while the Kufur Qari elementary school is distinctive in its democratic governance and the communal process it went through to establish that singularity. There have taken place other local initiatives that redefine the perspective of Arab-Palestinians on their citizenship: for instance, in December 2011 Ar'ara's high school students took part in the annual human rights march in Tel Aviv organised by more than a hundred civil society organisations. As it was reported in *Haaretz*, 'The students carried signs against racism and house demolitions, and in favour of peace and Arab–Jewish cooperation' (Nesher 2011a). As a reaction to this act of civil engagement on the part of the school, the Ministry of Education sent a letter of reprimand to the school's board. The school was required to give explanations regarding the participation of the students in the march. 'A thousand civic education lessons cannot provide what the students gained in that march,' said the head teacher in response. For the students, this was the first time they had the chance to take part in a public act together with Jewish youth. Isn't the Ministry of Education's fury the ultimate proof of the character of the state and of what *the teacher* is expected to deliver?

§ The last discussion highlighted various directions from which the official Zionist curriculum is actually confronted, sometimes by forces arising from civil society, at other times urged by parents, and occasionally by the individual actions of students and teachers. The motivational standpoint of these forces is no less important: reflecting on the Nakba, focusing on civil, democratic and multicultural values, bringing the Mizrahi viewpoint to the surface, and answering Palestinian families' concerns about their children's education. In the next chapter, a feminist standpoint brings the reader to critically reflect on the role of militarism in parenthood. Pick your struggle and profane. Better, make diagonal connections across struggles. Even better, make diagonal connections and proliferate the platforms of those struggles. Why? Because in these profanations lies the secret of weakening the constructive reverberations of *logics, mechanisms and affections* generated throughout different series of practices, discourses and content in Zionist education. In these profanations we find the power to shake the consistency of *the teacher*, to reconstruct their subjectivity. The point of these heterotopias – or counter-sites – is to create discontinuities, to puncture the general structure of power relations 'in such a way to suspend, neutralize or invert the set of relations, designated, mirrored, or reflected by them' (Foucault 2008: 17).

For the hegemonic common sense to arise and circulate, connections across these different series of practices, discourses and content need to be manufactured, operated and maintained. At times, these connections will be made possible only by the conscious intervention of committed teachers, educators and educational functionaries. That includes fighting against transformational interventions, as, for instance, when the Municipality of Tel Aviv required the Kedma branch in the city to close down five years after it was founded (Dahan and Levy 2000: 436). At other times, these connections emerge from proximities and intersections that bring together formally different areas of knowledge, for example the connections naturally woven by the Gadna and the citizenship education curriculum. Principally, these connections blur the boundaries between subject matter and distinct educational practices, enabling the learning experiences of students and teachers to feel like one imperial territory. But it is precisely because of these connections and the conscious and unconscious commitment of the Zionist teacher that the sort of profanations we discussed here become all the more important and urgent.

3 | THE PARENT

I didn't raise my son to be a soldier. (Women's campaign
against conscription, Australia, 1916)

Extrapolating from the conclusions of Charles Wells' brief and bril-
liant interpretation of Abraham's sacrifice, one could claim that at
the heart of any act of obeying a sacred rite lies a sin – in the case
of Abraham, the sin of disobeying God's basic body of laws. Wells,
however, proceeds to present Abraham's attempt to sacrifice his
only son as an act of citizenship that, despite all appearances, expresses a transgression, an act that in going against the fundamental
body of laws creates something new (2008: 75–8). The problem with
Wells' conceptualisation – and pardon me for moving the story into
the realm of love – is that it removes the horror that is central to
Abraham's sacrifice. This is an unreasonable train of thought when
intending to project the story onto a reading of zealous parental
support of children's military conscription in Jewish-Israeli society.

This parental support, the topic of this chapter, has in its own
Zionist genealogy a singular point that is worth examining in order
to begin to grasp the sentiment of Jewish-Israeli society towards
mandatory military conscription. This singular point is Operation
Betzer. On the night of 22 August 1948 and over the course of five
consecutive days – just three months after the declaration of independence of the State of Israel and in the midst of the 1948 war's
second truce negotiated by United Nations representatives – the
Israeli army blocked all exits from the city of Tel Aviv and imposed a
curfew on its inhabitants, a quarter of a million people, to be exact.
More than 3,000 soldiers were deployed on a military operation to
apprehend draft avoiders and deserters. Their mission was to recruit
and send them to reinforce army troops towards the third phase
of the war. 'Betzer', the operation's code name, is derived from the
Hebrew term *mivtzar*, meaning fortress, implying an operation both

to remove avoiders from their 'fortress' – or private shelter – and to fortify the army. Leaflets were distributed calling on people to inform on and give away individuals in hiding. By the end of the operation, the army had hunted down and arrested 2,764 men and women, of whom only about 900 were fully recruited into military service (Fireberg 2004).

In his beautiful book *Stone, Paper* (2011), Tomer Gardi offers a unique reading of Operation Betzer. Gardi delved into Israel Defense Forces (IDF) archives and used the minutes from trials conducted during the hunting of the draft avoiders to expose their stories. Gardi first refers to the ideological conscientious objectors who publicly negotiated with the IDF their recognition and exemption during the 1948 war. These few ideologues were members of the War Objectors' Association, and, as Gardi explains, they went to great lengths to stress the differences between the image of their refusal and that of those whom they dubbed frauds, who refused to serve for no real reason.

> They had the proper public stage upon which to voice their ideology; they wrote and spoke the official language of the rulers; they had their own stationery, secretary, chairman, and a principle; a strong and well-articulated principle. And very obedient refusal ... and between the lines they assured the government that since they are just a few, they pose no danger to society, to law and order, 'we are a sort of social club' – they affirmed – 'we are not going to disturb your business, we are not going to disturb ...' (ibid.: 63, my translation).

Gardi's discussion is not about these fellows. He is interested in other cases: a mother accused of having helped her son leave for America to study; a youngster who stayed at home to earn money and help his invalid parents and younger sister; cases where the defendants claimed to have been born on a different date than officially cited; cases of document forgery for avoiding the draft; people who pretended to be unfit for service, or who actually were; and people tried for having employed draft avoiders and for not turning them in to the army (ibid.: 53–68). Gardi is interested in the nonideological, the 'we-just-don't-want-to-serve-because-we-prefer-to-live' type of cases. It seems to me that this is a very interesting type of refusal, because it stems from circumstances of everyday life and a passionate commitment to life. It is not ideological but it is political, objectively political. Gardi's introspection goes even further, however. From his reading of the protocols of the Operation Betzer trials, he astutely manages to distil a certain sense: while men were judged for their avoidance of the draft, women were accused of betraying their future role in the new society, namely of not actively urging their partners and sons into the war (ibid.: 69).

The case of Mrs X is interesting. She had two sons, twins, late in life and was accused of helping them flee overseas for their studies. As Gardi describes the trial, she was treated as an accomplice to a crime (ibid.: 70–6). The prosecutor proves her complicity, aided by a series of letters written by Mrs X and provided to him by the censor. He then raises the question of whether Mrs X should be prosecuted as a traitor, beyond assisting her sons to avoid recruitment. *A traitor is the mother who helps her son to avoid being recruited to war.* This is the legacy of Operation Betzer, but it could not have transpired in the minds of 1948 Israelis without the unceasing development of militarism as a key element over the previous fifty years of the settler-colonial project (Ben-Eliezer 1998). Betzer leaflets intimidated Tel Avivians and pressured them to inform on their neighbours. The following was issued as an official letter distributed all over the city and addressing its near 300,000 inhabitants:

To the evader's parents!
Today we seek your son or daughter hiding for months from the public eye and its wrath. This is your last chance to redeem yourself from this shame. We do not aim at avenging our brave fellows who are fighting on the front lines, nor seeking revenge for the fallen. We have come to take your son to war. We come to him because he did not come to us. You have forced us to spare part of our forces for carrying out this despicable mission, as you were sure that this war is not yours, and you believe that your welfare and salvation will be achieved by others.

We have not come to judge you. Hebrew history will judge those who put out their heart and blood for the war of the people, and those who deserted and overburdened others. We came to redeem you of your own disgrace as it is also our own. This is your last chance to tell your son: Go! This is your last chance to atone for your visible sins against the people and your hidden crimes against parents who did send their sons to war as well as those who have been bereaved.

Remember! Today we will take your son to war. You have been given a brief hiatus to decide whether you align yourself today with those at the front or against them. At any rate: our role will be fulfilled; evasion will be uprooted.

(Army Commander for Tel Aviv Area, from Gardi 2011: 77, my translation)

Quite a disturbing document, even if issued in the midst of a war *perceived* by its protagonists as a struggle for survival. 'We have come to take your son to war.' *You will not take him*, I say. 'This is your last chance to tell your son: Go!' *You will not take him*, I say. This does not represent a dispute just between the institutions of the state and some of its citizens. More painfully, in Jewish-Israeli society such a dispute could tear families apart, and can still do so today. During those constitutive days of 1948, Tel Avivians were reproached for the fact that, while others were risking their lives and dying at the front, coffee shops and theatres in the city were teeming with young and healthy people. 'Tel Aviv should not be sheltering cowards! The faint-hearted! Every youngster should be in the army! At the front! ... Time for war! To victory!' (ibid.: 80). Other leaflets explicitly called upon people to inform on others: 'You who assist in exposing draft avoiders – remove shame from the city, hasten our victory!' (ibid.: 82). But some thousands of Tel Avivians avoided the draft during the 1948 war. So we must ask: What does this reveal? That in the midst of the nation's harshest test in history, at its founding sovereign moment, the impulses to live a civil life refused to be washed away, impulses that animated young people and parents. Yet these impulses were not rendered as the principles of the new Hebrew nation, far

from it. Sixty-two years later, in the right-wing tabloid *Israel Today*'s
newsletter of 18 May 2010, mainstream Israeli journalist Dan Margalit
called upon Netanyahu's government to launch a second Operation
Betzer: 'Year 2010 knows a similar phenomenon of draft-dodgers, but
without the shame, there is no disgrace anymore. They don't even
deny it. They don't hide anymore. Some even incite [others] not to
enlist. We need a strong government with an iron fist against the
draft-dodgers' (2010). The same Dan Margalit wished me and Michelle,
my partner in life, to be unsuccessful with our appeal to the Supreme
Court when he interviewed us in January 2003 on the television news
show *Erev Hadash*. Represented by the Association for Civil Rights in
Israel, we appealed to the Supreme Court to rule on my exemption
from serving in the military reserve force as I was the main caregiver
for our new-born daughter, Gefen (Supreme Court case 152/03). We
asked the court not just to rule on my exemption but also to issue
the army a general instruction exempting main child caregivers who
are males from military service. The fear of a legal precedent resulted
in the army releasing me, which in turn paved the way for the court
to reject our general petition (decision given on 4 September 2003).

To become an informer, even against your children – particularly
against your children – is the sad synthesis of the new nation, the existential territories of Jewish-Israeli fathers and mothers. The common
denominator is even larger and lower: enough to sympathise with the
suffering of Palestinians – not to mention to support their struggle – to
become a pariah within one's own family. Operation Betzer was the
event that expressed a principle already at work in Jewish society of
the 1940s. It did not sow the seeds of a new mentality. It only made
sure that *this kind of parenting* is the one around which that society
is tightly coiled. In 2011, Israeli Labour Party leader, MK (Knesset
Member) Shelly Yachimovich, told *Haaretz* how proud she was of her
son for serving in the army (Weitz 2011). But hers is just a standard
statement, no more than voicing the obvious, the voice of the cultural
infrastructure of Jewish-Israeli society. As Kimmerling rightly stated,
the military experience is the strongest, most continuous and most
widespread sociological common existence of all Jewish-Israelis (1993:
124; see also Ben-Eliezer 1998; Carmi and Rosenfeld 1989). 'Whether

we like it or not – we are a profound militarist society, and this militarism is also the central organising principle around which the Israeli society moves, acts, defines its boundaries, its identity and its customary rules of the game' (Kimmerling 1993: 124).

Parenthood becomes Abrahamic as long as it does not withdraw from the social obligation to turn progenies into soldiers-to-be. The foetus has almost no chance. The first garrison is the hospital and the first narrative is nationalist pro-natalism (Sperling 2010). As Enloe says, 'militarizing motherhood often starts with conceptualizing the womb as a recruiting station' (2000: 248). Conceived as a corporeal contribution to the general national project, the act of giving birth is closely supervised by the state's maternity policies. In that vein, legislation in Israel awards a 'birth grant' on condition that the mother is hospitalised. Moreover, as Morgenstern-Leissner explains, 'by covering the medical costs of only those women who give birth in hospital, the Law rendered out-of-hospital birth alternatives out of reach to all but the few who could afford to pay for their own care ... in this system, it is difficult to describe hospital birth as anything but *obligatory*' (2006: 215, emphasis added). Thus, the new-born child has the hospital as its first mandatory station.

The foetus has almost no chance because Abrahamic parenthood requires nothing, just to go with the flow. The Abrahamic type of parenthood is therefore silent, ordinary, self-evident, obvious. It is not a task you need to be aware of in order to execute it; no decision is needed. It is part of Jewish-Israeli parental wiring. For instance, parents' silence in the face of the intense military indoctrination at school, explains Mazali, only reflects the degree to which the army and war are normal phenomena in Jewish-Israeli society (2005). Ordinary chats at home about experiences in the military – generally initiated by the males in the family – are another everyday occurrence that play a dangerous role. These stories sow in the children curiosity, enthusiasm and eagerness to become protagonists in similar stories. Ezrahi speaks of these stories as the 'poisonous milk', the tales fathers tell their children about the military; however, contrary to Ezrahi, I do not think these stories become poisonous only when they are about 'the great heroic wars they or their fathers fought, in which glorious warriors sacrificed their lives' (1997: 118). The poison is transmitted to the children by the *telling* itself, regardless of its glorious content. A story fragment from basic training, an anecdote about the friends we made in the service, an explanation about weaponry we learned to operate – anything is good enough to do the work, to pass on to the children our world of images and sounds of which they will partake in their turn, just like the other roles that children are socialised to perform in their adulthood. It is the telling itself, the speech act, that instils in the children the sense that *they are the next in line*. These stories bestow on children's minds and bodies new attributes, new anxieties and new expectations; their participation in these family chats transforms children into subjects who absorb – both consciously and unconsciously, with both enthusiasm and fear – a social obligation that wasn't theirs before. The stories, along with other related components, establish a pattern of uninterrupted succession through which a particular sense of society subsists. Importantly, these are family talks, but inseparably enveloped by a social character (Deleuze and Guattari 1987: 79–82) – in other words, as much as they shape children's vocabulary, including the use of acronyms and slang characteristic of the Israeli army, imagery and a specific set of meanings, they help to re-create the social world of the interlocutors. What turns this telling of military experiences into a regular life routine is the combination of: 1) *its taking place at everyday moments* – in the course of a family meal or a rest, while driving, or during leisure time; and 2) *its being told along with stories about everyday moments* – a talk about what has happened on that particular day at school or at work, or interrupted by some murmuring about utility bills, or raised while discussing the argument we had yesterday with our neighbour. Absolutely nothing is extraordinary about the circumstances in which these military tales fill the rooms of the house with their concealed violence.

Eventually, the military stories and the conversations about the army become just another component in the general menu of life. They become part of what is regular and normal for Jewish-Israelis. The same can be said about the impact of annual military reserves duty. As Helman explains, 'the reserves system is considered one of the central mechanisms that enable the Israeli army to maintain a reservoir of trained soldiers while routine civilian activities are pursued' (1997: 310). In many Jewish-Israeli homes, children see their fathers almost every year leaving for periods ranging from a week to a month to serve in the army reserves.[1] They see them coming back with their uniform and weapon; as they pathetically wrap themselves up in the role of hero, their children witness their unambiguous expectation to be indulged with care and attention when back home on leave; they see the responsibility for accepting, adapting and cooperating with the convulsion that reserves duty inflicts upon the family's normal routine frequently falling solely on their mother's shoulders. But there is more to that gendered division of labour than meets the eye. 'Patriotic mothering', to use Cynthia Enloe's expression (2000), cannot be disjointed from the fact that most secular Jewish women in Israel serve a period of two years in compulsory military service. 'Mothers of male soldiers and women as soldiers can converge in the minds of male military manpower planners' (ibid.: 244), to form one more category to peddle recruitment. In spite of the fact that their service is considered to be of less value than that of males, the fatal significance of their service is that it makes military service not the exclusive business of the macho figure. 'Mum has served in the army, you know?' Women's conscription normalises military service in the sense that it demystifies the military as a space belonging only to courageous, muscular young men, and it does this enough to make it a place for all. 'If mum has also served in the army, you can serve too, like everyone else, you know?' Enloe, again, states that 'principally, militarizers seem to believe that if women cannot be controlled effectively, men's participation in the militarizing enterprise cannot be guaranteed' (ibid.: 294). Simply put, the militarisation of women and of their roles as mothers is crucial for the whole process of militarisation to root itself as a normal way of existing.

> Yet, when motherhood's militarization is resisted, when mothers refuse to believe that mothering is made easier by their child's fascination with real or make-believe weapons, then militarization within a society becomes very difficult to achieve (ibid.: 10).

Children do not necessarily admire the image of their father as a soldier, and uniforms and weapons do not necessarily incite their imagination positively, but if they accept their fate as eventually following in their fathers' and mothers' footsteps, it is not necessarily because of the glory and the grandeur with which these militarist images are imbued; rather, a more precise explanation would be the images' regularity and predictability. As Enloe says, 'militarization is such a pervasive process, and thus so hard to uproot, precisely because in its everyday forms it scarcely looks life threatening' (ibid.: 3). Eventually, children understand that the army is just another normal circle of life in their society.

One does not need to become an informer in the strict sense, as in Operation Betzer, to hand one's children over to society. We betray them on a daily basis when we silence our voices in the face of the countless practices of military indoctrination at school and in the youth movement, when we repeatedly comply with military nostalgia and with the annual tours of duty, either as fathers-soldiers or as mothers who accept their role of keeping alive the familial system that enables the males to serve. As the Israeli feminist journalist and critic Tsafi Sa'ar asks:

> How is it possible that mothers who carry [their child] in their womb for nine months, give birth to him and raise him with love and more than once with fear, become sad on many occasions when he is sad, and joyful when he is happy – do not strongly oppose when he reaches eighteen, when he enlists in the army? That is to say, how is it possible that they do not oppose their child being sent to that place where there is a real risk to his life? Why do they not struggle, scream, do whatever it takes to avoid it? (2011).

But the whole cycle of Israeli life is infected with processes through which children become subjects malleable enough to comply with military obligation, at the same time becoming increasingly stratified in ways that prevent their engagement in a civil imagery of refusal. Reflecting on her son's conscription, Rela Mazali unbinds her torment:

I held myself guilty, deeply and irreversibly guilty, for creating part of the conditions leading to his choice to enlist. To join a military that stood to endanger him his life his body his soul unjustifiably and unnecessarily. To enlist in an army that is doing a deed which I believe to be immoral. My conviction that he was consenting to a useless, mindless risk was only a case I could plea, spell out, repeat. He even agreed with me to some extent but opted for the army anyway. Just days before his conscription date, in a conversation about his choice, he said with an ironic smile, 'Ima, what a motivational talk you're treating me to'. Understanding and rejecting simultaneously. But I could still go on openly bringing up my belief that the army was doing immoral wrong throughout his term of duty (2011: 190–1).

Children are symbolically recruited before their actual recruitment: 'before they officially join the army, they are designed to feel that they are really in the army and are being prepared for combat' (Givol et al. 2004: 17). Kimmerling defined these symbolic and affective routine sociabilities using the term 'cognitive militarism', in an attempt to explain the penetration of militarism into the cultural state of mind of a society (1993: 129–30). But I would like to emphasise that the real challenge Israeli militarism poses resides in the fact that its location within the Jewish-Israeli cultural state of mind cannot be pinpointed, as its roles and significances have become indistinguishable from all other everyday social roles and significances. Militarist behaviour, attitudes and dispositions are not something one acquires by attending specialist workshops at school; one does not need to incorporate them through special training; they just grow in most Jewish-Israeli bodies together with all other fundamental kinds of behaviour and capacities. In other words, the strength of militarism in Israel rests on its capacity to be unfelt, to become imperceptible. Unlike Kimmerling and other critical Israeli sociologists (such as Ben-Eliezer 1998), I prefer not to define Jewish-Israeli society as a 'mobilised society'. The problem with this perception is that it retains the idea of mobilisation not as a process but as an act, attributed to a particular moment and in order to accomplish an exceptional and irregular social task, as if they were claiming that 'we are now mobilised, we are now assembled together to cope with a particular reality imposed on us; this is not what we do regularly'. This perception of mobilisation implies that the process is relatively reversible and that its mutability might be accelerated, for instance, by liberal and neoliberal openings in civil society (see, for example, Ben-Ari et al. 2001; Peled and Ophir 2001). I believe it is more accurate to speak of Jewish-Israeli society as a social body that in the continuing reconstitution of its normality and stability has so far managed to assimilate civil society governmentalities and practices into its military axiomatics. Furthermore, 'mobilisation' here works to hone a non-existent distinction between the military and civil society. My point is that the adoption of the military–civil society split as a prism for looking at changes is simply misplaced. The litmus test is *normality* and *continuity*, how this pair is constituted and how it is challenged.

Recent studies try to show that two factors – individualism and the family's growing involvement in the Israeli military – are shrinking the pervasiveness of militarism in Israeli society. Family involvement is analysed mainly from two directions: on the one hand, by looking into calls for greater civilian observation of the process of conscription and of the mandatory service itself; and, on the other, through the voices of political groups calling into question the army's military war choices (Herzog 2004). As part of the first category, a wide range of practices has emerged: draft guides written by fathers and representatives of the military, books written by mothers, call-in radio programmes, organised visits to military bases, providing children with services and support that are supposed to be made available by the military, and so forth – all of which illustrate the unwillingness of families to blindly trust the army's professionalism (ibid.: 11–23; see also Katriel 1991). However, I claim that this growing involvement of parents in the military cannot be seen as a challenge to the infrastructure of and the commitment to conscription. Rather, it attests to an increasing negotiation of roles in the performance of functions that produce soldier subjectivities. Katriel, for instance, rightly claims that these parental practices of involvement and support neutralise potential political issues relating more generally to the service or the army (ibid.: 71–91). This involvement, perhaps as Herzog claims, blurs to some extent the boundaries of the traditional division of labour between the army and the family; however, the important point is that these exchanges built around care and support deepen our attachment to military life and to the military bond by multiplying the points of subjectivation within the matrix of relationships that produce soldier subjectivities. These changes are therefore no more than internal negotiations that are not primarily aimed at challenging the general structure of conscription. Similar claims can be made about the argument that individualism is shifting the military bond from one of compulsion into more contractual waters (see, for example, Levy et al. 2007). This claim has been refuted (see, for example, Sasson-Levy 2006), the argument being that Israeli militarism adapts itself to developments coming from society at large and hence survives. I am not criticising parental care for children in the army; rather, I am trying to say that the actualisation of parental care as a neoliberal and individualist mechanism keeps at bay any negotiation of the structure of conscription itself. Therefore, it sophisticates and does not contest the type of social relationships working at home prior to conscription: love and care for children are concomitant with – and accomplices of – Israel's militarism. This is the essence of Abrahamic parenthood.

Parents prepare their children to go into the army as they prepare them for school, as they care for them as they attend social activities, as they love them in everyday life, as they play with them. 'One day you will be a soldier' (*I thought I already was one*). It is Abrahamic because such everyday parental care urges the child's body to engage in a transformation, a becoming that places the body on the altar. Only circumstances determine whether that placing on the altar will fully materialise as a carnal sacrifice or merely impose a psychological and behavioural toll. Either way, the point is that we walk them into what is perceived as merely one more customary thing we do as parents in our society. Parents are 'the army's secret task force', as Ruth Hiller, a New Profile activist put it: 'they are probably the largest indoctrinated sector of Israeli public and work very hard at perpetuating the war machine whether they realize it or not'.[2] During my life in Israel I have had the chance to meet many left-wing Zionist activists for peace who, unlike Ruth Hiller, felt assured that as long as we were still working to bring about peace, it would be reckless to renounce the military. The way in which the latter precludes the former always escaped their minds. It is Abrahamic because it uses children as agents through which Jewish-Israeli society 'reinforces the social cohesion of its adult, parent members' (Mazali 1998). Children on the altar of the military continually reaffirm society's *munus*, the 'substance that is produced by their union' (Esposito 2010a: 2). Children on the altar establish a reciprocal bond between those staging the sacrifice and the future generation, forming a union and so founding a people. By placing them on the altar, parents enact 'their practical acceptance of the rules and the underlying principles implemented through such social constructs' (Mazali 1998).

Parents do not escape the shadow of the altar: it is always present. On the one hand there is the natural parental fear for the son or daughter who serves in an army that for about six decades has entertained society with wars, ethnic cleansing and oppression. On the other hand, these parents submit to a rite that is carefully constructed, construed and introjected as a natural debt to the nation. As long as the latter takes precedence over the former, nothing will save us. As Mazali explains, 'parents who have to consent to endanger their sons' lives must be motivated by the beliefs and myths of their society' (1995: 694). It is Abrahamic because, in this parenthood, fear about the child's fate does not beget a retreat, an act of refusal. Rather, this fear is internalised in the form of another fear, motivated by state machinery that makes us all feel insecure, fearing the fact that 'we' are surrounded forevermore by enemies, and hence we must remain committed to our military obligation. Thus, parents conserve and experience a continuous dread relating to the military service of their children, but this fear is blurred by and confused with the nationalist-induced imagined fear of the Arabs inculcated in our minds and bodies for a whole century. Therefore, it is through the transposition of fears that the natural parental desire to protect our children dissipates, and, as a result, any vestiges of our refusal to comply with the state and the army are stifled. There are active Abrahamic parents, while others are more passive. The former explicitly shove their children not only into serving but also into giving 'significant service'; blind and irresponsible enthusiasm qualifies their attitude. Others just let it be. Through different emotional routes, both forms enhance the chances of having their children recruited. In more ways than one, both forms feed upon the kind of education they can count on to make their children's bodies flexible enough to bend. Education and parenthood make the communal obligation to multiply its magnetic power and to keep moving forward into a *historical storm* that refuses to be quelled.

> We prepare them by teaching them that Israel can only survive if it has the strongest army. We teach them that the Arab nations are always our enemy and that their strongest desire is to push us into the sea. We teach them that heroism in the name of Israel is the highest aspiration. We teach them that a dead soldier is always a hero. We glorify this loss of life and intertwine it in our folksongs and literature. We turn our monuments to the fallen into active community centers for encouraging culture and sports activities. Instead of learning from these painful experiences and how to preserve life, we commemorate and exalt death (Ruth Hiller, New Profile).[3]

This last text helps stress the claim that the abstract division between public and private is superfluous at best, and ideological at worst. Paraphrasing Louis Althusser from his *Lenin and Philosophy and Other Essays* (1971), the distinction between the public and the private is a distinction internal to dominant groups and valid in the domains in which hegemony exercises its authority. This is what distinguishes modern life: the state functions as a 'resonance chamber for private as well as public powers' (Deleuze and Guattari 1987: 536, note 6). As far as they concern the production of nationalist and militarist subjectivities in Jewish-Israeli society, the social spheres of the family, education and the army need to be seen through their prolific cooperative relationships of resonance: the waves (expressions) they generate superimpose and intensify the general penetration and impact of the system. The theoretical insistence on understanding society through the divisions between the public (education and the army) and the private (the family) ignores the realm of production of subjectivities that brings all these spheres together. The private is an extension of the public, just as the public is an extension of the private. They come into contact and merge through the functions that produce subjects. The two realms operate according to different discourses, practices and gestures, but their cooperative political industry of subjectivities is what synthesises their relationships. We do not move from home to school to army in discrete segments; we inhabit all these spheres simultaneously because of their concentric association. We may think we are at school or at home, but we are becoming soldiers; we are becoming exclusivist citizens – 'Chosen People' – we are becoming Zionists. Perhaps it is time to update the feminist axiom 'the personal is political' and to state that 'the complicity of social spheres is political'. This is why, strategically, the subversion of gendered relations of power (or any sort of relations of power) must take a broad spatial account of practices across all social spheres.

§ Corporal Gilad Shalit was captured by a Hamas commando in June 2006 and released back to Israel in October 2011. During his captivity, people were divided on the subject of the 'price' that the Israeli government should pay for his release. Apart from the ritual opposition of bereaved families to exchanging captive soldiers for Palestinians who were found guilty of killing Israelis, many thought that Shalit was not a proper combat fighter and literally surrendered without a fight, implying that he was less worthy than others of redemption. In August 2009, Gilad's sister Hadas, reaching the age for mandatory conscription, joined the army. Her parents did not hide their pride, nor did her friends or other relatives. The Hebrew-speaking media applauded. Noam, her father, said on the day of her recruitment: 'We did not want to let Gilad's abduction harm our other children; they continue with their lives, excel at their studies, and they do what other children do at their age.'[4] But this is mere appearance. The abduction *did* change the Shalits' life. The period of Gilad's captivity was a nightmare for them; everything changed in their everyday lives. And yet why didn't you, Noam, want Gilad's abduction to change your parental care and priorities regarding the military? Shouldn't it have affected you in ways that made you rethink those priorities? One child captive and nothing seemed to prevent another from conscription: the sacred – conscription into the Zionist army – thus remained sacred for the Shalit family. At the time when Hadas was recruited, the Israeli government seemed not to be making all possible efforts to negotiate Gilad's release with Hamas; Hadas' conscription therefore needs to be seen as a ratification of Gilad's sacrifice. What exactly does an average Jewish family in Israel need to experience in order to slide through the crack that makes refusal a possibility, and in turn makes non-militarist parenthood a possible route? Nevertheless, 'the pressure to see good mothering as patriotic mothering is difficult – and even risky – to resist' (Enloe 2000: 11), and the same can be said about the perception of good fathering in Jewish-Israeli society. So another option was possibly at work in the Shalit case. We may assume that the Shalits were indeed affected by their son's abduction in ways that traumatised their social beliefs. Some of this was even made explicit during the five years of pressure they exerted through their lobbying of the Israeli government. The public campaign to negotiate Gilad's release turned more confrontational from July 2008, after the coffins of two Israeli soldiers who had been held captive in south Lebanon were returned to Israel. Helped by a public relations firm, the Shalits intensified their protest; the media covered it extensively and supported their campaigns. Many acts of public support were organised, including the pitching of a protest tent opposite the prime minister's home at the culmination of a twelve-day march in which approximately 200,000 people participated. Noam and Aviva (Gilad's mother) lived in the tent for a year, until the government authorised the deal with Hamas that brought about Gilad's release. Protest was explicit. In one interview in 2010, Gilad's mother commented that 'no one teaches mothers what to feel and how to react when their son is abducted' (Weltzer 2010). Nevertheless, the Shalits supported their daughter's conscription. We might speculate that going against the grain in the case of Gilad's sister's conscription would have compromised the public support that the family received while pressuring the government to pursue a deal with Hamas. We might speculate that remaining loyal to Zionist lunacy – that is to say, giving their daughter to the military – was the proper price for the Shalits to pay. Fear of public ostracism and critique in the media that might delay negotiations with Hamas are perhaps the explanation for the family's attitude – in this alternative script – towards Hadas' conscription. One reporter put it quite well: 'Aviva Shalit will remain at the heart of the Israeli consensus as long as she keeps her media profile low-key' (Magen 2011). The problem is that in both scripts – the Shalits being committed to the militarist ethos, and the Shalits *playing their part* as being committed to the militarist ethos – Jewish-Israeli society is the source of that undisputable militarism.

In January 2013, Israeli singer Daniela Spector released her single *Abraham* (my translation):

> Abraham, do not touch this child
> He does not belong
> Don't you see?
> There's no time left
> > Don't go blindly
> > After the pillar of smoke
> > It's just an old story
> > Wake up!

The child does not belong: he does not belong to your covenant, he has no part in it. He does not belong to you, nor to your little stories and their little ghosts, the godly or military pillars of smoke, the fears, the threats, and the terror. Your only responsibility is to protect him. The covenant with the nation and the army is yours, not his, not hers. It is up to you to follow it or to break it. *Leave the child alone, do not recruit him.* In 2004, New Profile prepared a report on child recruitment in Israel, issued simultaneously with a report prepared by the Palestinian organisation Defence for Children International in Palestine examining the recruitment of Palestinian children (Givol et al. 2004). Both reports were prepared with the support of the international organisation the Coalition to Stop the Use of Child Soldiers. The New Profile report is based on the definition of 'child' by the international Convention on the Rights of the Child, and on the definitions of 'child recruitment' and 'child soldier' according to the *Cape Town Annotated Principles and Best Practice on the Prevention of Recruitment of Children into the Armed Forces and Demobilization and Social Reintegration of Child Soldiers in Africa* (1997).[5] As the writers of the report state, the great virtue of these definitions lies in their inclusiveness. 'There is more to being a soldier than carrying weapons and committing hostilities' (Givol et al. 2004: 7), and thus the New Profile report adopts three criteria for examining who is a recruited child in Israel: official membership in an armed force; promoting or supporting the actions of an armed force; and undergoing practical or theoretical training specifically designed and intended to develop abilities to assist in the actions of an armed force (ibid.: 7–8). I believe that by this point the reader is already able to see how Israeli life literally animates all three categories.

The report is worth reading in its entirety.[6] It surveys most areas of Israeli life, certainly the various practices in the educational arena, which, as shown in the previous chapter, is a major space of militarist subjectivation. The number of cases in this study is too great to quote here, but a non-exhaustive list would include the following: discussion of the legal preliminary system of conscription that places children aged sixteen and a half to seventeen under the conscription law, obliging them to follow orders and warrants issued by military personnel; the military high schools in Israel in which pupils are required to wear military uniforms while in school and where some form of military training is part of the curriculum; participation in private training courses for special combat units; child labour on military bases; children in the civil guard; children guarding the Jewish settlements in the West Bank; child soldiers in Jewish extreme right-wing militias; and the use of Palestinian children for military purposes. Another report that investigated child recruitment in Israel, issued in August 2012 by Child Soldiers International (formerly the Coalition to Stop the Use of Child Soldiers), practically repeats the range of infringements that we find in the 2004 New Profile report and calls on Israel to implement the Optional Protocol to the Convention on the Rights of the Child on the involvement of children in armed conflict.[7] The very talk of child recruitment in the context of Israel probably annoys many Jewish-Israelis. They will not argue with New Profile that these are indeed practices that are very common in everyday Israeli life; they will only complain that 'you don't understand; this is how we build social cohesion and communal support, so there is nothing wrong with it'. But this is not just a matter of discourse: the unambiguous and ample evidence of child recruitment practices in Israel provided by New Profile proves the relevance of the category of Abrahamic parenthood. It is much easier for Jewish-Israelis to demonise Palestinian parents by pointing to the participation of their children in stone-throwing and their *hutzpah* (gall) in confronting Israeli soldiers.

§ On the community level, mobilization devalues lives. When a society chooses a particular cohort of people – defined by age and sex – to endanger themselves in its service, when it goes on assigning this type of service to successive cohorts over an extended period, it's effectively saying that this category of people is relatively expendable. It's saying that society as a whole (not individual families) can cope with the steady loss of some members of this group ... By implication their possible loss is comparatively bearable for the community. (Rela Mazali, New Profile)[8]

Kibbutz Nahal Oz, near the border with Gaza, 30 April 1956. Roi Rotberg's funeral, killed a few days earlier by Palestinian refugees from Gaza. At the funeral, the legendary IDF chief of staff at that time, the man who became a symbol of Israel's militarism and modern Jewish regeneration, Mayor-General Moshe Dayan, took the trouble to make the trip south and give a eulogy that proceeded to be perceived by Jewish-Israeli society as a moral command:

Early yesterday morning Roi was murdered. The quiet of the spring morning dazzled him and he did not see those waiting in ambush for him, at the edge of the furrow. Let us not cast the blame on the murderers today. Why should we declare their burning hatred for us? For eight years they have been sitting in the refugee camps in Gaza, and before their eyes we have been transforming the lands and the villages, where they and their fathers dwelt, into our estate.

It is not among the Arabs in Gaza, but in our own midst that we must seek Roi's blood. How did we shut our eyes and refuse to look squarely at our fate, and see, in all its brutality, the destiny of our generation? ... Beyond the furrow of the border, a sea of hatred and desire for revenge is swelling, awaiting the day when serenity will dull our path, for the day when we will heed the ambassadors of malevolent hypocrisy who call upon us to lay down our arms.

Roi's blood is crying out to us and only to us from his torn body. Although we have sworn a thousand fold that our blood shall not flow in vain, yesterday again we were tempted, we listened, we believed.

We will make our reckoning with ourselves today; *we are a generation that settles the land and without the steel helmet and the canon's maw, we will not be able to plant a tree and build a home.* Let us not be deterred from seeing the loathing that inflames and fills the lives of the hundreds of thousands of Arabs who live around us. Let us not avert our eyes lest our arms weaken.

This is the fate of our generation. This is our life's choice – to be prepared and armed, strong and determined, lest the sword be stricken from our fist and our lives cut down. The young Roi who left Tel Aviv to build his home at the gates of Gaza to be a wall for us was blinded by the light in his heart and he did not see the flash of the sword. The yearning for peace deafened his ears and he did not hear the voice of murder waiting in ambush. The gates of Gaza weighed too heavily on his shoulders and overcame him (Dayan 1956, emphasis added).

'We are doomed to fight' – this is Dayan's legacy. Present editor-in-chief of the liberal Israeli daily *Haaretz*, Aluf Benn, said in May 2011 that the eulogy 'expressed the spirit of the times more aptly than any other text or speech prepared at the time. It continues today to articulate succinctly Israel's positions in its dispute with the Arabs' (2011). Benn adds, 'Though he understood the Palestinians' suffering, Dayan did not conclude that their demands had to be met. On the contrary: He called on Israelis of his generation to continue the fight, and not pull back,' as if the only way to maintain Jewish existence in the land of Israel is by means of the Zionist fist.

The late sociologist Baruch Kimmerling described the Rotberg eulogy as an unparalleled exemplification of Israeli militarism. In 1993, Kimmerling wrote that several codes essential to deciphering the truth about Israeli society could be identified in the eulogy. There were some voices that contradicted these militarist codes, Kimmerling argued, but on the whole the chords struck in Dayan's speech were those that fashioned the character of the society (ibid.).

Dayan's eulogy continues to inspire contemporary politicians. In his inaugural speech as a new MK, former journalist Ofer Shelach from neoliberal party Yesh Atid, part of Netanyahu's coalition, said on 19 February 2013:

What is the lesson that my youngest son, to be recruited to a combat unit next month, should carry with him from my personal and familiar military legacy? That as Moshe Dayan's words at Roi Rotberg's funeral, we are doomed to fight: everybody in his turn, everyone in his own generation, we are called to defend our piece of land with determination.[9]

Other figures, such as Ariel Sharon and Ehud Barak, waved Dayan's eulogy like a flag on many occasions. 'We are doomed to fight.' Are we doomed to fight? Who are doomed to fight? And for what purpose or for whose sake are we doomed to fight? Aren't we doomed to fight because we are told that we are doomed to fight? 'Doomed to fight' bears a message not about an exceptional historical situation that compelled us to fight back then, or just now, but we are doomed to fight – sentenced by history to fight. Literally, 'doomed to fight' means that *we today* and *the people of tomorrow* are all condemned to the same fate – to fight. The pivotal connection is 'generational continuity', a sort of key biopolitical command. As we are 'doomed' to grow, to study and to love, we are also doomed to fight. A society that adheres to this logic compels us to place the children we bear in a position that dooms them to fight: 'Go to the altar and fight!' Placing them in such a position assumes raising them to take that position. And raising them to obey such logic means that we are prepared – whether unconsciously or not – to devalue the lives of our children, to risk their well-being. True, in Jewish-Israeli society parents encourage and support conscription of their children, and their mouths water at the sight of their children all uniformed and armed. I do not for a single moment doubt the love of Jewish-Israeli parents for their children. But something is deeply disturbing about how this love unfolds, permitting itself to be blindly guided by forces of death.

According to Amos Harel, writer and *Haaretz* war correspondent, Dayan's eulogy has lost some of its magnetic power in the last few decades. Although this is a highly disputed point, in his view this is indicated by the general weakening of conscription commitment. For Harel, three main reasons have brought about the change: the Oslo process, which raised hopes for an end to the conflict with the Palestinians; the high number of fatal accidents in army training in the 1990s; and the occupation of south Lebanon that ended only in the year 2000 (2013: 220–2). Similar claims were made before by Levy et al. (2007). But, more precisely, Harel claims that Jewish-Israeli society is not as tolerant as it used to be of fatalities in military service and action. It seems to me that Harel does not distinguish between society's tolerance of its own casualties in war and its commitment to Dayan's legacy – to serve in the army. High sensibility with regard to the former might lead, for instance, to a more intense use of lethal weapons. Operation Pillar of Defence in Gaza in November 2012 showed exactly how the government lent an ear to public opinion: the IDF used unprecedented military power, particularly from the air, but kept its infantry and tank divisions outside the Gaza Strip to minimise Israeli military fatalities. The price was paid by the Gazans. The point, however, is that a society less tolerant of its own casualties is not necessarily a society less apt to recruit.

§ I want to thank you for supporting your son and thus allowing both him and us to perform our duties. (IDF commander to a group of parents during the Second Lebanon War, quoted from Rela Mazali, New Profile website[10])

Fight the Arabs and then we will accept you. (Ella Shohat, 1988: 31)

There are various ways to turn a cold shoulder to one's military obligation, some of them overt, others more implicit. In all cases, some sort of non-conformist attitude to both regular and reserves military service is at work. If we want to force a categorisation of refusal or avoidance on the diverse impulses of youth either to avoid complying with the rules of the game in the military or to entirely avoid conscription, four sorts of groups can be distinguished: there are those who manoeuvre the system to avoid either conscription or service in combat units, mainly by appealing to medical or psychological conditions, or are released by the army because they are defined as unfit to serve; there are those who struggle to be dismissed from service on the basis of explicit ideological and political reasons; there are those who refuse to adapt to the rules of the game, mainly from a position of social marginalisation – desertion being the extreme on this continuum; and there are those who are exempted by law on the basis of observing Orthodox Jewish life.

My classification is clumsy because it is not based on clear-cut variables or coordinates; instead, it is built upon various sources, such as motives, circumstances, the individual and the collective, in no particular order. But this inelegance reflects reality. There are refusers who might rely on medical conditions, but at times find themselves aligning with ideologues. Others, in their struggle not to adapt themselves to a system that has nothing to offer them, might resort to medical grounds to be rid of service duty once and for all; still others may claim to be a *Yeshiva* student just to evade recruitment but may find themselves running away from the military police. And on it goes. However, my classification aligns with what Shlomo Swirski defined as 'the shortcomings of the IDF as Israelizer' (1999: 126). By this, Swirski is referring to the role the army plays – through mechanisms of selection – 'in the reaffirmation of social lines of differentiation', that of gender, that of the nation, class, and the racial line (ibid.: 126).

News about the increase in numbers of draft-dodgers floods the front pages of daily newspapers every few months. But official information on the numbers and categories of unrecruited Israeli citizens is difficult to gather because the IDF keeps data about recruitment procedures and numbers as a military secret and releases it at its own discretion. Some information is released by IDF's personnel division officers in interviews to the press. Misinformation about the procedures and numbers of conscripts every year needs to be understood as a projection of society's anxiety in relation to the *potential erosion* of the hegemonic military ethos. 'Motivation crisis' is the code name for that anxiety. What transpires through these misinformation routines is that a tension around the question of conscription is kept alive, a tension that appears productive in the sense of feeding public opinion with concerns about conscription indices, which in turn induce new rounds of policies, mainly educational, that aim to improve youth motivation to enlist in 'significant' units. In other words, when a former IDF chief of staff publicly declares that military service no longer represents a core social value in Israeli society (Adres et al. 2011: 96), he is in fact saying that society should try harder to keep military service a core social value.

According to the Israeli Forum for Citizen Equal Rights and Obligations (an anti-religious civil society organisation that strives to change the law and have more Orthodox Jews enlist), every year about 50 per cent of eighteen-year-olds are not recruited, but this number takes into account Arab citizens (20 per cent of the general population), most of whom are not summoned anyway (Druze and Circassian young people are recruited by law, while only some of the Bedouins volunteer). Among the Jewish young, about 65 to 70 per cent enlist (75 per cent of males; 60 per cent of women). Roughly half of those *not* recruited are Orthodox Jews, who are exempted by law. This is the only sector that shows clearly increasing numbers of exemptions in direct proportion to the growth of this population, which is higher than that of the Jewish non-Orthodox sector. The others are not recruited because they either live overseas or are medically or psychologically exempted, or they are defined as being unfit to serve.[11]

The first group of refusers in my classification – many of whom are coded as 'Profile 21' by the IDF, permanently unfit for military service due to physical or psychological disabilities – is said to be on the increase. Although the IDF makes it impossible to gather exact data on the numbers in this group of refusers, the 'motivation debate' is an indicator that the military is aware of this growing phenomenon. For Rela Mazali, this group of youths, who deliberately attempt to fail medical exams so as to appear unfit for military service, express a sign of increasing alienation from the hegemonic identities and life pathways that mainstream Jewish-Israeli society has to offer (1997). 'We can say about this public that they don't believe anymore that "there is no choice"; and they are not interested in offering themselves as the choice, as the platter. They want to live their lives' (ibid.: 17). They no longer believe that their government puts their lives at risk because it is inevitable; they refuse to surrender to the paranoid narratives that coerce young people to blindly follow like lambs to the slaughter. 'A society which maintains an army regularly used in combat has to actively ensure the sufficient availability of soldiers; as it is unlikely that all recruits are born with a predisposition to risk their lives, such a society must be relying on some form of pressure or coercion' (Mazali 1995: 694).

Meir Amor defines 'social refusers' as those who express their non-conformism to recruitment by desertion or absenteeism, non-conformism derived from a more general discomfort with and protest against social marginalisation. Social refusers generally end up in military prisons, sometimes for months (Amor 2003). More generally, Kimmerling suggests a direct relationship between the inability to adapt (or rather the capability not to adapt) to army life and non-conscriptable groups on the one hand, and social marginality on the other (1979: 23). As Shohat explains: 'The overwhelming majority of army deserters is to be found in the Sephardi [Mizrahi] community, particularly among the very lower classes whose behaviour reveals a reluctance to "give anything to this Ashkenazi state"' (1988: 31). According to Amor, social refusal is an individual act of resistance, lacking in heroics and dramatic flavour. For Amor, the fact that these individuals find themselves experiencing the same social marginality in the army that they have known before conscription is a result of the IDF methodology of classification and categorisation of new conscripts. This system, explains Amor, despite presenting itself as universal and neutral, reproduces the disadvantages stemming from the social cleavage between Mizrahi and Ashkenazi Jews maintained by the educational system (Smooha 1993; Swirski 1999). This is because it relies on parental and familial attributes and capacities such as profession, education, housing and other socioeconomic factors in order to rank new conscripts. In fact, he rightly claims that 'IDF's logic of classification is a small-scale model of the methods of inclusion and exclusion that define Jewish-Israeli society' (Amor 2003: 2; see also Levy and Sasson-Levy 2008). In other words, by means of the classification of conscripts' individual competences and their categorisation into different roles in the service, the IDF validates the division between the dominating elite and dominated groups in Jewish-Israeli society. As Kimmerling explains, 'the possibility of using the value system to define participation in service as central (in accordance with particularistic interest and extra-military criteria) constitutes a specific type of power within the Israeli system' (1979: 24; see also Helman 1997: 306). The bottom line is that, whereas for the Jewish Ashkenazi hegemony military service has an intrinsic value that can be cashed in to fill the ranks of the elite after their completion of military service, it has almost no social value for the marginal groups – thus, social refusers refuse to participate in a very unrewarded experience, one that deepens their social marginality and therefore is perceived by them as an avenue of exploitation (Amor 2003: 3). For these refusers, there is little value in what in normative terms is held as a privilege, namely military service. In their acts of non-conformism, social refusers put the blame on the very structure of racial relationships within Jewish-Israeli society; what arises from their actions in particular is a voice of protest against the continuing systems of inequality between Mizrahi and Ashkenazi Jews (Adva Center 2012: 21; Haberfeld and Cohen 2007). Their imprisonment in military jails, as Amor reads these acts, resonates loudly with alienation and protest, but in a voice that does not get to keep its non-conformist tone when it reaches society at large; its sad fading is just another expression of hegemonic power as much as an expression of a missed opportunity for further acts of revolt. Yet a question lies at the heart of social refusal; that is, 'why is military service a social norm?' (Amor 2003: 8). In other words, why accept the normativity of a system that exacerbates inequality and marginalisation? On the one hand, these acts of dissent illustrate, on a small scale, why the interests of the original social groups of social refusers – mostly Mizrahi – contradict the interests of the white Jewish-Zionist hegemony. On the other hand stands the question regarding the potential of these acts of dissent to connect themselves with refusal and protest against other oppressive facets of military service, and more generally of militarism and Zionism. Undoubtedly, realisation of the potential connections has always been a hard nut to crack. It relates to the question of how hegemonic Jews can disentangle themselves from their own privileged position as much as it relates to the question of how Mizrahi Jews might extract themselves from their loyalty to Zionism, imposed on them by a white Jewish regime that needed them to populate and produce but did not really want them because of their Arabness (Massad 1996; Shohat 1999; 2003). This particular loyalty has developed in ways that are apparently best manifested in hatred towards Arabs, particularly Palestinians, fuelling in turn the aggressiveness of the same military system that reproduces their marginality. The point is that the disjunction between different forms of refusal and non-conformism in relation to military service enhances the chances to deepen and widen the cracks in Israeli militarism.

There is another important aspect to social refusal. As Amor explains, this refusal casts a shadow upon privileges earned by military service, and upon those who enjoy those privileges – mostly Ashkenazi males and the few Mizrahi males who manage to pass the test of conformity and loyalty (2003: 8). In fact, rather than casting a shadow, social refusal illuminates the poisoned connections between race and class belonging and the sorts of social capital that military service paves the way for these people to appropriate, opening up the higher echelons of all spheres of life in Israeli society (Izraeli 1997; Kimmerling 1993; Levy et al. 2007). The case of retired senior professional military men is particularly striking: these men retire at the age of forty-five, which makes it possible for them to launch a new career while receiving a pension that equals their corpulent taxes-paid salary.

> Retired senior military officers effortlessly gain access to the top echelon of the political system, the economy and public administration. For example, all three predecessors of the current Chief of Staff became senior government ministers within less than a year from their retirement ... following the last round of municipal elections in Israel, *Tsevet* – The Journal of IDF Career Service Pensioners, proudly published a table listing all the retired career officers ... who remained or became mayors, heads of municipalities or heads of regional councils in Israel ... Other retired senior officers seek and easily get the top jobs in public administration, become the top executives or directors of the largest companies in the Israeli business sector or, if they are merely Colonels or Majors, make do with jobs of a more plain character, like becoming school principals (Givol et al. 2004: 14).

These people are literally venerated and glorified by their neighbours, their family and their friends. They are perceived as the loftiest embodiments of the Jewish national project, the ones who have chosen to invest and risk their lives in the army for the sake of the nation. *You see, son? Dani is a high-ranking officer in the paratroopers. Would you like to be in the paratroopers when you join the army?* They capitalise on their long service in the army by taking their place in the social, economic and political elites, 'translating their military dominance into legitimate social dominance' (Levy et al. 2007: 130). Thus, their privileges are considered well deserved, while in truth they are bestowed on them in the name of the nation but at the expense of others while reproducing a whole unequal system of twisted social relations. Precisely for that reason, social refusal is significant – by not surrendering to the symbols, allocations and military machine's complicity with existing social hierarchies and exploitations, it ridicules the militarist ethos.

Not much has been written about social refusers, unlike conscientious objectors, about whom much academic writing has been published. As a topic it also attracts quite a lot of journalistic attention in the Hebrew media. Algazi (2004) outlines a sort of history of refusal. Chief among Algazi's list are the conscientious objectors. I would like to cite some of this list here in order to abstract the main features of the kind of refusal labelled conscientious objection. To begin with, let me say that ideological-political refusal developed in Israel as a practice of insiders: that is to say, a refusal that does not necessarily de-legitimise the general commitment to serve in the army or to serve the nation. As an example of an organised effort, it is worth mentioning what is known as the open letters by the 'Sheministim' (twelfth graders, high school seniors). In 1970, these students sent a letter to then-Prime Minister Golda Meir, expressing their reservations about serving in the West Bank and Gaza and what they perceived as the government's reluctance to negotiate peace. This was the first Sheministim letter, and similar letters have followed since, until the last one appeared in 2005 (others were sent to the government in 1979, 1987 and 2001). In all these letters, the main reservation was about serving in the West Bank and Gaza and taking part in the continuing oppression of the Palestinian people. The letters were anchored in a discourse of human rights, democracy and peace. In contrast to individual cases of ideological refusal or disobeying orders in the field, the Sheministim letters were characterised as both organised and collective acts of refusal. Another wave of refusal arose during the first Lebanon war (1982–2000); nearly 200 soldiers were prosecuted and sent to military prison for refusing to serve in Lebanon (Algazi 2004; Helman 1997). A similar selective act of political refusal emerged in 2002 during the onset of the Second Intifada with the organisation Courage to Refuse calling for the refusal to serve in the areas termed 'the Occupied Palestinian Territories'.[12] In general, ideological-political refusal has so far been articulated in relation to a particular manifestation of war or acts of open hostility, namely as selective refusal. As the above implies, at the basis of this refusal lies a narrative of belonging to the Zionist community to which the refusers present their claims and their disillusionment (see Chacham 2003: 9; Svirsky 2012a: 141–2). Thus, this type of political refusal has mostly been articulated by excluding the option of opting out of the system. Helman, for instance, has shown the presence of this discourse about 'changing the system from within' in her studies on refusers in the first Lebanon war (1997: 319). Furthermore, this selective political refusal has been explained by its actors as a special right reserved only for those who serve in the military.

Explicitly or indirectly, studies of conscientious objection in Israel show a strong correlation between this type of refusal and the racial affiliation of the refusers, most of them Ashkenazi middle-class males (see, for example, Chacham 2003; Helman 1997; Linn 1986). More generally, the protest against war and militarism emerged mainly from the Ashkenazi middle class, while Mizrahi Jews sought ways to enhance their incorporation into the state and its missions. The common explanation for this white genealogy of ideological-political protest and refusal is that members of dominant groups can afford to renounce certain aspects of their hegemonic membership in the systems that benefit them. They can do so not only because they can afford to sacrifice something they already have, but also because to a great extent their place is assured in spite of their acts of disloyalty, as it is their racial affiliation that opens the way back into the fold, 'the club'. 'The white club does not like to surrender a single member, so that even those who step out of it in one situation can hardly avoid stepping back in later' (Ignatiev 1997: 6). Privilege is granted to secure the club's supremacy; thus that privilege will always be there, expecting the club members to return, despite one or another subject's attempts to dis-identify with that club (Leonardo 2004: 137). This is not to say that conscientious objectors do not pay a high personal price for choosing to opt out of their military obligation. Once prosecuted and sentenced, they are sent to military prison, sometimes for long periods, and they do not always enjoy the support of their families or peer group (Algazi 2004). Those refusing mandatory recruitment altogether risk facing difficulties in the employment market: in Israel, although the law forbids employers interviewing work candidates about their army service (Employment

Equal Opportunities Law 1988, Article 2a), the candidate is very easily
profiled as having served or not. Just a few years ago, Shani Werner,
a former New Profile activist, refused to serve in the military. As she
explained to me, 'I volunteered for National Service [*Sherut Leumi*, a
civil alternative taken up mainly by women exempted from military
conscription] because there are almost no jobs for young people who
have no employment experience, so this is why I volunteered, to get
some experience' (interview, 13 November 2012).

Importantly, we can hardly say that nothing has changed in the
narrative of conscientious objectors. The clear-cut, all-encompassing
Zionist commitment in the selective actions of the conscientious
objectors during the Lebanon war, as well as of those who refuse to
serve in the West Bank nowadays (the Courage to Refuse group), has
not been prominent in the political discourse of the young objectors
of recent years – those who signed the 2001 and 2005 *Sheministim*
letters – choosing to confront the system and refusing to enlist in
regular mandatory service. New elements have appeared, significant elements. To begin with, the new objectors do not brandish
their belonging to the Zionist community in order to express a disillusionment of sorts; quite the contrary. In their discourse in court,
in the press and in various articles they publish, the horrors of the
military occupation of the West Bank and Gaza serve to illustrate
a rotten society. Furthermore, whether they anchor their refusal in
the particularities of the occupation or in pacifism or feminism, a
different vapour has been rising from the latest rounds of refusal,
one that highlights the links between the militarisation of society
and the preclusion of the emergence of life without violence or
hierarchies (see Algazi 2004; New Profile website). Without in the
least detracting from the merits of these refusers and their significant
political positions regarding the Zionist project, their vectors still fly
in spaces not crossed by other refusers, those who have been led to
dissent by social marginalisation.

However, from the point of view of the anti-colonial struggle,
I believe that the theoretical distinction between social and ideological-political refusal, avoidance or objection to military service is
fundamentally detrimental to the general cause of undermining the

militarisation of life. This distinction reproduces the image of racial cleavage between Mizrahi and Ashkenazi Jews, as if the former – in their act of refusal or avoidance – are only reacting to their material and symbolic exclusion from hegemony; whereas the latter – accustomed to basking in its pleasures – can afford to betray hegemony by engaging in a rationalistic discourse of rights in order to voice their refusal of military service. In this cataloguing of groups, Mizrahi refusal is portrayed as expressing reproach, while Ashkenazi refusal transcends their own conditions. So one is essentially embittered, the other a leader. Or it is as if the former is incapable of abstract thinking while the latter is detached from their social circumstances – quite a Platonic semiotisation of society. In my view, this whole distinction is wrong. This is not to say, however, that 'we are all people', that liberal hyper-racist approach that makes experiences and particularities evaporate in the name of a false universalistic stance. Moreover, this distinction between social and ideological refusers reflects the broader schism that characterises public struggles in Israel, between pursuing peace and social justice – the former embodied mainly by the pseudo-leftist Ashkenazi middle class, the latter disregarded by them. This schism has affected feminist activism as well. As Helman explains: 'The creation of a political space for women and the attempt to forge a voice of their own on issues of peace also had some unintended consequences such as the silencing of the identities of Mizrahi and Palestinian women' (2009; see also Abdo 2011). The main objection of Mizrahi feminists was to 'the one-dimensional agenda of the women's peace movement and its disregard of the connections between war, peace, class and ethnicity, or the disengagement between peace and social justice' (Helman 2009).[13]

However, the distinction between social and ideological refusers is profoundly reactionary, mainly because it entrenches a bipolar world and 'doesn't allow us to recognise that subjectivity has a composed, elaborated, manufactured character' (Guattari and Rolnik 2008: 97). As long as the political analysis respects that world of dichotomies, all we are left with is a partisan struggle that is blind to its potentialities and connections and keeps cranking up the celebration of identities, while these figures are precisely those we must venture beyond to make the struggle structurally unsettling (ibid.: 112). Besides, all refusals are social; they all have social impulses. Just like any other political attitude of resistance, refusals of military service are manufactured as particular outcomes of the constant encounter between the social realm and the body, which is in itself a site of social construction. Therefore, different bodies with different life experiences synthesise their positions and the changing social circumstances in different ways every time. Conscientious objectors arrive at their decision as a result of the particular ways in which society affects them, which are different from the ways society affected Amor's social refusers. By attributing a social reason to one form of refusal and a rationalistic and ideological one to the other, discourse helps re-territorialise ethnic divisions and, in so doing, hails dogmas that underwrite already segregated and hierarchised subjectivities. We do not refuse because we are led by ideological discourse. We refuse because something about life has become untenable, has affected us to the point where it moves our bodies to adopt – both unconsciously and consciously – that courageous Bartlebian stance 'I prefer not to' (Melville 1986). Agamben explains that there is a difference in quality between two types of potentiality, between to be and to not be: the first 'has as its object a certain act' (1993: 34), in our case the act of conscription; the second is 'a potentiality that has as its object potentiality itself' (ibid.: 35). Refusal, avoiding, being disinclined to serve in the military is about taking up the choice to not be the type of subject we were trained to be. In so doing, we open potentiality anew and carry the body into new adventures and compositions. Refusals to serve or to adapt to military service – regardless of whether those refusals are manifested in desertion, absenteeism or total avoidance – are all alternatives to the loyalty and conformism that breed militarism. They are alternatives to the normal and devoted Zionist subjectivities.

There is no need to embark on a common programme, but, as Guattari rightly suggested, we need 'corridors of passage' (Guattari and Rolnik 2008: 102), in our case corridors of communication between the Mizrahi–Ashkenazi issue and the anti-militarist one, between the 'loyalty to Zionism' issue and the social question, between the possibility of a Palestinian–Jewish shared life and the issue of Jewish paranoia, and between the feminist issue and all these other questions. *Transverse connections are what we need to 'after Israel'.* The big question, though, is how to create new resonances between the partial renunciations of hegemonic privilege expressed in the refusal to be recruited and the non-conformism and alienation expressed in the avoidance of complying with the norms and hierarchical games of the military. Accomplishing structural changes is all about constructing new social resonances.

If there is any organised struggle that recognises and promotes these alternatives, it has been carried out since 1998 by the activists and supporters of the feminist and anti-militarist movement New Profile. Its activities create a space in which to practise non-Abrahamic parenthood. New Profile is a feminist movement of men and women working towards a new profile for Israeli society, one that is demilitarised and civil-oriented rather than military-oriented (New Profile 2011: 3). It is part of an impressive feminist tradition of anti-war activism in Israel. Its predecessors, Mothers Against Silence, Women in Black and Four Mothers – though each addressing a different issue – have each in their distinct affirmations paved the way to begin framing the political protest against war without keeping the communal commitment to the army and the Zionist narrative in place (see Emmett 1996; Gillath 1991; Helman 1999; Helman and Rapoport 1997; Herzog 1999; Jacoby 1999; Lemish and Barzel 2000; Zuckerman-Bareli and Benski 1989). As Gadi Algazi succinctly describes:

> The activity of New Profile ... is of enormous importance ... [It] has transformed public discourse on refusal by placing it within a feminist perspective. Besides supporting both men and women refusers of all types, the activists of New Profile have raised fundamental questions regarding the presence of the military and of warfare in Israeli social life and its implications in every aspect of existence. If the focus of refusal was formerly the occupation, the army, obedience and democracy, new modes of action have now emerged, such as anti-militarist education and the development of

civil alternatives to military service, towards building a truly civil society in Israel (quoted in Mazali 2008).

The distribution of New Profile's written and visual material reaches hundreds of followers through email listings thanks to the work of about thirty activists; interestingly, in 2011 alone, their website was viewed by more than 150,000 visitors (New Profile 2011: 6). As they state in their charter, 'our position aims to change the mind-sets that have been perpetuating war in Israel for many decades'.[14] The movement maintains a vast network of relations with other organisations – both in and outside Israel – all working on different aspects of anti-militarism, anti-occupation, social change and feminism. In a successful attempt to build bridges with Egyptian anti-militarist activists, in April 2013 New Profile and the Egyptian organisation No to Compulsory Military Service signed a joint statement that confirms the support of both organisations for conscientious objectors in Egypt and Israel.[15]

On Monday 12 November 2012, I met Diana Dolev and Ruti Kantor (RK) in Tel Aviv, both central activists in New Profile for many years. Our conversation, continued later through emails, was also joined by one of New Profile's founders, Rela Mazali. As Diana explains, 'our focus is not just on the army but on the society; we direct our efforts at society' (interview, 12 November 2012), precisely because it is in everyday society that we witness 'how the militarist contents penetrate our lives, the visibility of militarism everywhere, in schools, in kindergartens, supermarkets, in people's small talk, at the university, practically everywhere' (RK, interview, 12 November 2012). New Profile's work centres around three main projects: educational work with youth; raising awareness of militarisation in Israeli society; and support for young people who choose to avoid military service in Israel (New Profile 2011: 4). Both Diana and Ruti stress that New Profile does not call upon people not to serve because of the legal implications and sanctions, among other reasons. Rather, New Profile urges people to think before conscription.

DIANA: In our work with the youth we do not always talk about conscription. We focus our work on critical thinking; thus, in the youth camps we talk about globalisation, ecology, sustainability and feminism.

RUTI: People find it hard to understand the relation between feminism and anti-militarism. But by means of feminist facilitation, we try to convey critical contents and then it happens that, from there, youngsters arrive at other topics that more directly tackle hierarchy, the army, power, hegemony and women (interview, 12 November 2012).

In 2001, New Profile established a counselling network to support young people who are beginning to consider avoiding military service. As it said in its 2011 report, New Profile is 'the only organizational structure in Israel, and one of only a handful in the world, that supports draft resisters of all kinds' (2011: 5). 'Counselling is provided by phone, e-mail, in face-to-face meetings, and via a web forum … In 2011, we estimate that approximately 1,500 people approached New Profile's counselling network to obtain information about possible venues for exemption from military service' (ibid.: 5). Legal aid is another avenue of action: New Profile is helped by several lawyers and law firms to provide legal support and counselling to conscientious objectors and other refusers. 'An important aspect of the legal network's function is to visit refusers incarcerated in Israeli military prisons … In 2011, NP supported many refusers. One case we supported was the Druze refuser Ajwad Zidan who served 7 terms of imprisonment. Another case was a 27-year-old medicine student who was to start his military service after a deferral for studies' (ibid.: 5).

DIANA: The education team assembled a portable exhibition we call 'Making Militarism Visible'. Every single item in the exhibition is part of the existing everyday situation in Israel … quotes from school textbooks, articles from the press, images from advertising, the visibility of soldiers in the streets and of weapons in playgrounds for children … with the aim to show how civil space here produces militarist ways of thinking. We took the exhibition to Tel-Aviv University, to the Hebrew University

THE PARENT | **167**

– Jerusalem, to teachers' colleges, and many other places ...
(interview, 12 November 2012).[16]

Militarism in Israel is pervasively visible, so it 'does not and cannot
pass unnoticed by children in Israel. The military is present everywhere. Anyone who ever visited Israel could not help notice the great
number of soldiers on the streets and in other public places' (Givol et
al. 2004: 14). At any one moment, roughly half a million individuals
are in active service (mandatory service, professionals and reserves
combined), so civil life is not just constantly disrupted by the olive-
green colour of soldiers carrying rifles and pistols – rather, it is woven
through with these 'disruptions'. In fact, rather than being perceived
as disruptions, they are the very material that makes up Israeli spatial
reality.[17] As ordinary pedestrians on Israeli streets and as consumers in
shopping malls, at cinemas and in coffee shops, on public transport
and in university classrooms and lecture halls – soldiers are everywhere; there are no purely civil spaces in Israel. 'Weapons are also to
be found everywhere. Old tanks, machineguns and even fighter jets
are placed in public places, quite accessible, sometimes especially
accessible, to children' (ibid.: 15). For many years, an Israeli fighter
plane has been placed in the main outdoor display area at the National
Museum of Science in Haifa, where I worked; without a doubt, the
plane is the most attractive exhibit for the thousands of children who
visit the museum every year. Israeli militarism is not only visible, it
is also pervasively audible, since cultural landscapes have visible and
audible aspects. The strident rightfulness of key mainstream radio
and television personalities that shapes the boundaries of public
deliberation; the ever stormy political discussions at school and in
universities, at home with family or friends; the distress caused by
the sounds of the Remembrance Day siren and the collective sense of
grief and sadness enhanced a thousand-fold by the unceasing torment
of war songs that for twenty-four hours tell and re-tell of human loss
and sacrifice; the sirens in the big cities that drill the civilian population every few months – together, all of these assemble a time and
space of unavoidable sounds that nail us deeper and deeper inside
a culture with very few moments of civilian life.

Since 1999, New Profile has operated youth groups, some meeting on a regular basis, currently in Jerusalem, Haifa and Tel Aviv. As Ruti explains, these groups have coordinators and the topics of discussion are very diverse, although they are all engaged to trigger critical thinking. 'You see, these young people have no other place to discuss these issues, not at school, nor in the youth movements' (RK, interview, 12 November 2012). In 2011 the organisation opened a bilingual and binational group in Haifa for local Jewish and Palestinian young women, which needs to be seen as building another layer of bridges and connections as a basis for stronger assemblages of resistance. Since 2004, New Profile has played a major role in an alternative summer camp for young people aged fifteen to twenty; the number of participants varies from year to year but is typically around eighty to a hundred (New Profile 2011: 8). In all these groups and events, beside more general topics of globalisation, ecology and sustainability, the youth discuss more specific issues such as discrimination against the Palestinian citizens of Israel, the Nakba, women in Israel, sexual harassment in a militarist society, neoliberal policies and other relevant themes of social justice in Israeli society. The following extract is from the testimony of a participant in one of the weekly groups:

> I attended meetings of New Profile's youth group for 16 weeks.
> I feel that in 16 weeks I learned much more than in 12 years of
> school. At first glance, it might seem like we are not a very diverse
> group because almost all of us come from the same part of the
> political spectrum but after every meeting I was surprised to know
> how much I learned from my friends and how many sides, which
> I didn't even think about, each subject has. We discussed sensitive
> issues which are mostly not discussed in 'ordinary' groups, such
> as: Is it right to go to the army? Is police brutality legit? Abortion
> and surrogacy, nationalism and collective memory. When I first
> decided not to enlist, New Profile was the first address I appealed
> to for support. I can tell with full confidence I feel more confident
> about my decision after I met more youth, who are not going to
> the army either, and after we discussed this subject from different
> perspectives (ibid.: 7).

Shani Werner (SW), today a social worker and a former activist in New Profile (when she was between the ages of sixteen and twenty), says that 'when I first met them, New Profile gave words to the thoughts I had at that time ... it was a home for me' (interview, 13 November 2012). Shani applied to the IDF Conscience Committee to be released, and like most young women who applied at the time, she got her exemption. In other words, the committee is very flexible with women but completely the opposite with men: that is why most male political refusers end up in jail. According to Shani, today there are other feminist organisations voicing political discourses similar to those of New Profile, such as Isha L'Isha (Woman for Woman) and the Coalition of Women for Peace. 'What is interesting about this discourse New Profile initiated is that it does not focus on what the army does to others but on what it does to us, to the society; it looks at the prices each of us pay for living in a society that sanctifies militarist values' (SW, interview, 13 November 2012). The conversation with Shani corroborated and even sharpened my thoughts about the different, sometimes limited aspects of the question of refusal. According to Shani:

> The discourse on conscription and refusal is not necessarily relevant to all. To refuse is a sort of privilege; the very political consciousness is a sort of privilege. People at the margins feel that society disregards them completely; they feel society does not give them anything so they do not want to give back ... and there are people who just can't afford to serve in the army as they need to work to help their families. In addition, there are people for whom the army is an opportunity to gain some social capital, to finish their high school matriculation, a chance to belong, a chance to leave a problematic home (interview, 13 November 2012).

Shani's analysis takes us back to the question of how to traverse segregations so as to connect across the various oppressive aspects of Israeli society – perhaps the most pressing question in the life of transformational activism in Israel. Shani agrees with New Profile's political agenda, but she asks us to be aware of the nuances surrounding the issue of conscription and refusal: 'anyone who can choose not to rely on the military to escape from some kind of hardship, of course that will be better, but there are many for whom this path is just not accessible' (SW, interview, 13 November 2012).

New Profile activists are more than aware of these complexities.[18] From my exchanges with the activists, I gather that the movement has gone to great lengths to try to avoid the ways in which the discourse of political refusal usually limits itself and steers away from social groups who, as Shani Werner put it so clearly, perceive conscription differently. As Rela Mazali explains, years ago the movement initiated an intellectual relationship with academic Meir Amor to articulate the phenomenon he later defined as 'social refusal'. In the past, New Profile established communication and organised cooperative activist work with groups that identify themselves as Mizrahi, such as Women for a Peace Culture and the Mizrahi Democratic Rainbow Coalition. In addition, New Profile's legal aid project allocates resources to help incarcerated social refusers (according to Amor's definition), including legal advice and channels of communication with the outside (correspondence, 14 July 2013).

In our conversation, Shani also illuminated another tricky situation that demonstrates the inescapability of collective military thinking, even for those who choose to refuse, as well as relating to gender. When Shani refused, a group of young men were being court-martialled for refusing to be recruited.

> Gender divisions suffered almost no change: in the same manner that our military service is regarded less seriously than that of boys, so is our refusal, because while we get exemption they go to jail. It is just more glorious. And when they went to jail, we sent to them letters, gift parcels, and also organised 'jailing parties' for them that looked pretty much the same as the 'recruitment parties' people get who enlist (SW, interview, 13 November 2012).[19]

These 'recruitment parties', as well as 'discharge parties', are integral to the rite of conscription, integral to the passages relating to military service. This is not to say that the refusers carve similar subjective territories as those of the recruited. Rather, the infiltration of these practices (farewell and welcome parties) into the refusers' experience tells of the difficulty of isolating the events, emotions and discourses that shape new constructions of subjectivity. Particularly striking is the reproduction of gender relations here. Surely, given the ways in which the Israeli military deals with refusal, it is unlikely that young refusers will be able to traverse the gender relationships characteristic of society at large and the ways in which these relationships reverberate in the military. Nevertheless, it is imperative to find means of demilitarisation 'that avoid privileging masculinity' (Enloe 2000: 4).

§ The IDF response to what seems to be a definite increase in the numbers of those who intentionally avoid recruitment fluctuates between refraining from making these facts a too visible phenomenon, and being alarmed enough to induce new forms of consent through aggressive persuasion. As we saw in the previous chapter, the state invests time and money in its educational system to keep alive high levels of youth motivation. The important question here is how a new form of parenthood and the phenomenon of non-recruitment can be linked. We, as parents, must take note of this rhizomatic growing phenomenon. Studying it might provide insights into how we can create new ways to support young refusers of all sorts – conscientious objectors, social refusers, religious refusers, medical/psychological avoiders and deserters. Their numbers are still small compared with the cultural strength of the militarist commitment in Jewish society, and there is no overarching anti-militarist project that connects them. But these existing routes for evading and avoiding military service invite parents to consider alternatives to their Abrahamic practices. It is another biblical figure, not Abraham but Bithiah, Pharaoh's daughter, risking her position by saving the child from drowning in the Nile, who must illuminate our parental imagination.

New Profile offers us real practices, texts and images of how to experiment with non-Abrahamic parenthood, presenting new ways in which to constitute ourselves out of Jewish militarist and nationalistic subjectivities. Their protagonists refuse to animate the scripts that Jewish-Israelis are expected to perform, refuse to voice the world views Jewish-Israelis are expected to hold. This transformative protagonism disconnects itself from the Zionist patriarchal organism, an abandonment that damages its very organisation; as it detaches itself, it leaves behind zones of chaos and disorder. However, we never fully leave the bodies in which our oppressive subjectivities were cultivated, and so, rather than being a simple act of abandonment, non-Abrahamic parenthood bifurcates the body, causing a split between submitting to Zionist codifications and entering – through experimentation – new phases that are free or partially free of those codifications. As the mind–body is enriched with new accounts of the world, consciousness is bifurcated (Bailey 1998). Crucially, non-Abrahamic protagonism does not dwell in the unseen margins of society. Its significance resides in the fact that it consciously dwells alongside mainstream Zionism – or even in its very midst. *It has become possible for Jewish-Israelis not to perform in Zionist ways.*

These positive developments have not escaped the controlling eye of the state. On 15 September 2008, the Attorney General of Israel, Mr Menachem Mazuz, ordered a criminal investigation of New Profile to be opened for incitement to avoid military service. The decision was made following a request from the Military Advocate General, Brigadier General Avichai Mendelblit. The penal code establishes that whoever incites people not to serve or to desert from the military can be sentenced to between five and fifteen years in prison. A few months later, on 26 April 2009, the Tel Aviv police arrested seven New Profile activists; they were interrogated for hours and their personal computers were confiscated. All along, New Profile's position was to insist that the movement does not incite refusal but provides legitimate information and support to those who have decided to avoid military service or to those who have been punished by the military system for being unable to adapt to it. In November 2009, the Tel Aviv police informed the court of its decision to close the case because of a lack of evidence. One wonders what sort of evidence the police needed on which to base a prosecution. One surely lacks any kind of sense if one does not see the connection between Operation Betzer and the police raid on New Profile activists' homes. In both instances, security forces were after people who were suspected of disloyalty to military service. In both, they were looking to apprehend people who refuse to adhere to the Abrahamic script. In Jewish-Israeli society, there are mothers and fathers who raise sons and daughters to become soldiers, and there are also mothers and fathers who raise sons and daughters.

> The soldier is applauded who refuses to serve in an unjust war by those who do not refuse to sustain the unjust government which makes the war; is applauded by those whose own act and authority he disregards and sets at naught; as if the state were penitent to that degree that it hired one to scourge it while it sinned, but not to that degree that it left off sinning for a moment. (Henry David Thoreau, *On the Duty of Civil Disobedience*, 1849)

4 | THE VOTER

What is the political regime underlying the electoral system in which Israeli citizens participate? What does this political regime encompass in terms of populations and territories affected by the policies issued by its elected officials? These two questions are important for determining the nature and goals of participation in the Israeli national electoral process. Azoulay and Ophir offer a series of important theoretical distinctions on which I shall rely to address these questions. One distinction highlights the four different 'governed groups' in ethnic nation states such as Israel: 'citizens who are members of the nation that "monopolizes" the state; other citizens of the state, conceived as "minorities"; non-citizens who are governed but hardly counted'; and 'a fourth group of indigenous population expelled through ethnic cleansing which is associated with the state by being entirely excluded from it' (2013: 190–1). With specific reference to Palestinians and Jews, naming these groups in Israel's case, they are: the Jewish-Israelis; the Palestinian minority within Israel proper; the Palestinian population living under Israeli military occupation in the West Bank, Gaza and East Jerusalem; and the Palestinian refugees expelled in 1948 and their descendants.[1]

Of the four categories, the last is the least obvious, as it means that the 1948-expelled Palestinians and their descendants – or some aspect of their lives – are also governed by Israel. This needs some clarification. To begin with, all these groups are governed populations of Israel in the sense that Israel rules directly or indirectly over the lives and systems of opportunities of these peoples, *all of whom have claims* to the political, material and symbolic space administered by Israel's ruling apparatuses in the geographical region that lies from the Mediterranean Sea to the Jordan River. In the case of the Palestinian diaspora, the association with the State of Israel is actualised in the form of the historical exclusion that expedited the formation of the state in the first place. It thus created a space of reclamation that Israel has tried to extinguish, preventing by law and physical erasure the return of Palestinian refugees to their lands and assets. This continuing prevention, however, actually serves to keep alive the political association between the two entities. The same can be said of the symbolic prevention of the Palestinian return and the avoidance of any mention of the Nakba in education and popular culture in Jewish-Israeli society. In other words, there are laws, policies, strategies and techniques that Israel has developed that have the Palestinians in exile as their object. The very control of the ways in which all aspects of that past have a bearing on the present makes that past a time that is continuing, expressing a state of affairs that is incomplete yet still in progress. Beyond the direct prevention of return for the original refugees and their families, the continuation of this prevention, and therefore the political association between the refugees and Israel, has several anchors. First, by means of the ongoing deed: the ethnic cleansing in 1948 was phenomenal in its scale, but, as a technique for governing non-Jews, Israel has never relinquished the logic of displacement that animates ethnic cleansing. Only recently (on 24 January 2013), the Knesset passed the Prawer-Begin Bill, which legalises the mass expulsion of Arab-Bedouin communities in the Negev desert in the south of Israel. The bill authorises the destruction of thirty-five Bedouin villages and the forced relocation of 40,000 to 70,000 Arab-Bedouin citizens of Israel into existing Bedouin townships that have suffered severe discrimination for decades. By forcibly displacing the Bedouin population, Israel wished to put an end to their claims to their historical lands, taken over by the state in the 1950s. A massive protest against the Prawer-Begin plan, which included international criticism, brought Netanyahu's government in December 2013 to the decision to cancel the plan.

The point is, however, that the logic of displacement, which is at the heart of the Zionist historical project and implemented by Israel to this very day, keeps alive and perpetuates its past crimes of displacement, and therefore also keeps alive the calls for justice. Second, the political relationship between the Palestinian exile and the State of Israel is also expressed in the fact that Palestinian representatives have been rightly reluctant to remove the refugee question from the negotiations agenda; this forces Israel to be part of future decisions to reopen the issue, and thus have an impact on the expectation of the Palestinians in exile with regard to their return. Third, another anchor confirms the view of the Palestinians in exile as a group governed by Israel; Israeli prevention of Palestinian return needs to be read as being linked to Israel's Jewish 'law of return' that grants diaspora Jews *latent* citizenship. This means that, even more than having the potential to become citizens by reason of certain ascribed qualities, Jews outside Israel are assigned by Israeli law an innate Israeli citizenship that exists congenitally in a concealed form as long as it is not activated through immigration. This inverted diasporic link that Israel has established in law and practice with Palestinians and Jews outside Israel is a fundamental axiom of the Zionist regime. It is a link that further confirms the view that the Palestinian diaspora is governmentalised by Israel.

Together, the four governed groups make up about 15.5 million people, only half of whom are Israeli citizens (the first and second groups).[2] What needs to be established now is how much each of these four groups shares in the political navigation of the ship of state, because 'the differences between the groups and the mobility from one group to another are among a state's most important characteristics' (ibid.: 191). Azoulay and Ophir also distinguish between two planes of power: 'being governed' and 'sharing government and partaking in governance' (ibid.: 200). Groups in the governed population are positioned differently in these two categories. With regard to the plane of power of 'being governed', Palestinians in the West Bank are governed by means of a military tyranny, whereas Gazans are besieged by that same army; the Palestinians in exile are governed by preventing their return to the land and to their native political space and by denying them access to the continuing revenues produced from their robbed assets; and the Palestinians in Israel proper, 'however severely deficient their civil status is', share with Jewish-Israelis the same category as citizens (ibid.: 204). As for the 'sharing government and partaking in governance' plane of power, a further separation takes place that relates to the ethnic character of Israel as a Jewish state: in spite of their citizenship and their partial representation in the Knesset and other official institutions, the Palestinian minority in Israel is structurally excluded from sharing government and partaking in governance at the national level, which in turn impairs a priori their chance of improving their well-being. Importantly, Arab and Arab-Jewish political parties in the Knesset have been factually banned from participation in governmental coalitions. So, despite the fact that on one plane of power (citizens versus non-citizens) Palestinian citizens have a 'relative equality' with Israeli Jews, their structural exclusion on the ethnic plane (in government and governance) makes that relative equality as citizens a matter for reinterpretation; in other words, the current state of affairs invites us to consider how such crippled citizenship can be put to work to challenge the regime that cripples it. As Azmi Bishara put it: 'We do not drink at separate water fountains or sit at the back of the bus. We vote and can serve in the parliament. But we face legal, institutional and informal discrimination in all spheres of life' (2007).[3] Although there is a difference between the Palestinian citizens of Israel and all other Palestinian groups in their status as governed people, that difference is seriously blurred because of the ethnic exclusion in sharing government and partaking in governance. I will return to this important point later.

In summary, from the perspective of ethno-national lines, Israeli citizens participate in an electoral process that enthrones representatives who, since 1948, have enacted laws and have issued policies that *systematically and ideologically* – though differentially – impair the well-being, rights, interests, assets and structure of opportunities of all the governed subject groups except the Jewish-Israeli. From a racial standpoint, this is not entirely correct, as official institutions do little or nothing to reverse the historical and structural marginalisation of Mizrahim or to avoid discrimination against Ethiopian Jews. But again, ethno-national lines do exist, and this is exactly what makes Israel a Jewish state. Voting in parliamentary elections in Israel: 1) takes place alongside and because of the impossibility of the regime's Palestinian non-citizens voting – West Bankers,

Gazans and refugees in the diaspora; and 2) has demonstrated no affirmative structural bearing on the chances of Palestinian citizens accessing participation in government and radically improving their material and symbolic well-being. This is exactly what makes Israel a Jewish state.

What really happens when we go to vote in Israel? At the polling station we choose a ballot paper to cast our vote in the box. Most of us have already made that choice in advance. In the Israeli parliamentary elections, each ballot paper represents a political party using one or more letters of the alphabet with the name of the party in a much smaller font directly below. Sixty grams is the weight of the small ballot paper, a rectangle of 7 by 10 centimetres, with black print on a white background. We might see these little ballot papers as encapsulating the political platforms of the parties. They also condense our political dreams for change, whatever we imagine that change to be. But this is not all. After registering at the desk of the polling station, we go behind the curtain, pick a ballot paper, and, before placing it in the envelope and casting it into the box, for an instant we stare expectantly at our party's letter and name. We hold it for a brief moment, and then we cast it. We certainly do not inspect it, examine it as a legal document, or turn it to see its flip side. We assume that everything is in its right place. And we truly believe that we are voting for those letters, as nothing else seems to appear on that little piece of printed paper. But if only we had more time and clearer vision, if we could have a closer look or even zoom into it, we would notice that within the letters and between its pixels, *something else* is written on the ballot paper, on all of the ballot papers. And by throwing that piece of paper into the box, we are definitely voting for that as well. All ballot papers have the very same *something else* written on them: this is the *hidden curriculum* of voting. It is carried with the ballot paper and draws another breath of life as the little piece of paper finds its way into the box. And by participating in voting we inevitably cast our vote for it. Like it or not, we vote for that hidden curriculum. It always gets an absolute majority of votes – 100 per cent, not one vote less. With regard to the act of voting, it has no competition. It needs no coalition, no political bargaining to rule. It rules and we confirm its reign by our participation. Rather than sneakily inculcating values and norms – which is how it assumes its function in education, from which I borrow the term – the main function of this sort of hidden curriculum is to drain *the voter*'s energy. This energy provides the electoral system and the political regime that sets it in motion with an aura of legitimacy. Significantly, this is not the legitimacy that the results of a particular election grant to the winning party to allow it to establish a new government and pursue a specific political agenda; nor is it the legitimacy that every new government draws on as it pretends to act on behalf of all of its governed subjects: 'I will be *everyone's* prime minister,' they reiterate. The kind of legitimacy and consent that participation in the electoral system endows anchors the political organism in itself and animates and grants validity to its democratic image.

By curriculum I mean the programmes or projects that the political regime pursues at a historical level: they are continuous and manifest society's chief dispositions. As Azoulay and Ophir explain, in the modern state 'a project exists at a level of organization higher than that of instruments, techniques, and modes of operation: it is a set of policies coordinated to achieve what may be described as an end that justifies its means; only rarely does it need further justification' (2013: 195). But in order to become a project of the state that is operated and actualised by the regime, it should attain some stability and operational continuity over time. Israeli society has developed a series of such projects, all related to its aspiration to create an exclusivist Jewish state: the prevention of Palestinian return; tyrannical military oppression of Palestinians in the West Bank, Gaza and East Jerusalem; the internal exclusion from governance and full equality of the state's Palestinian citizens; and the structural inhibition of Arab-Jewish collaborative life (Table 4.1). The silhouette cast by these national projects is, in fact, *the curriculum of the state*. The differential ruling of Israel's four governed populations is expressed in its four national projects. This is what makes Israel the state it is.

I call the curriculum instilled in the ballot hidden because its projects are not explicitly stated as the objectives of the state's official

TABLE 4.1 What is the Jewish state?

Israel's governed populations	Israel's national projects
Palestinians in exile	The prevention of Palestinian return
Palestinians in the West Bank, Gaza and East Jerusalem	Tyrannical military rule
Palestinians and Jewish citizens of Israel	Structural exclusion from governance and denial of full equality of Palestinian citizens, and structural inhibition of Arab-Jewish shared life

institutions. Their visibility surfaces only through the critical action of opposing political parties, bodies and individuals, and in fact no mainstream political party explicitly calls upon its voters to articulate a choice relating to these projects – they are the assumptions underlying the mainstream. It is a hidden curriculum not because its contents are unknown or barred from deliberation, or because it infuses itself through our veins in a devious or conspiratorial manner – nothing is devious here since *we* are its creators and executors, we are the people who sanction the everyday actualisations of these contents. Well, most of us. Rather, it is a hidden curriculum in the sense that the historical stability and continuity of its contents hold at bay the public's potentiality to 'touch' it in ways that might deform it or even destroy it. These all-Jewish projects, hidden inside the party letters on the little ballot papers, have other names as well. We may call them the social contract of society or its pillars, the spirit of the nation, or the mandate of generations. So as we pick out a ballot paper behind the curtain, that act of secrecy inevitably bears a public aspect, a *collective enunciation*. A ballot has two parts: one is our sincerest hope; the other its constraints. The relationship between the two defines the contours of political space. In the Knesset, political parties of the anti-Zionist left have courageously tried to redefine the state's curriculum; nevertheless, and inescapably so far, voting in parliamentary elections in Israel only serves to ratify the

continuation of Israel's national projects, namely the prevention of
Palestinian return; the tyrannical military oppression of Palestinians
in the West Bank, Gaza and East Jerusalem; the internal exclusion
from governance and full equality of the state's Palestinian citizens;
and the structural inhibition of Arab-Jewish shared life. Being that
voter is perhaps the only common denominator of Jews and Palestinians who actually vote.

§ Ask any political scientist at any comfortable university in the
Western world to choose just one principle or practice as the litmus
test of democracy. The overwhelming majority will say *fair elections*.
And they have the US Supreme Court on their side: 'No right is
more precious in a free country than that of having a choice in the
election of those who make laws under which, as good citizens, we
must live. Other rights, even the most basic, are illusory if the right
to vote is undermined' (Blomberg 1995: 1015). In another ruling,
the US Supreme Court determined that: 'The right to vote freely
for the candidate of one's choice is of the essence of a democratic
society, and any restrictions on that right strike at the heart of representative government' (ibid.: 1021). What transpires is a strong
correlation between the existence of the right to vote that feeds
into a free electoral system and the perception of that regime as
legitimately democratic.

One may expect a regime aspiring to be thought of as democratic
to be tested on the basis of the autonomy of its judiciary or, more
generally, with regard to its separation of powers, the implementation
of equality as a universal principle, the range and depth of other
individual and minority rights available to the public, or the existence
of an independent media or welfare system. Political scientists surely
mention these categories when offering a more substantial answer to
what democracy is about, but still, as Blomberg claims, 'little dispute
exists that no right is more fundamental that the right to vote' (ibid.:
1015). This wide consensus is reflected, for instance, in the way in
which popular empirical indices measure the presence and depth of
democracy. Freedom House places the electoral process as one of its
major categories for rating democracies; it even measures a narrower

concept, that of 'electoral democracy'. The Economist Intelligence Unit's 'Democracy Index', another distinguished gauge, also favours in its calculation of the index the qualities of the electoral system – defined as a 'critical area of democracy' (Economist Intelligence Unit 2012: 27). This is not the place to discuss the extreme bias of these organisations because of the way in which they construct their methods. These are fundamentally questionable mainly because they compare regimes with a particular image of democracy consistent with empire's neoliberal values and interests. In their ideological constitutive assumptions and methods, these empirical systems of measurement fail to rank countries such as Cuba and Venezuela appropriately, while at the same time they are blind to the different variables that should be taken into account when assessing regimes such as Israel's. This problematic has not escaped the attention of a few individuals: as Diamond explains, 'a growing number of scholars are questioning the tendency to classify regimes as democratic simply because they have multiparty elections with some degree of competition and uncertainty' (2002: 23). Nevertheless, Diamond, too, joins the chorus and categorises Israel as a liberal democracy.

How Western 'democracy indices' manage to avoid measuring the fact that for nearly half a century Israel has held under military occupation about 3.5 million Palestinians in the West Bank and Gaza, has kept Gazans under siege since 2007, and discriminates against its 1.6 million Palestinian citizens by ethnocratic means – this is a wonder that defies reason. Like a sleight of hand – now you see it, now you don't – this fact is no longer there to be measured. Israeli academia has certainly helped in this magic trick. For decades, in their assessments Israeli political scientists and sociologists 'did not overstep the boundary which considers Israel a democratic system' (Ghanem and Mustafa 2007: 53) and ignored the forms of ethnic discrimination and military occupation that Cuba does not need to have to be ranked as a non-democracy. The Israel Democracy Institute, established in 1991, is a mainstream think tank that also supports this trend. In its 2012 Israeli Democracy Index, Israel holds a comfortable centre position in most indicators, directly following the leading Organisation for Economic Co-operation and Development (OECD) countries (Israeli Democracy Index 2012). Thus, in spite of its historical and developed tendencies and all its bad habits of oppression, discrimination and dispossession, including the deep and wide infringement of rights, and in spite of its differential ruling of its four governed populations, Israel still stars on the international stage as a democracy. The pace of anti-rights and anti-equality legislation, particularly over the past ten years, makes right-wingers blush the world over. Nonetheless, with not an iota of shame and with admirable success, Israel brandishes its procedural democracy as its most evocative aspect. The problem is that this appellation and the image it semiotises have detrimental implications on our efforts to transform Israeli society. If an image hides the reality, then the failure to see through the image only aggravates that reality. No matter what the reasons for failure are, whether genuine or false, the final consequence is obfuscated judgement. In his discussion of the attempts to disqualify the Palestinian MK (Knesset Member) Hanin Zoabi from the 2013 elections to the Knesset, mainstream Israeli journalist Dan Margalit could not have explained it better:

> I hereby recommend that the Central Elections Committee reject the efforts to disqualify her [Zoabi] ... The other, main reason is that this move to disqualify Zoabi and the Arab parties will cause unprecedented damage to Israel's image in the West, right at the most sensitive time. Israel's enemies are trying to sabotage its status as the only democracy in the Middle East, and such a move can be used by them as proof that Israel is in fact not a democracy (2012).

Open and free democratic elections based on a formal multiparty political system that bans almost no one, an active judiciary, a plausible range of liberal freedoms for its citizenry and a regulated equality between Jewish and Palestinian citizens of the state are all parts of the Israeli democratic spectacle. Add to this series the neoliberal mindset and the ultra-modern commercialised landscape Israel takes pride in, and a *perceived Western democracy* is thus formed. It is therefore no wonder that Israel has managed to uphold a democratic self-image. It has almost all the necessary ingredients to do the trick, and in sustaining that image it matters little that the particular combination of these ingredients is toxic for the consumers (elements matter only for the relationships they establish). In the production and marketing of the democratic image 'for export', it is imperative for Israel to hold up its citizens as active participants in its democratic procedures. There are always reluctant participants, but voter turnout rates at Knesset elections have been quite high since 1949. Until 1999 these rates were around 80 per cent. Since then they have been in decline, numbers having stabilised at around 65 per cent – but high enough to retain the image, particularly if we bear in mind that voting in Israel is not compulsory.

Voters of what in Israeli terms is perceived as the far left eagerly aim to change Israel's curriculum. As Ghanem and Mustafa say about the Palestinian political parties that 'run in the Knesset elections, they have adopted a "serious citizenship" mode of trying to achieve equality, even to the extent of hoping to change the nature of the state and to turn it into the state of its citizens' (2007: 54). Voters in this honest left, particularly, do not see themselves as part of the electoral system that elects the ruling power responsible for the tyrannical rule beyond the Green Line. They see their participation as a way to possibly change that state of affairs. For most people wanting to influence and bring about change, nothing seems more appealing and straightforward than elections. So we end up believing in our intervention regardless of the constraints forced on the political space by the state's curriculum. The problem is that Israel has developed a curriculum that makes the lives of half of its governed groups unbearable by compelling the other half to actively participate and believe in the production of that deprivation of life. The bottom line here is that, in Israel, allowing political culture to grip us as tightly as cogs in a participatory electoral mechanism produces the momentous side effect of incorporating us as active cogs in that mechanism – rather than letting us become the spokes we must throw into Israel's wheel to stop it. Over time, Israel's national projects were successful enough to develop and adapt to changing circumstances and thus to remain with us, deep in our lives – and to a far greater extent than all the subsequent parliamentary and civil society achievements in terms of rights, equality and transformation.

In addition, for many years Israel capitalised on the contrast with the late Arab authoritarian regimes. In the process, this gave rise to the infamous slogan 'the only democracy in the Middle East'. Why does Israel's democratic image in the international community matter for those working towards *after Israel*? Simply because it hinders change by supplying tacit support – in the form of the explicit abstention of criticism – reserved only for the members of the democratic club. Such membership is confirmed annually by the 'democracy indices' and by the images and discourses that the club's members skilfully disseminate about themselves. In that respect, apartheid in South Africa could not attain that support because it never invested in representing itself as a legitimate regime in the eyes of the international community. Its racism was bluntly gauche, not sophisticated. Apart from that difference, another significant obstacle preventing the international community from placing Israel in the same category as apartheid South Africa is a misconception of who the governed people of Israel are. In the case of South Africa, the international community perceived all inhabitants of the regime as 'the governed population' and hence concluded that South Africa was infringing on the rights and well-being of its own people. Although it took a long time to happen, finally, in the 1980s, the boycotts and sanctions against South Africa gained momentum. The case of Israel could have been construed in a similar manner, but so far it has not been. This is, I claim, because what frames the political mindset of the international powers that have had a say in the Israeli–Palestinian case so far is not the relationship of oppression that must be ended unconditionally but the right of self-determination. In the international political discourse about the region, the latter has been prioritised over the former and thus the preoccupation with oppression has been conditioned on the right of Jews and Palestinians to each have their own state. This conditioning, however, first benefits the side that already has a state of its own – because negotiations between the parties are only about agreeing on the right of the other to have a state. Second, prioritising self-determination endorses forms of oppression that actualise Israel's exclusivism. Let us disarticulate this claim.

To begin with, the case of the Palestinian refugees has been deliberated at the United Nations and a series of resolutions accepted that favour their return (particularly resolution 194 of 11 December 1948, as well as General Assembly Resolution 169 and Security Council Resolution 237). However, neither Israel nor the world see the Palestinian refugees as a governed population of Israel in the sense I have claimed above. The international powers involved in the Israeli–Palestinian negotiations have so far allocated resolution of the refugee issue *not within* Israel's final geographical borders. As for the Palestinian citizens of Israel, their position as 'governed' people is not disputed. However, their structural exclusion has never been considered by international mediators and the media as needing to be placed as an integral part of the agenda of these negotiations. Again, as with the refugee issue, the international consensus on the question of the Palestinian minority in Israel is drawn from the principle of Israel's right to self-determination; in other words, these attitudes affirm the right of Israel to Jewish exclusivity. In recent years, the Palestinian non-governmental organisation Adalah (the Legal Centre for Arab Minority Rights in Israel) has been investing in international advocacy, mainly by targeting specialist committees on human rights in the European Union (EU), the US Congress and the United Nations. The main goal of these activities is to hold Israel accountable for its official commitments to human rights and to report on its infringements of rights. Despite this and other welcome initiatives, the world – like Israel itself – sees the condition of the Palestinian minority as an internal matter for Israel. This certainly does not add any splendour to the Israeli regime, even in its own eyes. Nor does it, however, fatally vitiate the image of Israel as a vibrant democracy. Precisely because of this state of affairs, as twisted as it might seem, political participation in elections by Palestinian citizens has more value for Israel than participation by its Jewish citizens. This is because, although their political influence is structurally restricted due to their being Arabs, their very participation as Arabs is what increases Israel's democratic shares on the global market. Self-defeat by voting.

The only Palestinian governed population whose condition attracts the world's attention is that of Palestinians in the West Bank and Gaza, and, to a lesser extent, the Palestinians in East Jerusalem. Until recently, the occupation was treated by the international community as an unintended addendum to Israeli democracy that would soon be removed from Israel's supervision. As the occupation nears its fiftieth anniversary, the world's attitude towards it is shifting. Most notably, in mid-July 2013 the EU decided to label products from Israeli settlements in the West Bank as being distinct from goods imported from Israel proper. This decision came a week after the EU issued its directive to prohibit investments in or funding of entities that operate in the settlements. Israel retaliated by announcing that it will not cooperate with EU human rights organisations helping Palestinians on the ground. The point is that the world has eyes solely for the Israeli occupation of Palestinian territories – this *is the only point* it addresses in the Israel–Palestine context. According to this approach, the refugee issue is not Israel's problem and structural discrimination of the Palestinian minority in Israel proper continues to be set aside as a non-problem, as do the segregative policies that keep Jewish and Palestinian citizens apart. Europe, the United States and the international community at large do distinguish between the governed populations of Israel in their assessments and approaches, but the result of that separation is that Israel's exclusivist Jewishness is respected.

§ Voters in Israel – Jews and Palestinians alike – endorse the Israeli political system by default and by proxy, vitalising the regime that produces the four national projects. Through their participation they reinforce Israel's democratic image as well, in turn helping to make the world see the separation of Israel's governed populations as perfectly logical, even though such separation entails the continuation of the Zionist exclusivist project in the region.

These conclusions are not news for many among the Palestinian minority in Israel and for the few Jews who, in the past fifteen years or so, have been abstaining from and boycotting the electoral system. However, this position – though gradually expanding – has not been held by the majority of the Palestinian citizenry in Israel. Since 1948 the Palestinian discourse has followed a strategy by which their citizenship in Israel should be taken as seriously as possible as part of their struggle for equality and to raise issues of Palestinian concern; participation in the electoral system and in Israeli politics was therefore considered mandatory. Simply put, 'in order to reform the regime we must take part in its institutions'. But something dented the appeal of this discourse during and since the riotous events of October 2000, when the Israeli police killed thirteen Palestinian citizens demonstrating in solidarity with the Second Intifada in the West Bank and Gaza, a demonstration that quickly turned into a major protest against the continuing structural discrimination of the Palestinian minority (Bishara 2001; Svirsky 2012a). As I have explained elsewhere, a new political culture of resistance transpired, causing the October events to become an open and conscious challenge not only to Zionist state policies but also to paradigms in Palestinian politics, still traditional up until the October events. Strictly in terms of political activism, two major developments took place following these events: one was the assertion of Palestinian indigenous politics (Jamal 2011) and the second was the radicalisation of forms of Arab-Jewish collaborative activism that left behind those forms that for decades had benefited the status quo (Svirsky 2012a: Chapter 3). These effects continued to propagate and affect more and more realms of thought and civil action; one of these developments is the re-evaluation of the traditional Palestinian discourse of citizenship (Ghanem and Mustafa 2007: 54–5).

This should not surprise anyone. It was just a matter of time until more and more people would realise the significance of the fact that '[t]he Israeli regime did not intend real and equal citizenship on any occasion and this remained as it was in the past' (ibid.: 54). Once the penny dropped, it was only logical to expect high degrees of scepticism regarding the advantages and real effects of participation in the Knesset electoral system. This was highlighted in a recent study commissioned by the Abraham Fund Initiatives (AFI – a high-profile and well-funded organisation promoting co-operation between Arab and Jewish citizens) to explore behavioural

TABLE 4.2 Palestinian turnout in Knesset elections (%)

Year	Palestinian turnout	General turnout	Palestinian boycotters
1949–99	75–85 (approx.)	75–85 (approx.)	15–25 (approx.)
2001*	19	62.3	81
2003	62	67.8	38
2006	56	63.2	44
2009	53	65.2	46
2013	56	67.7	43

Note: * Results for prime ministerial elections only.
Source: Most data in this table are taken from Ghanem and Mustafa 2007.

patterns of Palestinian citizens in elections (2012). This 'showed that even when Arab politicians are elected to the Knesset, their constituents see their power as marginal ... [and] if Jewish leaders were to include Arabs in running the nation's affairs, it would increase the likelihood of voting' (Prusher 2012). 'No single factor can explain the Palestinian minority's diminishing investment in national politics,' states journalist Jonathan Cook (2013). In fact, a mix of structural reasons and circumstantial triggers explains the increasing withdrawal of Palestinian citizens from voting in Knesset elections. The cumulative awareness that the structural exclusion of the Palestinian minority impedes significant transformation of the Zionist regime is undoubtedly paramount among the reasons shaping the refusal to participate. Other reasons include concerns that may be termed 'national', such as the continuing occupation of the West Bank, Gaza (in its siege actualisation since 2007) and East Jerusalem and the Jewish settlements on these lands, as well as the obstinate Zionist refusal to discuss the Palestinian right of return. As already stated, circumstantial triggers are also at work, particularly war events of differing orders of magnitude against Palestinians, either within Israel proper or beyond the Green Line. Other factors are more specific to the electoral system, such as the recurrent attempts of right-wing parties to disqualify individual Palestinian MKs and Arab political parties. Taken together, this series of reasons explains the drastic decline of Palestinian voter turnout in the past decade or so, as shown in Table 4.2, defined by some as an 'unprecedented and historic change' (ibid.; Ghanem and Mustafa 2007: 68).

From the first Knesset elections to the 1999 campaign, the percentage of Palestinian voters resembled that of Jewish voters. The change in the Palestinian turnout began right after October 2000. But it would be wrong to align this declining voter turnout with a parallel decline, though less pronounced, in Jewish turnout (as in Rudnitzky 2013). Everywhere in neoliberal spaces we find an increase in political indifference, but the increase in the withdrawal of Palestinian voters has other local explanations as well. The sharp decline in Palestinian turnout in Knesset elections was, in fact, what drove AFI to launch its study. A close look at it reveals that, at its core, this study is devoted to dealing with potential strategies to reduce abstention, so it would not be inexact to claim that the AFI research was designed in the first place to encourage the participation of Palestinian citizens in general elections to the Knesset. As AFI's co-directors Amnon Be'eri-Sulitzeanu and Mohammad Darawshe confess:

> We are very disturbed by the consistent fall in the level of participation of Arab citizens in various spheres of society, and particularly in the political system ... This decline is a recipe for social instability and for a profound social and ethnic rift that will not easily be repaired in the future. We are interested in seeing expanded participation in the elections, each voter according to his or her conscience ... (Prusher 2012; see also Table 4.3).

It is worth looking at the ways in which AFI justifies its call to Palestinian citizens to participate in Knesset elections, beyond the more general assumptions of the benefits of political participation. To do so, let us focus on two of the three categories explaining the refusal to vote, as adopted by Ghanem and Mustafa (2007), and on which the AFI study seems to base its conceptual platform. (The third category, which is of no interest for my analysis, is 'technical' abstention and relates to a general indifference to politics and other personal reasons.) Of these two categories, one is labelled 'ideo-

TABLE 4.3 Critical analysis of the AFI's co-directors' speech

'We are very disturbed by the consistent fall in the level of participation of Arab citizens ... particularly in the political system ...'	Why are the AFI co-directors disturbed? Their concern is a reaction to Palestinian voters evacuating the 'voting territory'. By perceiving active voting as the only legitimate relationship to this territory, they rule out other political avenues. To shape their concern, AFI's co-directors must minimise the significance of the material, affective and symbolic conditions that cause Palestinian citizens not to vote.
'This decline is a recipe for social instability and for a profound social and ethnic rift that will not easily be repaired in the future ...'	Using illegitimate 'scare tactics', AFI's co-directors accuse voting refusers of causing social instability and profound social and ethnic rift.
'We are interested in seeing expanded participation in the elections, each voter according to his or her conscience ...'	Pleading for social stability and normative political behaviour, disregarding the structural exclusion of the Palestinian minority.

logical' and is based on the idea that 'participation in elections gives legitimacy to the state's democracy and it cannot change the situation of the Palestinian in Israel' (ibid.: 59). Traditionally, this position is endorsed mainly by two political movements: the leftist secular movement Abnaa al-Balad ('Sons of the Land') and the Northern Branch of the Islamic Movement. The other trend is tagged as 'political' and mainly 'expresses a political protest against the situation of the Palestinians in Israel on one hand, and the inability of the parliamentary arrangement to make the desired change in this situation on the other' (ibid.: 59). In 2007, Ghanem and Mustafa reported that ideological boycotting in the previous decade accounted for about 10 per cent of Palestinian non-voters, according to opinion polls (ibid.: 59). Five years later, during the election campaign of

2013, the AFI study reports that 17 per cent of respondents boycotted the elections for strictly ideological reasons, a rate that for AFI's co-directors Be'eri-Sulitzeanu and Darawshe was a source of relief: 'The low level of "ideological abstainers" is an encouraging finding' (Prusher 2012).

However, I find the conceptual differentiation between 'ideological' and 'political' factors for refusal or abstention from voting problematic in more ways than one. Its ends are essentially political. For instance, while Ghanem and Mustafa (2007) use this categorisation to depict what seems to reflect the internal diversity of the Palestinian public discourse on the topic of voting for the Knesset, the AFI study uses this categorisation to disqualify ideological boycotters and to launch a general call to Palestinian citizens to go out and vote. It does so by anchoring the distinction between 'ideological' and 'political' in a value system with a negative pole as its point of reference. In the AFI study, 'ideological' is the negative model against which AFI suggests acting. By 'ideological' the study assumes an irrational, ideology-based, self-ostracised and detached-from-reality attitude to participation in the Israeli national political system as a whole. In other words, the AFI understands 'ideological' to mean 'not political' – as if embedded in a sort of Platonic ideal understanding of the world, ultimately proving unproductive, unhelpful and harmful as it weakens Palestinian representation and political power in the Knesset that might counterbalance the centre-right. At the other end of the spectrum, a large proportion of the Palestinian respondents in the AFI study (2012) ascribed their preference for not voting to reasons such as 'lack of confidence in the Israeli democracy' and 'the inability of Arab MKs to affect the political agenda'. In line with Ghanem and Mustafa (2007), the AFI study defined these reasons as 'political'. I believe that by 'political' the AFI study means that issues in this category should be addressed politically, that is to say, through formal politics by means of participation in Knesset elections.

To me, both sets of arguments seem to reflect a realistic and practical understanding of 'the reality of the Jewish state, the ethnic nature of this state and its role in blocking the horizon of political work' (ibid.: 54). When 'ideological' refusers claim that 'participation in elections ... cannot change the situation of the Palestinian in Israel' (ibid.: 59), they do not anchor the argument in ideal representations but in actual politics. The only difference between the two sets of arguments is that the 'ideological' position anticipated the 'political' position both chronologically and in discourse. One might claim that people who have only recently refused to vote and explain their refusal as 'political' have given the Israeli political system a period of grace of which Israel never made use. Therefore, the distinction between 'ideological' and 'political' seems to substantiate a drift that does not really exist and that has essentially served as a platform to attack the 'ideologues' and back those perceived as more pragmatic *because they do vote*. However, this distinction does not reflect a deep dissonance. Ultimately, what tips the scales is the growing understanding that the Jewish state never sincerely intended to embrace equality or meet Palestinian interests. Devoid of this understanding, the AFI study fails to interpret the underlying cracks revealed by the general pattern of Palestinian political participation in elections, which since the events of October 2000 has declined drastically.

Although, in the past, calls to boycott the elections were met with apathy by the Jewish population and the Hebrew press, the dramatic fall in Palestinian voter turnout has been drawing increasing attention. So, in the run-up to the 2013 Knesset elections, the AFI study was not alone in its efforts to influence Palestinian citizens to vote. As Abu-Rass reports, just one day before the elections 'several Israeli newspapers have run opinion columns ... calling on Arabs to vote' (2013). The *Haaretz* newspaper took an unusual step of printing an editorial in Arabic encouraging Arabs to vote. Labour party leader Shelly Yachimovich began an extensive last-minute campaign on Arab websites and Arabic-language social media networks, also hoping to grudgingly extract a few more Arab votes. In a publicised web chat with citizens a few days before the 2013 elections, Zahava Gal-On, chairperson of Meretz, a small Ashkenazi liberal and Zionist-left party, called on Israel's Arab citizens: 'Don't despair, don't be part of the "hopeless party", and don't give up. Go out, vote and influence!' (Lior 2013).

What was the panic about? Why does the Zionist left rush out to recruit Arab voters? Is it just the assumption that more Arab voters will increase its chances for more leftist seats in the Knesset? It is not only that. Beyond and above this political interest, there are other forces aiming to keep Arab citizens and their representatives in the Knesset tight within the political system. These forces are not explicitly expressed in everyday politics and nothing is said about their vectors on political platforms or in speeches or interviews – but what is revealed by the acts of these forces is their desire not to let Palestinian citizens and Jewish dissidents opt out. This voice resonates along such lines as 'You are part of the society, so you should vote to influence that society' – even though this voice grows louder by silencing the fact that the Palestinian minority is *a part that plays no part*. What is the panic about, then? The Zionist left is horrified at the image of a Knesset without Palestinian representatives. Their presence in the Knesset is the corpus delicti of this particular variety of leftists, the physical evidence of the crime that provides their discourse with a corporeal silhouette. Their subtext goes more or less as follows:

> *Honourable Chairman of the Knesset, members of the Knesset, these are my Arabs. [Please, would you come closer, my dear Arab, so I can show you here to my colleagues?] They suffer discrimination. And you should all know that the actions inflicted by our brave soldiers on their families in the territories are simply inconceivable. Members of the Knesset ... Please, don't interrupt me, let me have my say. I shall not let you violate my rights. I have rights ... as a Jew in the Jewish state I have rights! I am asking not to be interrupted ... [Please don't go away, my dear Arab, wait just a minute, I have more to say ...]*

As Cook explains, 'unlike the right wing, the centre-left fears that were the Knesset no longer to represent Palestinian citizens, due either to boycott or a right-wing ban, Israel's rule over its Palestinian minority would look increasingly illegitimate and more like a variety of apartheid. In such circumstances, the centre-left's role in defending Israel abroad – its chief selling point to its constituency at home – would be in danger of becoming redundant' (2013). So as long as 'Ahmed mixes the mortar and keeps silent' (Lavih 2013) or, in other words, as long as Arab citizens keep voting in spite of the fact that they are invisible to Jewish society and never really had the chance to influence or change the regime, the political system can go on with its democratic carnival.

The 2001 prime ministerial election[4] campaign witnessed the emergence of the Popular Committee for Boycotting the Knesset Elections as a direct response to the October 2000 events. Its success was unparalleled, with 81 per cent abstention among the Palestinian electorate. According to Azmi Bishara, the boycott intended to make the right to vote more meaningful (2001: 67). The Popular Committee has appeared again ever since in every Knesset election. It comprises movements such as Abnaa al-Balad as well as academic, public and media personalities in Palestinian society in Israel. In February 2006, during the electoral campaign of that year, 'the committee issued a pamphlet in which it asked Palestinians in Israel to boycott the parliamentary elections' (Ghanem and Mustafa 2007: 62). Interestingly, as Ghanem and Mustafa explain, the pamphlet merged ideological and political reasons and principles, and in so doing stressed their interdependence. Its main contents are quoted below:

First: the central national principle which means not playing an effective political role in supporting the highest Israeli institution, the Knesset, by voting for it and supporting its legitimacy ...

Second: the inability of Palestinian representatives to be effective through parliamentary work. They become a consistent opposition after the elections. They neither have any worthy option nor do they have any possibility to participate in decision making ...

Third: the situation of Palestinian parties: the revision of the situation of Palestinian parties that participate in the Knesset game indicates that these parties were converted into hostages, 'the need to stay in the playground' ... [while there are] racist Zionist attacks against our people ...

Fourth: in the height of the failure ... to achieve our daily and national-political rights through the Knesset, and the role of this institution as a source of racial legislation for the 'Jewish State' against Palestinian citizens ... we suggest the implementation of a programme of reforming and rebuilding all our Palestinian institutions in Israel by electing higher national bodies to represent our public (The Popular Committee, 14 February 2006; quoted in Ghanem and Mustafa 2007: 62–3).

Let us briefly summarise these principles of the boycott: 1) target: the Knesset's legitimacy; 2) fact: the inability of Palestinian MKs to exert influence; 3) interpretation: Palestinian MKs and political parties help create the stage for Israel's policies; and hence, 4) action: Palestinian citizens need to consider alternative forms of representation and the setting up of new institutions. We may arrive at this political programme from a sensible demand: participation in elections to the Knesset should be subject to a test that measures the effects of our representatives in substantially changing the four historical Zionist projects.

§ During the 2013 campaign, and particularly while the formal petition to disqualify Palestinian MK Zoabi was being submitted by right-wing parties in the Knesset, Palestinian scholar Nadim Rouhana called upon Palestinian citizens in Israel not to vote: otherwise, he said, 'they will be doing Israel a favour' (2012). In addition, Rouhana claimed that the disqualification of Zoabi would open up a new political era for Palestinian citizens. Firstly, Israel's image in the world would be seriously damaged, and, as a result, Palestinian citizens would be able to organise themselves to lead a civil struggle against a regime acknowledged as non-democratic. The fact that, as expected, MK Zoabi was not disqualified matters little. What matters is the inclusion of a growing number of Palestinian intellectuals and public figures in this call. Rouhana, in fact, was adding his voice to the call sounded by the Popular Committee for Boycotting the Knesset Elections in 2012.

It is time to revise this call. More precisely, it is time to expand it. Common political positions might be adopted by people of different political leanings and ascribed identities. What, then, would be the reasons for those Jewish voters who are already associated with progressive politics not joining the call to boycott the Knesset elections? I have repeatedly heard the claim that Jews of the left must not refuse to vote because that refusal would overemphasise the point that their right to vote is worth more than the right to vote of Palestinian citizens. I find this claim sheer nonsense, a sort of racialised justification of the fear of opting out. First of all, as I have shown above, large parts of the Israeli political system and civil society are already in a panic because of the increasing withdrawal of Palestinian voters. Their act of refusal is certainly gaining attention and concern, even if for the wrong reasons. No one really expects Jewish citizens to adhere to this withdrawal, but joining it would enhance that attention rather than lead to a shift away from it. Second, similar reservations were raised when Jewish citizens of the left began supporting the Boycotts, Divestment and Sanctions movement (BDS). 'Do not interfere, this is a Palestinian struggle,' some Jewish activists claimed. But this counter-effective argument was proved wrong. Boycott from Within, the Israeli branch of BDS, has been praised for its contribution to the anti-colonial struggle (Barghouti 2011). Third comes the argument that Palestinians and Jews should adopt political positions according to their ascribed identities in a sort of division of activist labour; it is one thing to accept this division as a result of real constraints on the ground, but quite another to conceptualise this division as a desired strategy. In the second case, this division mainly reinforces the ethnic caesura upon which Zionism built the project of colonisation of Palestine (Svirsky 2014). My claim is that joint action by Palestinians and Jews boycotting the Knesset elections is significant in that it institutes another dimension in the common political ground that activists have been struggling to create (Svirsky 2012a). Let us expand on this last point.

As Ghanem and Mustafa explain, one important change resulting from the Palestinian boycott of the elections is that 'the protest against the position of the Palestinian in Israel … is no longer expressed by participation, but by abstaining and boycotting' (2007: 68). Amal Jamal defined this transformation in terms of 'abstention as participation' (2002). In other words, abstaining and boycotting are conceived as a particularly active actualisation of the right to vote. There is no fundamental or practical reason why Jewish voters should not embrace a similar transformation for themselves by adhering to the call for a boycott. Not voting in this sense has nothing to do with political indifference or social ostracism; quite the contrary. Moreover, the Popular Committee for Boycotting the Knesset Elections does not target a particular state of affairs. There is a difference in the quality of political participation between abstention as a vehicle for expressing dissatisfaction with a particular political state of affairs, a specific set of policies or a given set of candidates on the one hand, and refusal to vote as an active form of participation expressing political delegitimisation of the entire parliamentary political work and of the regime itself on the other hand. In the latter, by targeting Israel's highest political institution, the problem we raise is not an unqualified candidate or a corrupt policy. The refusal to vote, rather, addresses the unqualified regime and the deprivation of life this regime has caused and maintained.

By withdrawing from voting to the Knesset, voters might be able to partially deplete the source of consent, without which Israeli political rule would be exposed as what it actually is – domination. *The voter that arises is the non-voter.* Therefore, boycotting the Israeli Knesset elections also contributes to the erosion of the image of Israel as a democracy, with a parliament that engenders such rejection among its citizenry. An entire crisis of legitimacy is thus achieved. Think of the restrictions the Israeli political system has been implementing to ban Palestinian parliamentarians and parties from participating in government and the attempts to disqualify Palestinian MKs and parties from running for the Knesset; think, more generally, of the media propaganda machines demonising Palestinian politicians. We must see these restrictions as belonging to all – not only as restricting Palestinian politicians and the political horizon of the entire Palestinian community. Rather, I suggest seeing them as restrictions per se that significantly hinder the possibility of democratic life for all. I am not claiming that a particular act of political protest – such as boycotting the elections – can reverse or wash away the differences between privilege and marginalisation of the different groups of boycotters. But by means of perceiving parliamentary restrictions as limitations that have the entire political community as their object, we engage in political alliances. The fact that the Popular Committee for Boycotting the Knesset Elections addresses its call to Palestinian citizens is merely a reflection of past experiences and commitments; it is really not news that the groups most affected by oppression are always the first to raise the voice of dissent. The others should follow.

Essentially, boycotting elections is another opportunity to establish common political ground. If we stop voting, our bodies move away from a practice that brought us, before, to be intimate with and part of the political system. Importantly, the political change of heart I am suggesting occurs at a very different level compared with more common expectations in relation to voting, such as the view voiced by the Israeli pseudo-left since the late 1970s with regard to Mizrahi voting. During the 1977 political campaign, Mizrahim massively backed the major right-wing political party Likud, and, for the first time since the establishment of the state, Labour was overthrown. Ever since, and because of the strong neoliberal mindset of the right wing in Israel (of which Labour is not exempt), Mizrahim have been criticised for voting against their political interests. They were expected, allegedly, to realise that their real interests lay with Labour, with the Zionist left. Scholars have provided explanations for this Mizrahi right-wing preference. An amalgamation of three of these accounts seems relevant. Firstly, as Ella Shohat claims, the political behaviour of the Mizrahim should be seen as a reaction to years of Ashkenazi oppression (1988: 14). Secondly, against this background, the Mizrahi politics of resistance 'from the events of Wadi Salib to *Kedma*', as in Sami Shalom Chetrit's (2004) account, portray an anti-hegemonic genealogy that explains to a large extent the political, social and emotional impossibility of aligning with left-wing Zionism. And thirdly, as Dani Filc explains, the legacy of Menachem Begin – who, as the Likud leader in 1977, knew how to include the excluded Mizrahim in his agenda – is still in force (2011). Drawing on Bourdieu, Filc claims that the Likud – based on its populist politics and leadership – continues to enact the political habitus of inclusion towards the Mizrahim that was originated by Begin, regardless of the fact that after Begin, and during their many years of rule, the Likud has not even attempted to transform the structural constraints that continue to reproduce Mizrahi marginalisation. 'And habitus,' as Filc states, 'persists because habitus endows agents with "durable dispositions capable of surviving the economic and social conditions of their own production". Voting patterns and political preferences are thus less prone to change' (ibid.: 234). Therefore:

> The support of the lower classes for leaders who combine a populist rhetoric with neo-liberal policies is not the result of their irrationality, their primitiveness or their manipulation by unscrupulous leaders, but the result of the continued weight of the past experience of partial inclusion as well as the absence of true inclusive alternatives (ibid.: 236).

It would be more than naive to expect that, despite the fact that the call to boycott Israeli elections to the Knesset and Mizrahi right-wing support have in common the rejection of the white Zionist project, these two avenues can easily meet. For the anti-Zionist agenda to offer a truly inclusive alternative, the issue of the racialised absorption of Mizrahim and other Jewish minorities, such as the Ethiopians, should be just as much at its core as the ethno-national exclusion of the Palestinians, the social differentiation of women and the impossibility of building a shared and equal life for Jews and Palestinians. There exists a mutual conditioning between these issues that gives no priority to any one of them, but it exists only circumstantially – this mutual conditioning is in fact Zionism in practice. In other words, it is time to stop stipulating everything that needs to be redone once 'the Israeli–Palestinian conflict' is resolved. Everything depends on everything. Make transverse connections and profane.

§ To turn displacement away from the Knesset into a productive withdrawal, an internal political migration of sorts should follow suit. We migrate into political territories that have yet to be constructed, and hence into transitions. Old understandings of citizenship and political community are to be discarded. Much can be learned in this respect from the Zapatista experience. Indeed, what is needed is a sort of Zapatista enclave in Israel–Palestine: an adjacent political space in which to incubate thousands of forms of collaboration between segregated subjectivities. When the Popular Committee for Boycotting the Knesset Elections calls to establish alternative forms of representation and new institutions, we should all see this call as an open public invitation. The realisation that political reform in Israel has no future of its own must lead us to invest in cultural and political prefigurative work *within* the state but not *with* it.

A THOUSAND PROFANATIONS

'The political, ethical, social, philosophical problem of our days is not to try to liberate the individual from the state, and from the state's institutions, but to liberate us both from the state and from the type of individualization linked to the state. We have to promote new forms of subjectivity through the refusal of this kind of individuality that has been imposed on us ...' (Michel Foucault, 1983)

'The only acceptable finality of human activity is the production of a subjectivity that is auto-enriching its relation to the world in a continuous fashion.' (Félix Guattari, 1995)

I have tried hard to convince readers that the production of subjectivity is more important than the production of tanks and fighter planes that sow fear and terror; more important than the production of microchips and gadgets that help the Israeli army control the lives of Palestinians; more important than the production of the components and elements that together create separation barriers and checkpoints; more important than the production of separate roads for Jews and Palestinians. This is because, as Félix Guattari so lucidly explained, *the production of subjectivity is the raw material for any and all production* (Guattari and Rolnik 2008: 38).

This is not to say that the production of subjectivity establishes linear relationships of causality with other forms of social and cultural production. Social production involves circular interactions simultaneously producing the infinitesimal psychic, corporeal and affective veins and organs that form our subjective bodies in this world on the one hand; and the social, cultural, economic and political wholes we animate on the other hand. These two levels have been defined as the micropolitical and the macropolitical, or the molecular and the molar (Deleuze and Guattari 1987). The two levels affect each other; they redefine each other. Life lies in the outputs of the continuing interactions between these two realms. Subjectivity is produced in the midst of social, cultural, economic and political processes, and yet *subjectivity is the infrastructure of social production*. As a productive social phenomenon, oppression cannot be enacted without trained torturers, militant minds and executors. Therefore, the point of transformation is *how not to reproduce dominant subjectivities* premised on fear, hatred and exclusion in our daily activities and thinking. Through experimentation we struggle to transform our subjectivities, but this internal struggle and the external struggle to defy social institutions is one and the same. To deprive the torturer from the points of subjectivation, the chains of significance and the principles that organise his body as a torturer, is the aim of the revolutionary struggle as much as it is the subversion of the law, the institutions and the social relations that complement and enable his functions.

Israel's nationalist and militarist projects should not be taken at face value but as productions concomitant with the evolution of specific Israeli subjectivities and modes of being. This productive association – between projects and subjectivities – anchors and deepens the everyday commitment of Zionist practitioners; these projects and these modes of being become instilled within their bodies, conveying instructions for the development of social life. Without that produced level of cohesiveness across Jewish-Israeli subjectivities, no one would occupy, oppress or segregate anyone. But they do, and have already done so for a century, and this is why Zionism is not just an ideology and a political plan but has become a hegemonic *historical bloc*. How does this function? In each social sphere, logics, mechanisms and techniques of subjectivation are produced, but, as we have seen throughout this book, they share a reservoir of centres of subjectivation – myths, ideas, events and passions that coil bodies and minds around themselves – making Zionist subjects actual practitioners. From the point of view of the minute subjective constructions, each social sphere shapes itself by articulating particular uses of centres of subjectivation – of the Jewish holocaust, of the right to the land, of the idea of return, of the 'other', of democracy, military violence, sacrifice, nature, citizenship and so forth. At the next level, social spheres become less distinguishable due to the different combinations of these uses. For instance, as I have shown, Zionist hiking does not rely on Arab victimisation or on the holocaust but draws its subjective gravitational forces from the territorialisation of land and military violence; the latter, together with nationalist uses of the holocaust, is also strongly present in educational subjectivation. In turn, processes of subjectivation in education and voting share the inculcation of a duplicitous conceptualisation of citizenship and democracy that makes possible the image of Israel as 'the only democracy in the Middle East'.

At a further level of analysis, the use of the same reservoir of centres of subjectivation and their function within the different social spheres establishes a concentric relationship between those spheres, enhancing their reciprocal connectivity without them totally losing their own distinctiveness. This connectivity is the *resonance* of the system, its expressive coherence. Centres of subjectivation are nurtured reciprocally through the functions they perform within the different social spheres. This amplification of the presence and significance of centres of subjectivation in social life is expressed en masse in the particular contents of our common sense. Noam Chayut, one of the founders of Breaking the Silence, described this relationship as follows:

> I can't live here at ease; on the other hand, I'm here. I feel good here, I like the weather, I like people here, I like my language, I write in my language, but the fact that I live here obliges me to erect all sorts of barriers between myself and this place. One of them is the Arab-Jewish bilingual school ... I just can't send my son to a Jewish public school here. Why? Today I find it bizarre ... *they will take him on those holocaust trips to Poland, they will tell him that the Jews had a terrible life in Europe and therefore we need to slaughter the Arabs here ... all these dogmas I grew up with, they are just criminal ...* (interview, 6 November 2012, emphasis added).

Noam's transformative moment took place on one of his obligatory tours of duty in the West Bank as an Israel Defense Forces (IDF) officer during Operation Defensive Shield in 2002. His secure world crumbled on the day 'his holocaust' was 'stolen' by a single Palestinian girl staring at him, terrified. Of all the children, men, women and elderly people, it was that Palestinian girl: 'Only you waited there,' Noam narrates in his memoir, 'staring at me for another shuddering moment. Then you shook yourself out of your frozen stance, turned silently – a scrawny girl in light-coloured clothes – and ran off, not looking back. You ran and disappeared among the olive trees, appeared again, and then disappeared into the village alleys, forever' (Chayut 2013: 59). And she took with her Noam's own holocaust, as he says, 'the belief that I was avenging my people's destruction by absolute evil, that I was fighting absolute evil' (ibid.: 63). In her eyes, Noam, the IDF officer ravaging her village and her life, embodied absolute evil – a role reserved for Zionism's constitutive others, the Nazis and the Arabs. And at that moment, as Noam says, 'the absolute evil that had governed me until then began to disintegrate' (ibid.: 63). We all need someone to steal our holocausts.

The impressive success of Zionism lies not in the territories it has seized or its technological might, but in having fabricated a Jewish society with strong ties of meanings, interpretations and dispositions that tightly knit together distinct social spheres. As a teacher, a hiker, a parent or a voter, Zionists feel secure in their own territory: expectations are met with regard to their general interpretations of life. Zionists resonate between themselves so that 'several voices seem to issue from the same mouth' (Deleuze and Guattari 1987: 97). The same mouth is the 'we'. When functioning as Zionists, Jewish-Israelis rarely speak as individuals. But 'we' is not only *us*; it does not point just to belonging. Rather, 'we' is above all an acronym of '*without others*' – 'we', the exclusivist pronoun par excellence. Jewish-Israeli society is not unique in having a strong sense of 'we-ness'. But it is a viscous, racist, ferocious, obstinate and unmistakable 'we'; it is a 'we' that emerges out of the conjugations between all the Zionist social codifications – and in Jewish-Israeli society, everything is a target for social codification, nothing is left to chance. This is why the major threat that terrifies the State of Israel and its Jewish majority is the increasing number of activist collaborations between Palestinians and Jewish-Israelis. These collaborations run counter to everything Zionism means, making more palpable the danger of the deluge, the danger of social fluxes that escape codification, pouring over Zionist heads with rage, those fluxes that drown the existing Zionist codes.

Indeed, I have also tried hard to show that it is possible to develop dissident modes of subjectivation *against* the Zionist subjectivity-producing machines. You see, 'ruling groups never engineer consent with complete success' (Lears 1985: 570), or, in a more Gramscian view, consent and dissent always coexist – that is one fundamental principle of hegemony. My aim in this book was not to reduce Jewish-Israeli society to a completely uniform, closed and unified social system or identity. Rather, I wanted to stress the strength of Zionist hegemony from the point of view of subjectivity, namely how human agency implicates subjects in domination as well as how that position is confronted. In Israel, the language of opposition exists: Zionist legitimisation is not all-encompassing, not always, and not by Jewish-Israelis as a whole – there are always escapes. Dissident modes of subjectivation are singular ways of existence that dare to reject, perforate and profane pre-established Zionist identities, associations, political dispositions and habits. These singularities map their targets and erode their cohesiveness by myriad strategies, such as simulating majoritarian functions but eventually overturning their coherence; by refusing existing practices, thus wearing away the cogs of the dominant forms of legitimacy; by creating adjacent existential territories into which to migrate; and by overwhelming assumed knowledge with discourses that have been silenced so far. In one fell swoop, collaborative alliances that cross segregated subjectivities expose and emplace the form of life against which Zionism built its own life. For instance, refusing to vote in the Israeli parliamentary elections offers an opportunity to participate in the creation of a new collaborative territory. On 18 November 2012, in Tel Aviv, I meet with Udi Aloni, the Israeli-born filmmaker and writer. Every minute with Udi became a visualisation of a universe of struggle. For Udi, collaborative alliances rest on two premises: one is that the means of struggle of the oppressed are respected; and the other is to offer new spaces – namely that alliance can offer affirmative constructions.

I couldn't agree more. It is never enough, explains Udi, to support the Boycotts, Divestment and Sanctions movement (BDS) or to bring down the wall or fence separating the Jewish state from the West Bank. One must construct something in their place. And yet, '[f]idelity to the oppressed and his struggle is the first act,' adds Udi, 'upon which one can then suggest new theories and new constructions' (interview, 18 November 2012).

Why cultural transformation? Simply because the very subjectivities that owe their historical existence to war and to the deprivation of life cannot take part in the reconstruction of society. They must go; it is not enough to prevent their ingress into the new society. We must make them go, make them disintegrate into the past. Jewish-Israelis tend to think that, just as they are, they have what is necessary to bring about peace and social justice. But they continually bring about war and injustice. Jewish-Israelis nonsensically believe that only he who has experienced war is able to make peace. But they have stubbornly showed that he who has experienced war has committed himself to infinitely repeat war.

Cultural transformation is the missing link in our thinking about the future, a future that has been colonised and shrunk by the image of 'the occupied territories' in ways that avoid considering Jewish-Israeli society itself in transformative terms. The fact that the oppression of the Palestinians in the West Bank and the siege of the Gaza Strip make Israel's other cruelties inside the Green Line pale in comparison, the expectations that any agreement with the Palestinians will be based around some form of withdrawal from the occupied lands of the West Bank, and, lastly, the fact that international opposition to Israel from civil society focuses on the occupation – together, these factors help keep Jewish-Israeli society safe from serious criticism. If Israel is criticised, and if the BDS call for boycotts is gaining more and more support, it is mainly because of the occupation. To put it in another way: what does the world want from Israel? Answer: *To end the occupation*. Almost nowhere in the international critique do you see a connection between current thinking about the occupied territories and the kind of society inside the Israel of the Green Line. The occupation overwhelms the

perception of international activists, and rightly so. But the infrastructure underlying what has been going on in the territories for so
long lies within the Green Line, in the production of the collective
subjectivity of Jewish-Israeli society itself. In fact, BDS refers to that
complexity by demanding equality for the Palestinian citizens of
Israel, but most BDS supporters around the world are unaware of this.

Surely, focusing on the occupation is the right thing to do in the
sense that this oppression must be ended immediately. But, as a
by-product, it enables Israel to represent the occupation as the only
'problem' that needs a solution – the only topic to be put on the
negotiating table and about which Israel claims to be ready to make
'sacrifices'. It is no secret that the refugee problem is Israel's red
rag, but only because the refusal to negotiate the refugee problem
is the flip side of the definition of Israel as a Jewish state, which
in turn points also to the question of the status of the Palestinian
citizens of Israel. This is why Israel insists on being recognised as a
Jewish state as a precondition for reaching any agreement with the
Palestinians. This demand reveals Israel's deepest collective desires.
Being recognised as a Jewish state means closing down the future. It
means legitimising the way of life that begot and enjoys the results
of one of the major ethnic cleansings of the twentieth century; the
way of life that feeds into and is fed by the regime of occupation; the
same segregationist way of life that denies equal citizenship for the
Palestinian minority – a way of life that is incapable of generating
anything but segregation, dispossession and social injustice.

Any 'solution' to the occupation of the West Bank, East Jerusalem
and Gaza will always be a partial one unless it is closely tied up
with the refugee question and the status of the Palestinian citizens
of Israel – in other words, unless it is part of a larger process of
transformation in which Jewish-Israelis take part. This is exactly
what I meant in the introduction to this book when I claimed that
no political solution will save us, not until a process of cultural
transformation gets under way. The secret lies not in the holding of
such or such territories but in the processes that produce the means
of production of Israel's domination and oppression, and these processes are those that produce Zionist modes of being. Oppressors

must change; their modes of being in this world must change. That historical event will not be staged on the lawn of the White House, nor will it be broadcast live to all corners of the globalised world. Cultural transformation works slowly, away from the limelight.

However – and extremely importantly – this is not to say that people suffering as a result of the Zionist will to continue with nationalistic, militarist and territorial projects should wait for a cultural transformation in Jewish-Israeli society. I insisted only that the expectations of an Israeli–Palestinian agreement on lands and sovereignty lack any understanding of the role of subjectivity and culture; however, the anti-Zionist struggle has gone on for decades, and in this book I have chosen to investigate only one important aspect of it. There are at least two interconnected realms of resistance: the historical Palestinian struggle and the politics of Palestinian–Israeli collaboration, which has recently been on the increase; and the efforts to culturally transform the subjectivity of the oppressor. These realms are interconnected because – from the point of view of transformation – one is unthinkable without the other. In itself, traditional struggle (generally based on some form of nationalism) might be able to put an end to some forms of oppression and may even achieve political autonomy or independence, but the cultural infrastructure that originally put in place those forms of oppression and dispossession and made them functional is generally left intact. I believe that this is the response we should be giving to Patrick Wolfe's observation that 'settler colonialism is relatively impervious to regime change' (2006). If the 'regime' is understood as in the ancient Greek tradition, as being the political as much as the cultural constitution of society – 'constitution' expressing both process (the continuing formation) and form (the stable stages of that continuing formation) – it cannot really be changed without a deep transformation of its ways of life.

And this is also why engaging in a process of self-transformation cannot unfold as an egotistic adventure. If Jewish-Israelis choose to make changes to their lives just to 'feel better with themselves' or because they see these changes as something that is in 'their best interests' – these interests being perceived from a tribalistic point of view – they should rescind. Nothing transformative can come out of such a disposition. Any line of separation that is imposed between the transformation of the oppressor's subjectivities on the one hand and the general project of de-settlerisation led by the oppressed on the other is a line that reflects settlerism. In other words, for self-transformation to happen, Jewish-Israelis must embrace the goals and aspirations of the Palestinian struggle as their own, carefully accommodating themselves and functioning in that struggle in consultation with their Palestinian partners.[1] Truthfully transforming Jewish-Israelis' subjectivities should be about engaging with the general anti-settlerist Palestinian struggle to rid the region and its people of the burden and the cruelty of Zionism. This huge historical enterprise necessitates the agitation of forces from within – cultural transformation and collaborative struggle among them – as much as the support and pressure of forces from the international community. Of the latter, the BDS is nowadays the most encouraging and promising of all.

And yet, with regard to cultural transformation, we need more and more strategies to help us identify blockages, points of co-optation and mechanisms of capture and to implant them with *a thousand profanations*. A thousand profanations every day are needed in our confrontation with Zionist hyper-subjectivity. This is the way to put behind us the sort of identities and ways of being that still maintain the Zionist machine. In turn, this is the way by which we may be able to construct a new beginning in historical Palestine. But you will need to be alert, and not drop your guard even for a second. Relax your vigilance and you risk being seized – by holocaust imagery, by biblical nostalgia, or by militarist passions that overwhelm your profanatory thoughts and actions. You will sense those images coming nearer and nearer as you dare engage with *the after*. They emerge from any crevice in which they were sown. But in any crevice we can find the chance to embark on a journey of self-transformation. The newsletter sent from our children's school, a protest we spot driving on our way home, a comment made by a friend, an article we just read in the newspaper – anything can become the incubator of our voyage into new affective horizons, anything can hold the key to begin noticing everything we were bound not to.

NOTES

Introduction

1 The Mizrahi Jews are Jews of Middle Eastern descent or from Muslim-majority countries, also known as oriental Jews or Arab-Jews. The Ashkenazi Jews are Jews of European descent.

2 Mizrahim is the plural form in Hebrew for Mizrahi Jews. I would like to thank Orly Noy for her help in articulating my thoughts in this passage.

3 Ashkenazim is the plural form in Hebrew for Jews of European descent.

4 Generalising from Nahla Abdo's claim regarding the status of women in Israel, I totally agree that 'citizenship status in Israel can best be comprehended in terms of the presence of two different processes operating simultaneously within the Israeli state: one of exclusion and racial separation, which affects the Palestinian citizens at large; and another of racialized (and ethnicized) inclusion, to which Palestinians and Mizrahis (especially women) are subjected' (2011: 40).

5 So, as Abdo explains: 'For most Mizrahi scholars, including feminists, Zionism represents the position of only some European Jews, who brought the ideology and movement from the West and implanted them in Palestine; further, it only speaks for them' (2011: 87). The longing to see this conscious disengagement inundating the hearts of those who see themselves as Mizrahim is just that, a longing and not a reality. Sadly, this position is shared by only small circles of academics and activists, and even if at some unconscious level the antagonism towards white Zionism is still effervescent, those secret desires continue to be overwhelmingly repressed in the form of the factual commitment of the vast majority of Mizrahim to Zionist practices of hate and dispossession.

6 I would like to thank Ian Buchanan (University of Wollongong) who helped me with the ideas in this section.

7 I could not have articulated these conceptual differences without the help of Christopher John Muller (Cardiff University).

8 See, for example, Azoulay and Ophir 2013; Ghanem 2001; Gordon 2008; Jabareen 2008; Jamal 2011; Kimmerling 1983; Lustick 1980; Yiftachel 2006.

9 See www.themarker.com/career/1.558123 (accessed 11 November 2013) (in Hebrew).

10 See www.handinhandk12.org/. My support of these shared educational frameworks should be read in tandem with the critique I have expressed that rests on some segregative procedures these schools have adopted, in spite of their initial collaborative impetus (see Svirsky 2011; 2012a; Svirsky and Mor-Sommerfeld 2012).

11 See www.newprofile.org/english/.

12 See http://zochrot.org/en.

13 See www.breakingthesilence.org.il/.

14 Since the late 1990s, Israeli feminist discourse has been revised in regard to the omission of the role of race and class in the constitution of womanhood in the Jewish society (see, for example, Abdo 2011; Lavie 2011; Motzafi-Haller 2001; Shohat 1996).

15 In our lifetime, it is practically

impossible to reach a two-state condition because the Israeli electorate will never elect an assertive government with sincere plans to end the military and economic occupation and to dismantle the Jewish settlements in the Palestinian territories – measures without which any two-state implementation would only entrench Palestinian dependency. Simply put, a national interest invested in engaging with a peaceful situation has never been constructed. It is also practically impossible if not extremely difficult to reach a two-state condition because any attempt at dismantling the Jewish settlements in the West Bank will face fierce armed resistance and possibly insurrection within the Israel Defense Forces, which might unleash bloodshed in the entire region. In terms of territorial coherence, the two-state condition is geographically hampered by the physical separation between the Gaza Strip and the West Bank, not to mention the Jewish settlements that have dotted the entire West Bank, thus preventing Palestinian territorial continuity.

16 To be precise, Grinberg places responsibility for making the given reality fit within his political model in the hands of 'research centres and think tanks', to then be passed on to the respective Israeli and Palestinian leadership. Again, we are left with another top-down approach that fails to take account of ordinary changes.

17 Abnaa el-Balad is a secular movement founded in the late 1960s as a political movement for Palestinian liberation with a Palestinian political programme. It comprises mainly Palestinian members with a few activists of Jewish origin.

18 Information on the activities of the Jaffa Group for One Democratic State is available at http://yaffaods.

wordpress.com/2013/04/25/announcement-on-the-establishment-of-the-jaffa-group-for-one-democratic-state/.

19 Social reports on equality can be found at www.adva.org/default.asp?PageId=102&ItemId=15&type=tag.

1 The hiker

1 *Tiyulim* is hikes in Hebrew (plural). The singular is *tiyul*.

2 'Sephardi' means 'from Spain'. It refers to Jewish families who emigrated from Spain during the Inquisition. In terms of religious practice, 'Sephardi' also encompasses Jews from the Muslim countries of North Africa and the Middle East. In Israel, after 1948 the term 'Mizrahi' replaced the use of 'Sephardi'.

3 The Ministry of Education geography curriculum (1998) carries more than merely the traces of early pioneering desires. It states in its official aims: 'The development of affinity, involvements and responsibility towards the natural and cultural landscapes of the Land of Israel and loyalty towards the State of Israel' (see Bar-Gal and Bar-Gal 2008: 59).

4 Neumann went as far as to describe the relationship woven between the pioneer and the land in terms of a carnal relationship (2011). Although his explicit purpose is to legitimise Zionist colonisation by anchoring discourse in an erotic type of narrative that stresses the pioneers' passion and physical love for the land of Israel, it is precisely this passionate narrative that sheds light on the raping character of this particular form of colonisation, as it seems that the new Jewish masculinity could be achieved only through an all-male corporeal assault on the land.

5 A neighbourhood in West Jerusalem founded in 1926.

6 For a comparative analysis of these two institutions as regards their

connection to the erasure of Palestinian villages, see Kadman 2008: 87–8.

7 For a brief history of these changes in the pre-state period, see Almog 2000, Stein 2009 and Dror 2011.

8 See the *Shelah* programme on the Ministry of Education website: http://cms.education.gov.il/Education-CMS/Units/Noar/TechumeiHaminhal/Shelach/masaisraeli.htm (in Hebrew).

9 See the *Shelah* programme on the Ministry of Education website: http://cms.education.gov.il/Education-CMS/Units/Noar/TechumeiHaminhal/Shelach/masaisraeli.htm (in Hebrew).

10 See www.newprofile.org/english/node/215 (accessed 1 July 2013).

11 As Ella Shohat compellingly narrates: 'Despite these obstacles, Sephardi revolt and resistance has been constant. Already in the transient camps there were "bread and jobs" demonstrations. David Horowitz, then General Director of the Ministry of Finance, during a political consultation with Ben Gurion, described the Sephardi population in the camps as "rebellious" and the situation as "incendiary" and "dynamite". Another major revolt against misery and discrimination began in Haifa, in the neighborhood of Wadi-Salib, in 1959. Israeli authorities suppressed the rebellion with military and police terror. The Labor Party (Mapai), furthermore, tried to undermine the political organization that emerged from the riots by obliging slum residents to join the Party if they hoped for a job. Another large-scale rebellion broke out again in the seventies, when the Israeli Black Panthers called for the destruction of the regime and for the legitimate rights of all the oppressed without regard to religion, origin or nationality. This alarmed the establishment, and the movement's leaders were arrested and placed under administrative detention. At that moment, the Black Panthers launched demonstrations which shook the entire country. In a demonstration that has since become famous (May 1971) tens of thousands, in response to police repression, went into the streets and threw Molotov cocktails against police and government targets. The same evening, 170 activists were arrested, 35 were hospitalized, and more than 70 policemen and officers were wounded. Taking their name from the American movement, the Black Panther revolt was led by the children of the immigrants, many of them delinquents who passed through rehabilitation centers or prisons. Gradually becoming aware of the political nature of their "inferiority", they sabotaged the myth of the "melting pot" by showing that there is in Jewish Israel not one but two peoples. They often used the term *dfukim veshehorim* (screwed and blacks) to express the ethnic/class positioning of Sephardim and viewed the American Black revolt as a source of inspiration. (The choice of the name "Black Panthers" also ironically reverses the Ashkenazi reference to Sephardim as "black animals".) More recently, in December 1982, riots broke out in response to the police murder of an Oriental slum resident whose only crime was to build an illegal extension to his overcrowded house' (Shohat 1988: 29–30).

12 As Abdo explains: 'Zionism needed (Arab) Jews for several reasons: demographically, they were needed to legitimize the state as Jewish; geographically, they were necessary for the Judaization of the land; economically, they were needed to supplement and strengthen the emerging market; and finally, Mizrahi Jews (especially males) were needed to shore up Israel's military power' (2011: 88–9).

13 In his article, Yochai Oppenheimer analyses the works of Shimon

Ballas, Sami Michael, Kobi Oz, Yosi Sucary, Dudi Busi, Albert Suissa, Ronit Matalon and others.

14 See research conducted by a student at the Hadassah College in Jerusalem at https://spreadsheets. google.com/spreadsheet/formResponse?formkey=dHVEZjRVVmJfX2JIcoZyZkp1 MUtSZ2c6MQ&ptok=1871249207529915 882&ifq and other, very similar, research conducted by a student at the University of Haifa at https://docs.google.com/ spreadsheet/viewform?fromEmail=true& formkey=dHZBbThadkVCZjhhYXEwTod4 SkNsZ1E6MQ (both sites in Hebrew).

2 The teacher

1 See: www.newprofile.org/english/ node/224 (accessed 23 December 2012).

2 'As Natural as Mother's Milk – Impregnating Society with Militarism'. Available at: www.newprofile.org/ english/node/215.

3 The full dossier (in Hebrew) is available at: http://cms.education.gov. il/EducationCMS/Units/Noar/Katalog Pirsumim/HachanaLezahal/ogdan.htm.

4 See 'The New Profile Report on Child Recruitment'. Available at: www. newprofile.org/english/node/249.

5 Since then, and until 2008, I was in charge of the programme and taught the compulsory courses.

6 See, for example, these articles in the Hebrew press: Yisrael Harel, 'Gideon the teacher teaches civic education', *Haaretz*, 30 April 2009; Ben-Dror Yemini, 'Let the Palestinian refuse', *Maariv*, 9 May 2009; Efrat Zemer, 'Change the curriculum of civic education', *Maariv*, 25 November 2009; Yaheli Moran Zelikovitz, 'Civic studies are leftist', *Ynet*, 25 November 2009; Hagit Sasar, 'Citizenship against Zionism', *Makor Rishon*, 22 January 2010.

7 See the guide's units on the Zochrot website: http://zochrot.org/en.

8 See the Zochrot website: http:// zochrot.org/en.

9 http://www.haaretz.com/news/ national/.premium-1.569422.

10 On Shas' network of schools, see Dahan and Levy 2000: 431–7 and Schiffman 2005.

11 See: http://kedma-edu.org.il/ main/siteNew/index.php?page=83 (accessed 12 November 2013).

3 The parent

1 Periods of service depend on the unit in which men serve. This also determines when they serve until – generally no longer than age forty-five. Although, according to the law, women can be recruited up to the age of thirty-four if they are not married, 'their participation has been marginal' (Helman 1997: 310).

2 See www.newprofile.org/english/ node/215 (accessed 1 July 2013).

3 See www.newprofile.org/english/ node/215 (accessed 1 July 2013).

4 See www.nrg.co.il/online/1/ ART1/934/248.html (accessed 4 July 2013) (in Hebrew).

5 From the New Profile report: 'According to Article 1 of the Convention on the Rights of the Child, "a child means every human being below the age of eighteen years unless under the law applicable to the child, majority is attained earlier". The age of majority in Israeli law is 18. In the present report we adopt this definition. Thus a child, for the present purposes, is any person below the age of 18. Matters become less clear-cut when we come to define the term "child recruitment". The generally accepted definitions for the terms "child soldier" and "recruitment" in this context are found in the Cape Town Principles: "Child soldier" in this document means any person under 18 years of age who is part of any kind of regular

or irregular armed force or armed group
in any capacity, including but not limited
to cooks, porters, messengers, and those
accompanying such groups, other than
purely as family members. It includes
girls recruited for sexual purposes and
forced marriage. It does not, therefore,
only refer to a child who is carrying or
has carried arms. "Recruitment" encompasses compulsory, forced and voluntary
recruitment into any kind of regular or
irregular armed force or armed group'
(Givol et al. 2004: 7).

6 See www.newprofile.org/english/
node/249.

7 See www.child-soldiers.org/
publications_archive.php.

8 See www.newprofile.org/english/
node/287 (accessed 8 July 2013).

9 See http://yeshatid.org.il (accessed
8 July 2013) (in Hebrew).

10 See www.newprofile.org/english/
node/287 (accessed 8 July 2013).

11 See www.shivyon.org.il/Default.
asp?PageId=64679 (accessed 5 July 2013)
(in Hebrew).

12 I am intentionally refraining
from using the concept of 'Occupied
Palestinian Territories' because the use
of 'Occupied' attached to 'Palestinian
Territories', referred to as the West Bank,
Gaza and East Jerusalem, overlooks
the fact that the State of Israel in its
entirety is the product of a colonising
project of dispossession and ethnic
cleansing, as if there were a 'legitimate'
Israel within the international borders of
the Green Line. My position is that there
is no such legitimate state. The use
of 'proper' to denote the Israel of the
Green Line, as in Azoulay's and Ophir's
work, denotes a distinction between
governmentalities of domination. A
colonial history binds both together.

13 On this subject, see Dahan-Kalev
1997, Emmett 1996, Shadmi 2000 and
Shiran 1991.

14 See www.newprofile.org/english/
about_en/charter.

15 See www.newprofile.org/english/
node/316.

16 For information on the exhibition, see www.newprofile.org/english/
Exhibition.

17 I exclude here the few thousand
working for the Shabak (Israeli General Security Services) and the Mossad
(Israeli Intelligence Agency) who are not
'recognisable' in public spaces.

18 See the discussion at www.
newprofile.org/node/263 (in Hebrew).

19 In this discussion I am not
addressing the question of, as Lubin
framed it: Should feminists struggle
for the implementation of equal rights
in the army in the form of inclusion of
women in exactly the same roles and
functions as men, or is feminism about
dismantling all modes of violence, the
army included? (2002: 164). Personally,
I align with the latter position. On this
issue, see also Barak-Erez 2007.

4 The voter

1 Beyond the Israeli–Palestinian
ethno-national lines, migrant workers
and refugees living in Israel are part of
the third category.

2 According to the United Nations
High Commissioner for Refugees
(UNHCR), the Nakba has led 'to the
existence today of over four million
Palestinian refugees' (Lentin 2010: 9).
The Palestinian population of the West
Bank and the Gaza Strip, taken together,
is 3.5 million.

3 However, since 2003 the Egged
company's public buses that stop in ultra-
orthodox Jewish neighbourhoods (in
Jerusalem and Bnei Brak) force women to
get on the bus from the back door and sit
at the back. These are called 'Mehadrin
bus lines'. In 2011, the supreme court gave
its consent to the arrangement.

4 The Israeli public voted only three times in prime ministerial elections: in 1996, 1999 and 2001. The law regarding prime ministerial elections, and together with it the electoral reform, was cancelled in March 2001.

A thousand profanations

1 I have written on this issue in my *Arab-Jewish Activism* (2012a) and in the forthcoming 'Settler colonialism and collaborative struggles in Australia and Israel-Palestine' (2014).

REFERENCES

Articles, books and reports

Abdo, N. (2011) *Women in Israel: Race, gender and citizenship.* London: Zed Books.

Abu-Rass, T. (2013) 'Why Palestinian citizens don't vote in Israeli elections'. *+972*, 21 January. Available at: http://972mag.com/why-palestinian-citizens-dont-vote-in-israeli-elections/64332/ (accessed 23 April 2013).

Abu-Saad, I. (2006) 'State-controlled education and identity formation among the Palestinian Arab minority in Israel'. *American Behavioural Scientist* 49(8): 1085–100.

Activity Agreement (2007) *Activity Agreement for Preparation to the IDF.* Available at: http://cms.education.gov.il/NR/rdonlyres/33CFE0B8-6930-4D90-BB0F-23A97AF08AA0/105308/sherutsikum.pdf (Hebrew).

Adan, H., V. Ashkenazi and B. Alperson (2001) *To Be Citizens in Israel: A Jewish and democratic state.* Jerusalem: Ma'alot (Hebrew).

Adres, E., P. Vanhuysse and D. Vashdi (2011) 'The individual's level of globalism and citizen commitment to the state: the tendency to evade military service in Israel'. *Armed Forces & Society* 38(1): 92–116.

Adva Center (2012) *Report on Inequality 2012.* Tel Aviv: Adva Center.

AFI (2012) *The Political Participation of the Arab Citizens in Israel: Political attitudes towards the 19th Knesset.* Harey Yehuda: Abraham Fund Initiatives (AFI).

Agamben, G. (1991) *Language and Death: The place of negativity* (translated by K. E. Pinkus and M. Hardt). Minneapolis, MN: University of Minnesota Press.

— (1993) *The Coming Community* (translated by M. Hardt). Minneapolis, MN: University of Minnesota Press.

— (1995) *Idea of Prose.* New York, NY: State University of New York Press.

— (2000) *Means without End: Notes on politics* (translated by V. Binnetti and C. Casarino). Minneapolis, MN: University of Minnesota Press.

— (2007) *Profanations* (translated by J. Fort). New York, NY: Zone Books.

Algazi, G. (2004) 'Listening to the voice which says no'. In D. Chenin, M. Sfard and S. Rotberd (eds), *The Refuseniks' Trials.* Tel Aviv: Babel Publishing House, pp. 11–35 (Hebrew).

Almog, O. (2000) *The Sabra: The creation of the New Jew.* Berkeley, CA: University of California Press.

Althusser, L. (1971) *Lenin and Philosophy and Other Essays.* New York, NY: Monthly Review Press.

Amor, M. (2002) 'The epistemology of Mizrachiut in Israel'. In H. Hever, Y. Shenhav and P. Motzafi-Haller (eds), *Mizrahim in Israel: A critical observation into Israel's ethnicity.* Tel Aviv: Van Leer Jerusalem Institute and Hakibbutz Hameuchad, pp. 15–27 (Hebrew).

— (2003) 'The mute history of social refusal in Israel Defense Forces (IDF)'. *Sedek* 5: 32–41 (Hebrew).

Andrew, B., J. Keller and L. H. Schwartzman (2005) *Feminist Interventions in*

Ethics and Politics: Feminist ethics and social theory. Lanham, MD: Rowman & Littlefield Publishers.

Apple, M. (1993) *Official Knowledge: Democratic education in a conservative age.* New York, NY: Routledge.

ATG (2008) *Palestine and Palestinians: Guidebook.* Ramallah: Alternative Tourism Group (ATG).

Avidan, D., T. Ben-Yosef, M. Cohen, M. Rozenfeld, M. and E. Shaish (2007) 'Skills Workshop for Shelah – the sortie'. Eretz veDarkei Haaretz, Jerusalem: Ministry of Education (Hebrew).

Avishar, O. (2011) 'The development of the myth of the hike from the perspective of national Zionist education'. In G. Cohen and E. Shaish (eds), *The Tiyul (Hike) as an Educational Tool.* Jerusalem: Ministry of Education.

Azoulay, A. (2011a) 'Declaring the state of Israel: declaring a state of war'. *Critical Inquiry* 37(2): 265–85.

— (2011b) *From Palestine to Israel: A photographic record of destruction and state formation, 1947–50* (translated by C. S. Kamen). London: Pluto Press.

— (2012) *Civil Alliances: Palestine 47-8* (film).

— (2013) 'Thinking through violence'. *Critical Inquiry* 39(3): 548–74.

— and A. Ophir (2013) *The One-State Condition: Occupation and democracy in Israel/Palestine.* Stanford, CA: Stanford University Press.

Bailey, A. (1998) 'Locating traitorous identities: toward a view of privilege-cognizant white character'. *Hypathia* 13(3): 27–42.

Bar-Gal, Y. (1993) *Moledet and Geography in a Hundred Years of Zionist Education.* Tel Aviv: Am Oved Publishers (Hebrew).

— and B. Bar-Gal (2008) 'To tie the cords between the people and its land: geography education in Israel'. *Israel Studies* 13(1): 44–67.

Barak, M. (2005) 'Civic education in Israel'. *Adalah Electronic Monthly* 18 (Hebrew).

— and Y. Ofarim (2009) *Education for Citizenship, Democracy and Shared Living.* Educational Policy and Pedagogical Philosophy Series. Jerusalem: Van Leer Jerusalem Institute.

Barak-Erez, D. (2007) 'The feminist battle for citizenship: between combat duties and conscientious objection'. *Cardozo Journal of Law and Gender* 13: 531–60.

Barghouti, O. (2011) *Boycott, Divestment, Sanctions: The global struggle for Palestinian rights.* Chicago, IL: Haymarket Books.

Behar, M. (2011) 'Unparallel universes: Iran and Israel's one-state solution'. *Global Society* 25(3): 353–76.

Bell, J. (2009) *Deleuze's Hume: Philosophy, culture and the Scottish Enlightenment.* Edinburgh: Edinburgh University Press.

Ben-Ari, E., Z. Rosenhek and D. Maman (2001) *Military, State and Society in Israel.* London and New York, NY: Transaction Publishers.

Ben-David, O. (1997) 'The "tiyul" as an act of consecration of space'. In E. Ben-Ari and Y. Bilu (eds), *Grasping Land: Space and place in contemporary Israeli discourse and experience.* Albany, NY: State University of New York Press, pp. 129–46.

Ben-Eliezer, U. (1998) *The Making of Militarism in Israel.* Bloomington, IN: Indiana University Press.

Ben-Israel, A. (1999) 'The idea of the tiyul and its development'. In A. Peled (ed.), *An Anniversary of the Educational System in Israel.* Jerusalem: Ministry of Education (Hebrew).

Ben-Israel, T. (2007) 'The integration of physical education into the curriculum of Israel's pre-state education system'. *Israel Affairs* 13(3): 566–85.

Ben-Porath, S. (2006) *Citizenship Under Fire: Democratic education in times of conflict*. Princeton, NJ: Princeton University Press.

Ben-Yosef, T. and E. Shaish (2005a) *Derech Eretz veDarkei Haaretz: First year (exercises)*. Jerusalem: Ministry of Education (Hebrew).

— (2005b) *Derech Eretz veDarkei Haaretz: Second year (exercises)*. Jerusalem: Ministry of Education (Hebrew).

— (2006) *Derech Eretz veDarkei Haaretz: The curriculum*. Jerusalem: Ministry of Education (Hebrew).

Benn, A. (2011) 'Doomed to fight'. *Haaretz*, 9 May. Available at: www.haaretz.com/weekend/week-s-end/doomed-to-fight-1.360698 (accessed 5 March 2013).

Benvenisti, M. (2002) *Sacred Landscape: The buried history of the Holy Land since 1948* (translated by M. Kaufman-Lacusta). Berkeley, CA: University of California Press.

Bernstein D. (2000) *Constructing Boundaries: Jewish and Arab workers in Mandatory Palestine*. New York, NY: State University of New York Press.

Bishara, A. (2001) 'Reflections on October 2000: a landmark in Jewish-Arab relations in Israel'. *Journal of Palestine Studies* 30(3): 54–67.

— (2007) 'Why Israeli is after me'. *Los Angeles Times*, 3 May.

Blackman, L. J. Cromby, D. Hook, D. Papadopoulos and V. Walkerdine (2008) 'Creating subjectivities'. *Subjectivity* 22: 1–27.

Blomberg, J. (1995) 'Protecting the right not to vote from voter purge statutes'. *Fordham Law Review* 64(3): 1015–50.

Brecht, B. (1964) *Brecht on Theatre: The development of an aesthetic* (translated by J. Willet). London: Eyre Methuen.

Buchanan, I. (2000) *Deleuzism: A metacommentary*. Durham, NC: Duke University Press.

— (2013) 'Change'. In I. Szeman (ed.), *Fueling Culture: Energy, history, politics*. New York, NY: Fordham University Press (in press).

Campos, M. (2011) *Ottoman Brothers*. Stanford, CA: Stanford University Press.

Carmi, S. and H. Rosenfeld (1989) 'The emergence of militaristic nationalism in Israel'. *International Journal of Politics, Culture and Society* 3(1): 5–49.

Carroll, D. (1990) 'Foreword: the memory of devastation and the responsibilities of thought: "And let's not talk about that"'. In J. F. Lyotard, *Heidegger and the Jews* (translated by A. Michel and M. Roberts). Minneapolis, MN: University of Minnesota Press, p. ix.

Chacham, R. (2003) *Breaking Ranks: Refusing to serve in the West Bank and Gaza Strip*. New York, NY: Other Press.

Chayut, N. (2013) *The Girl Who Stole My Holocaust*. London: Verso.

Chetrit, S. S. (2000) 'Mizrahi politics in Israel: between integration and alternative'. *Journal of Palestine Studies* 29(4): 51–65.

— (2004) *The Mizrahi Struggle in Israel: Between oppression and liberation, identification and alternative, 1948–2003*. Tel Aviv: Am Oved (Hebrew).

— (2010) *Intra-Jewish Conflict in Israel: White Jews, black Jews*. London and New York, NY: Routledge.

Child Soldiers International (2012) *Report to the Committee on the Rights of the Child in Advance of Israel's Second Periodic Report under the Convention on the Rights of the Child*. London: Child Soldiers International.

Cook, J. (2013) 'Israel's rightward shift leaves Palestinian citizens out in the cold'. *Middle East Research and Information Project*. Available at: www.merip.org/mero/mero021313 (accessed 3 March 2013).

Dahan, Y. and G. Levy (2000) 'Multicultural education in the Zionist state: the Mizrahi challenge'. *Studies in Philosophy and Education* 19: 423–44.

Dahan-Kalev, H. (1997) 'Tensions in Israeli feminism: the Mizrahi Ashkenazi rift'. *Women's Studies International Forum* 24(6): 669–84.

Davidson, N. (2008) 'Nationalism and neoliberalism'. *Variant* 32. Available at: www.variant.org.uk/32texts/davidson32.html.

Dayan, M. (1956) 'Eulogy'. Available at: www.jewishvirtuallibrary.org/jsource/Quote/dayan1.html.

Deleuze, G. (1995) *Negotiations* (translated by M. Joughin). New York, NY: Columbia University Press.

— and F. Guattari (1987) *A Thousand Plateaus: Capitalism and schizophrenia* (translated by B. Massumi). Minneapolis, MN: University of Minnesota Press.

Diamond, L. (2002) 'Thinking about hybrid regimes'. *Journal of Democracy* 13(2): 21–35.

Diskin, A. (2011) *Regime and Politics in Israel: Principles of citizenship*. Tel Aviv: Maggie Publishers (Hebrew).

Dror, Y. (2011) 'Tiyulim as part of the national education'. In G. Cohen and E. Shaish (eds), *The Tiyul as an Educational Tool*. Jerusalem: Ministry of Education (Hebrew).

Eber, S. and K. O'Sullivan (1989) *Israel and the Occupied Territories: The rough guide*. London: Harrap-Columbus.

Economist Intelligence Unit (2012) *Democracy Index 2012*. London: Economist Intelligence Unit.

Edensor, T. (2000) 'Walking in the British countryside: reflexivity, embodied practices and ways to escape'. *Body & Society* 6(3–4): 81–106.

Emmett, A. H. (1996) *Our Sisters' Promised Land: Women, politics and Israeli-Palestinian coexistence*. Ann Arbor, MI: University of Michigan Press.

Enloe, C. (2000) *Manoeuvres: The international politics of militarizing women's lives*. Berkeley, CA: University of California Press.

Eqeiq, A. (2012) 'Not an epilogue'. In T. Gardi, N. Kadman and A. Al'abari (eds), *Once Upon the Land*. Tel Aviv: Pardes Publications, pp. 500–2.

Esposito, R. (2010a) *Communitas: The origin and destiny of community* (translated by T. Campbell). Stanford, CA: Stanford University Press.

— (2010b) *Immunitas: Protezione e negazione della vita*. Turin: Einaudi (Italian).

Evron, B. (1981) 'The holocaust: learning the wrong lessons'. *Journal of Palestine Studies* 10(3): 16–26.

Ezrahi, Y. (1997) *Rubber Bullets: Power and conscience in modern Israel*. New York, NY: Farrar, Straus and Giroux.

Filc, D. (2011) 'Post-populism: explaining neo-liberal populism through the habitus'. *Journal of Political Ideologies* 16(2): 221–38.

— and U. Ram (2013) *The Social Protest Forum*. Jerusalem: Van Leer Jerusalem Institute (forthcoming, Hebrew).

Fireberg, H. (2004) 'Wonderful generation'. *Et-Mol* 177: 14–6 (Hebrew).

Foucault, M. (1982) 'The subject and power'. In H. Dreyfus, P. Rabinow and M. Foucault (eds), *Michel Foucault: Beyond structuralism and hermeneutics*. Chicago, IL: University of Chicago Press, p. 208.

— (2008) 'Of other spaces'. In M. Dehanene and L. De Cauter (eds), *Heterotopia and the City: Public* space in a post-civil society. London: Routledge, pp. 13–29.

Gaard, G. and P. Murphy (1998) *Ecofeminist Literary Criticism: Theory, interpretation, pedagogy*. Champaign, IL: University of Illinois Press.

Gardi, T. (2011) *Stone, Paper*. Tel Aviv: Hakibbutz Hameuchad (Hebrew).

— N. Kadman and A. Al'abari (eds) (2012) *Once Upon the Land*. Tel Aviv: Pardes Publications (Hebrew).

Geiger, I. (2009) *Civics Studies: Education or unidirectional indoctrination?* Jerusalem: Institute for Zionist Strategies.

Ghanem, A. (2001) *The Palestinian-Arab Minority in Israel, 1948–2000: A political study*. New York, NY: State University of New York.

— and M. Mustafa (2007) 'The Palestinians in Israel and the 2006 Knesset elections: political and ideological implications of election boycott'. *Holy Land Studies* 6(1): 51–73.

Giladi, G. N. (1990) *Discord in Zion: Conflict between Ashkenazi and Sephardi Jews in Israel*. London: Scorpion Publishing.

Gillath, N. (1991) 'Women against war: parents against silence'. In B. Swirski and M. P. Safir (eds), *Calling the Equality Bluff: Women in Israel*. New York, NY: Teachers College Press, pp. 142–6.

Givol, A., N. Rotem and S. Sandler (2004) *The New Profile Report on Child Recruitment in Israel*. Israel: New Profile. Available at: www.newprofile.org/english/node/249.

Gluzman, M. (2007) *The Zionist Body: Representations of the body in modern Hebrew literature*. Tel Aviv: Hakibbutz Hameuchad (Hebrew).

Golan, G. (1997) 'Militarization and gender: the Israeli experience'. *Women's Studies International Forum* 20(5/6): 581–6.

Goodman, Y. and N. Mizrahi (2008)

'"The Holocaust does not belong to European Jews alone": the differential use of memory techniques in Israeli high schools'. *American Ethnologist* 35(1): 95–114.

Gor, H. (2005) *The Militarization of Education*. Tel Aviv: Babel (Hebrew).

Gordon, N. (2008) *Israel's Occupation*. Berkeley, CA: University of California Press.

Gratch, A. (2013) 'Masada performances: The contested identities of touristic spaces'. PhD dissertation, Louisiana State University and Agricultural and Mechanical College, University of North Carolina.

Grinberg, L. (2012) 'Neither one or two: reflections about a shared future in Israel-Palestine'. *HaMerhav HaTziburi* (*The Public Sphere*) 6: 142–54 (Hebrew).

Grunzweig, N. (2012) 'Burayr'. In T. Gardi, N. Kadman and A. Al'abari (eds), *Once Upon the Land*. Tel Aviv: Pardes Publications, pp. 447–52 (Hebrew).

Guattari, F. (1996) *The Guattari Reader* (edited by G. Genosko). Oxford: Blackwell.

— (2013) *Schizoanalytic Cartographies* (translated by A. Goffey). Bloomsbury: London.

— and S. Rolnik (2008) *Molecular Revolution in Brazil*. Los Angeles, CA: Semiotext(e).

Gur-Ze'ev, I. (2009) 'Book review: *Citizenship Under Fire: Democratic education in times of conflict*'. *Studies in Philosophy and Education* 28: 171–84.

Haberfeld, Y. and Y. Cohen (2007) 'Gender, ethnic, and national earnings gaps in Israel: the role of rising inequality'. *Social Science Research* 36: 654–72.

Harel, A. (2013) *The Face of the New IDF*. Tel Aviv: Kinneret Zmora-Bitan Dvir (Hebrew).

Harel, N. and E. Lomsly-Feder (2011) 'Bargaining over citizenship: premilitary preparatory activities in the service of the dominant groups'. In H. Alexander, H. Pinson and Y. Yonah (eds), *Citizenship Education and Social Conflict*. New York, NY: Routledge, pp. 187–98.

Harel, Y. (2009) 'Gideon the teacher teaches civic education'. *Haaretz*, 30 April (Hebrew).

Harmes, A. (2012) 'The rise of neoliberal nationalism'. *Review of International Political Economy* 19(1): 59–86.

Harrer, S. (2005) 'The theme of subjectivity in Foucault's lecture series L'Herméneutique du Sujet'. *Foucault Studies* 2: 75–96.

Harvey, D. (2005) *A Brief History of Neoliberalism*. New York, NY: Oxford University Press.

Hazony, Y. (2000) *The Jewish State: The struggle for Israel's soul*. New York, NY: New Republic/Basic Books.

Helman, S. (1997) 'Militarism and the construction of community'. *Journal of Political and Military Sociology* 25: 305–32.

— (1999) 'From soldiering and motherhood to citizenship: a study of four Israeli peace protest movements'. *Social Politics* 6: 292–313.

— (2009) 'Peace movements in Israel'. *Jewish Women: A comprehensive historical encyclopaedia*, Jewish Women's Archive. Available at: http://jwa.org/encyclopedia/article/peace-movements-in-israel (accessed 19 July 2013).

— and T. Rapoport (1997) 'Women in black: challenging Israel's gender and socio-political order'. *British Journal of Sociology* 48: 681–700.

Henderson, K. (1992) 'Breaking with tradition: women and outdoor pursuits'. *Journal of Physical Education, Recreation & Dance* 63(2): 49–52.

Hermann, T. (2012) *The Israeli Democracy Index 2012*. Jerusalem: Israel Democracy Institute.

Herzl, T. (1956) *Diaries* (edited by M. Lowenthal). New York, NY: Dial Press.

Herzog, H. (1999) 'A space of their own: social-civil discourses among Palestinian-Israeli women in peace organizations'. *Social Politics* 6: 344–69.

— (2003) 'Post-Zionist discourse in alternative voices: a feminist perspective'. In E. Nimni (ed.), *The Challenge of Post-Zionism: Alternatives to Israeli fundamentalist politics*. London: Zed Books, pp. 153–67.

— (2004) 'Family-military relations in Israel as a genderizing social mechanism'. *Armed Forces & Society* 31(1): 5–30.

Hever, H., Y. Shenhav and P. Motzafi-Haller (eds) (2002) *Mizrahim in Israel: A critical observation into Israel's ethnicity*. Tel Aviv: Van Leer Jerusalem Institute and Hakibbutz Hameuchad (Hebrew).

Hiller, R. (2001) 'As natural as mother's milk: impregnating society with militarism'. New Profile. Available at: www.newprofile.org/english/node/215 (accessed 1 July 2013).

Hoffmann, A. (2012) 'A better approach to aliyah'. *Haaretz*, 20 January. Available at: www.haaretz.com/print-edition/opinion/a-better-approach-to-aliyah-1.408261 (accessed 23 April 2013).

Howitt, P. (1998) *Sliding Doors* (film).

Ichilov, O. (1993) *Citizenship Education in Israel*. Tel Aviv: Poalim (Hebrew).

— (2005) 'Citizenship education in Israel: a Jewish and democratic state'. *Israel Affairs* 11(2): 303–23.

Ignatiev, N. (1997) 'The point is not to interpret whiteness but to abolish it'. Talk given at the conference 'The

Making and Unmaking of Whiteness', University of California, Berkeley, 11–13 April.

Isin, E. and G. Nielsen (2008) *Acts of Citizenship*. London: Zed Books.

Iton Gadol (2011) 'La Agencia Judía quiere maximizar la cantidad de jóvenes que tengan vivencias israelíes significativas'. *Iton Gadol*, 27 April. Available at: www.itongadol.com.ar/noticias/val/55793/%E2%80%9Cla-agencia-judia-quiere-maximizar-la-cantidad-de-jovenes-que-tengan-vivencias-israelies-significativas.html (accessed 12 March 2013) (Spanish).

Izraeli, D. (1997) 'Gendering military service in the Israel Defense Forces'. *Israel Social Science Research* 12: 1.

IZS (2012) *Teaching of Civics: Full follow-up report 2012*. Jerusalem: Institute for Zionist Strategies (IZS).

Jabareen, Y. (2006) 'Critical perspectives on Arab Palestinian education in Israel'. *American Behavioural Scientist* 49(8): 1052–74.

— (2008) 'Constitution building and equality in deeply-divided societies: the case of the Palestinian-Arab minority in Israel'. *Wisconsin International Law Journal* 26(2): 346–400.

Jacoby, T. (1999) 'Gendered nation: a history of the interface of women's protest and Jewish nationalism in Israel'. *International Feminist Journal of Politics* 1(3): 382–402.

Jamal, A. (2002) 'Abstention as participation: the labyrinth of Arab politics in Israel'. In A. Arian and M. Shamir (eds), *The Elections in Israel 2001*. Jerusalem: Israel Democracy Institute, pp. 55–103.

— (2011) *Arab Minority Nationalism in Israel: The politics of indigeneity*. London: Routledge.

Jameson, F. (1994) *The Seeds of Time*. New York, NY: Columbia University Press.

— (2005) *Archaeologies of the Future: The desire called utopia and other science fictions*. London: Verso.

— (2010) *Valences of the Dialectic*. London: Verso.

Janz, B. (2001) 'The territory is not the map'. *Philosophy Today* 45(4): 392–404.

Kadman, N. (2008) *Erased from Space and Consciousness: Depopulated Palestinian villages in the Israeli-Zionist discourse*. Jerusalem: November Books (Hebrew).

Karlik, A. (2012) 'Sólido vincula entre Israel y el mundo judío'. Available at: http://shalom.cl/?p=1083 (accessed 22 March 2013).

Kashti, O. (2009) 'Under the nose of the Ministry of Education, a leftist organisation disseminates to teachers educational material on the Palestinian Nakba'. *Haaretz*, 4 June. Available at: www.haaretz.co.il/news/education/1.1264209 (accessed 18 August 2013) (Hebrew).

Katriel, T. (1991) *Communal Webs: Communication and culture in contemporary Israel*. New York, NY: State University of New York Press.

— (1995) 'Touring the land: trips and hiking as secular pilgrimages in Israeli culture'. *Jewish Folklore and Ethnology Review* 17(1–2): 6–14.

Katz, S. (1985) 'The Israeli teacher-guide: the emergence and perpetuation of a role'. *Annals of Tourism Research* 12: 49–72.

Keller, D. (1997) 'Plot and characters in the text of educational ideologies'. In I. Gur-Zeev (ed.), *Education in the Era of Postmodern Education*. Jerusalem: Hebrew University Magness Press (Hebrew).

Kemp, A. (2002) 'State domination and resistance in the Israeli frontier'. In H. Hever, Y. Shenhav and P. Motzafi-Haller (eds), *Mizrahim in Israel: A* critical observation into Israel's ethnicity. Tel Aviv: Van Leer Jerusalem Institute and Hakibbutz Hameuchad, pp. 36–67 (Hebrew).

Khalidi, W. (2006) All that Remains: The Palestinian villages occupied and depopulated by Israel in 1948. Baltimore, MD: Port City Press.

Khazzoom, A. (2005) 'Did the Israeli state engineer segregation? On the placement of Jewish immigrants in development towns in the 1950s'. Social Forces 84(1): 117–36.

Kimmerling, B. (1979) 'Determination of the boundaries and frameworks of conscription: two dimensions of civil-military relations in Israel'. Studies in Comparative International Development, Spring: 22–40

— (1983) Zionism and Territory: The socioterritorial dimensions of Zionist politics. Berkeley, CA: Institute of International Studies, University of California.

— (1993) 'Militarism in Israeli society'. Theory and Criticism: An Israeli Forum 4: 123–40 (Hebrew).

Kovel, J. (2007) Overcoming Zionism: Creating a single democratic state in Israel/Palestine. London: Pluto Press.

Krawitz, C. (2009). 'Interview with Sami Shalom Chetrit on Mizrahim in Israel'. JVoices. Available at: http://jvoices.com/2009/03/15/interview-with-sami-shalom-chetrit-on-mizrahim-in-israel/ (accessed 13 October 2013).

Kremnitzer, M. (1996) To Be Citizens: Citizenship education to all Israeli pupils. Jerusalem: Ministry of Education, Culture and Sport.

Landau, I. (2012) 'Who is in favour of eliminating the Gadna?' (blog). Available at: http://idanlandau.com/2012/01/16/against-gadna/ (accessed 23 March 2013) (Hebrew).

Lardy, H. (2004) 'Is there a right not to vote?' Oxford Journal of Legal Studies 24(2): 303–21.

Lavie, S. (2005) 'Israeli anthropology and American anthropology'. Anthropology Newsletter, January: 9–10.

— (2011) 'Where is the Mizrahi-Palestinian border zone? Interrogating feminist transnationalism through the bounds of the lived'. Social Semiotics 21(1): 67–83.

Lavih, A. (2013) 'The left wants that Ahmed mix the mortar and keeps silent'. Forbes Israel, 8 January. Available at: www.forbes.co.il/news/new.aspx?Pn6VQ=M&or9VQ=GGLI (accessed 8 April 2013) (Hebrew).

Lazar, A., J. Chaitin, T. Gross and D. Bar-On (2004) 'Jewish Israeli teenagers, national identity, and the lessons of the holocaust'. Holocaust and Genocide Studies 18(2): 188–204.

Lears, T. J. (1985) 'The concept of cultural hegemony: problems and possibilities'. The American Historical Review 90(3): 567–93.

Lemish, D. and I. Barzel (2000) 'Four mothers: the womb in the public sphere'. European Journal of Communication 15(2): 147–69.

Lemish, P. (2003) 'Civic and citizenship education in Israel'. Cambridge Journal of Education 33(1): 53–72.

Lentin, R. (2010) Co-memory and Melancholia: Israelis memorialising the Palestinian Nakba. Manchester: Manchester University Press.

Leonardo, Z. (2004) 'The color of supremacy: beyond the discourse of "white privilege"'. Educational Philosophy and Theory 36(2): 137–52.

Levy, G. and M. Massalha (2012) 'Within and beyond citizenship: alternative educational initiatives in the Arab society in Israel'. Citizenship Studies 16(7): 905–17.

Levy, G. and O. Sasson-Levy (2008) 'Militarized socialization, military service, and class reproduction: the experiences of Israeli soldiers'. *Sociological Perspectives* 51(2): 349–74.

Levy, Y., E. Lomsky-Feder and N. Harel (2007) 'From "obligatory militarism" to "contractual militarism": competing models of citizenship'. *Israel Studies* 12(1): 127–48.

Linn, R. (1986) 'Conscientious objection in Israel during the war in Lebanon'. *Armed Forces & Society* 12(4): 489–511.

Lior, I. (2013) 'Gal-On to Haaretz surfers: Livni-Yechimovitz block is a spin'. *Haaretz*, 6 January. Available at: www.haaretz.co.il/news/elections/1.1898286 (accessed 3 May 2013) (Hebrew).

Lockman, Z. (1996) *Comrades and Enemies: Arab and Jewish workers in Palestine, 1906–1948*. Berkeley, CA: University of California Press.

Lubin, O. (2002) 'Gone to soldiers: feminism and the military in Israel'. *Journal of Israeli History: Politics, Society, Culture* 21(1–2): 164–92.

Lustick, I. (1980) *Arabs in the Jewish State: Israel's control of a national minority*. Austin, TX: University of Texas Press.

Magen, D. (2011) 'Aviva Shalit: the most public consensus it can be'. *Walla*, 28 September. Available at: http://touch.walla.co.il/ExpandedItem.asp x?WallaId=1//1862144&ItemType=101 &VerticalId=2 (accessed 6 April 2013) (Hebrew).

Mamdani, M. (2007) 'Good Muslim, bad Muslim: a political perspective on culture and terrorism'. *American Anthropologist* 104(3): 766–75.

Mandel, R. (2008) 'Demonstration in Tel Aviv: "IDF officers – not in our schools"'. *Ynet*, 26 March. Available at: www.ynet.co.il/articles/0,7340,L-3523799,00.html (accessed 23 December 2012) (Hebrew).

Mansfield, N. (2000) *Subjectivity – Theories of the Self from Freud to Haraway*. Australia: Allen & Unwin.

Margalit, D. (2010) 'The time for Operation Betzer No. 2'. *Israel Hayom Newsletter*, 18 May. Available at: www.israelhayom.co.il/site/news letter_article.php?id=6610 (accessed 3 July 2013) (Hebrew).

— (2012) 'An Arab-free Knesset?' *Israel Hayom Newsletter*, 11 December. Available at: www.israelhayom.com/site/newsletter_opinion.php?id=3035 (accessed 14 June 2013).

Massad, J. (1996) 'Zionism's internal others: Israel and the Oriental Jews'. *Journal of Palestine Studies* 25(4): 53–68.

— (2002) 'Deconstructing holocaust consciousness'. *Journal of Palestine Studies* 32(1): 78–89.

Mayer, T. (2000) 'From zero to hero: masculinity in Jewish nationalism'. In T. Mayer (ed.), *Gender Ironies of Nationalism: Sexing the nation*. London: Routledge, pp. 283–308.

Mazali, R. (1995) 'Raising boys to maintain armies'. *British Medical Journal* 311: 694.

— (1997) 'I refuse: three perspectives of one woman on the military and militarism'. *Noga* 32: 17–20 (Hebrew).

— (1998) 'Parenting troops: the summons to acquiescence'. In L. A. Lorentzen and J. Turpin (eds), *The Women and War Reader*. New York, NY: New York University Press.

— (2005) 'Recruited parenthood'. In H. Gor (ed.), *Militarism in Education*. Tel Aviv: Babel (Hebrew).

— (2008) *Parenting Troops: An introduction-in-hindsight for the Turkish version*. (No publisher details available.)

— (2011) *Home Archaeology*. Tel Aviv: Hakibbutz Hameuchad (Hebrew).

Melville, H. (1986) 'Bartleby the

Scrivener: a tale of Wall Street'. In H. Melville, *Billy Budd and Other Stories*. New York, NY: Penguin.

Ministry of Education (2008) *Shelah Core Programme*. Jerusalem: Ministry of Education (Hebrew).

Morgenstern-Leissner, O. (2006) 'Hospital birth, military service and the ties that bind them: the case of Israel'. *A Journal of Jewish Women's Studies and Gender Issues* 12: 203–41.

Morris, B. (2004) *The Birth of the Palestinian Refugee Problem Revisited*. Cambridge: Cambridge University Press.

Motzafi-Haller, P. (2001) 'Scholarship, identity, and power: Mizrahi women in Israel'. *Signs: Journal of Women in Culture and Society* 26(3): 697–734.

Muldon, P. and A. Schaap (2012) 'Aboriginal sovereignty and the politics of reconciliation: the constituent power of the Aboriginal Embassy in Australia'. *Environment and Planning D: Society and Space* 30: 534–50.

Nail, T. (2012) *Returning to Revolution: Deleuze, Guattari and Zapatismo*. Edinburgh: Edinburgh University Press.

Naor, M. (ed.) (1989) *The Youth Movements 1920–1960*. Jerusalem: Yad Yizhak Ben-Tzvi (Hebrew).

Nesher, T. (2011a) 'Education Ministry blasts Israeli Arab school for taking students to human rights march'. *Haaretz*, 30 December. Available at: www.haaretz.co.il/news/education/1.1604874 (accessed 14 October 2013) (Hebrew).

— (2011b) 'Poland trips boost Israeli students' opinions of the IDF, study finds'. *Haaretz*, 5 September. Available at: www.haaretz.com/print-edition/news/poland-trips-boost-israeli-students-opinions-of-the-idf-study-finds-1.382537 (accessed 9 May 2013).

— (2012) 'Israeli Arabs fume at plans to reward schools for IDF enlistment'. *Haaretz*, 14 November. Available at: www.haaretz.com/news/national/israeli-arabs-fume-at-plans-to-reward-schools-for-idf-enlistment.premium-1.477523 (accessed 22 May 2013).

— (2013) 'Arab teachers: we cannot teach the civil education text'. *Haaretz*, 7 April. Available at: www.haaretz.co.il/news/education/1.1986800 (accessed 14 October 2013) (Hebrew).

Netzer, D. (2008) 'Painful past in the service of Israeli Jewish-Arab dialogue: the work of the Center for Humanistic Education at the Ghetto Fighters House in Israel'. *In Factis Pax* 2(2): 282–91.

Neumann, B. (2011) *Land and Desire in Early Zionism*. Waltham, MA: Brandeis University Press.

New Profile (2011) *Annual Activity Report 2011*. Israel: New Profile.

Nimni, E. (2003) *The Challenge of Post-Zionism: Alternatives to Israeli fundamentalist politics*. London: Zed Books.

Nitzan, J. and S. Bichler (2002) *The Global Political Economy of Israel*. London: Pluto Press.

O'Sullivan, S. (2006) 'Pragmatics for the production of subjectivity: time for probe-heads'. *Journal for Cultural Research* 10(4): 309–22.

Oppenheimer, Y. (2010) 'The holocaust: a Mizrahi perspective'. *Hebrew Studies* 51: 303–28.

— (2012) 'Representation of space in Mizrahi fiction'. *Hebrew Studies* 53: 335–64.

Oz, A. (2000) *The Sabra: The creation of the New Jew*. Berkeley, CA: University of California Press.

Papadopoulos, D. (2008) 'In the ruins of representation: identity, individuality, subjectification'. *British Journal of Social Psychology*, 47: 139–65.

Pappe, I. (2006) *The Ethnic Cleansing of Palestine*. Oxford: Oneworld.

Pease, B. (2010) *Undoing Privilege: Unearned advantage in a divided world*. London: Zed Books.

Pedhazur, A. (2001) 'The paradox of civic education in non-liberal democracies: the case of Israel'. *Journal of Educational Policy* 16(5): 413–30.

— and A. Perliger (2004) 'The built-in paradox of civic education in Israel'. *Megamot* 1: 64–83 (Hebrew).

Peled, Y. and A. Ophir (eds) (2001) *Israel: From mobilized to civil society?* Tel Aviv: Hakibbutz Hameuchad (Hebrew).

Peled-Elhanan, N. (2008) 'The denial of Palestinian national and territorial identity in Israeli schoolbooks of history and geography 1996–2003'. In R. Dolon and J. Todoli (eds), *Analysing Identities in Discourse*. Amsterdam: John Benjamins Publishing.

— (2010) 'Legitimation of massacres in Israeli school history books'. *Discourse & Society* 21(4): 377–404.

— (2012) *Palestine in Israeli School Books: Ideology and propaganda in education*. London: I. B. Tauris.

Pinson, H. (2007) 'Inclusive curriculum? Challenges to the role of civic education in a Jewish and democratic state'. *Curriculum Inquiry* 37(4): 351–80.

Piterberg, G. (2001) 'Erasures'. *New Left Review* 10: 31–46.

Podeh, E. (2002) *The Arab-Israeli Conflict in Israeli History Textbooks*. Westport, CT: Bergin & Garvey.

Polisar, D. (2001) 'On the quiet revolution in citizenship education'. *Azure* 11: 66–104.

Prusher, I. (2012) 'Study: Arab sector sees no point in voting'. *The Jerusalem Post*, 28 October. Available at: www.jpost.com/National-News/Study-Arab-sector-sees-no-point-in-voting (accessed 12 July 2013).

Research and Information Centre (2010) *Report on Youth Movements 2010*. Jerusalem: Knesset Research and Information Centre (Hebrew).

Reynolds, H. (1998) *This Whispering in Our Hearts*. St Leonards, New South Wales: Allen & Unwin.

Rouhana, N. (2012) 'Making a favour to Israel'. *Maariv*, 27 December. Available at: www.nrg.co.il/online/1/ART2/425/076.html (accessed 23 May 2013) (Hebrew).

Rudnitzky, A. (2013) 'Arab politics in Israel and the 19th Knesset elections'. *An Update on Middle Eastern Developments* 7(4).

Sa'ar, T. (2011) 'The paradox: a soldier's mother'. *Haaretz*, 25 October. Available at: www.haaretz.co.il/gallery/mejunderet/1.1530529 (accessed 12 April 2013) (Hebrew).

Said, E. (1998) 'Israel-Palestine: a third way'. *Le Monde Diplomatique* (English edition), September.

— (2001) 'Time to turn to the other front'. *Middle East News Online*, 1 April. Available at: http://weekly.ahram.org.eg/2001/527/op2.htm.

— (2003) 'New history, old ideas'. In E. Nimni (ed.), *The Challenge of Post-Zionism: Alternatives to Israeli fundamentalist politics*. London: Zed Books, pp. 199–202.

Sasar, H. (2009) 'Citizenship against Zionism'. *Makor Rishon*, 22 January.

Sasson-Levy, O. (2006) *Identities in Uniform: Masculinities and femininities in the Israeli military*. Jerusalem: Hebrew University Magness Press (Hebrew).

Schiffman, E. (2005) 'The Shas school system in Israel'. *Nationalism and Ethnic Politics* 11(1): 89–124.

Schoken, R. (2012) 'Chilling effect of

the Nakba Law on Israel's human rights'. *Haaretz*, 17 May. Available at: www.haaretz.com/opinion/chilling-effect-of-the-nakba-law-on-israel-s-human-rights-1.430942 (accessed 19 September 2013).

Schwarz, O. (2013) 'What should nature sound like? Techniques of engagement with nature sites and sonic preferences of Israeli visitors'. *Annals of Tourism Research* 42: 382–401.

Segev, T. (2000) *The Seventh Million: The Israelis and the holocaust* (translated by H. Watzman). New York, NY: Owl Books.

Shachar, D. (2013) *Israel: A Jewish and democratic state*. Tel Aviv: Kinneret Zmora-Bitan Dvir (Hebrew).

Shadmi, E. (2000) 'Between resistance and compliance, feminism and nationalism: women in black in Israel'. *Women's Studies International Forum* 23: 23–34.

Shafir, G. (1989) *Land, Labor and the Origins of the Israeli-Palestinian Conflict, 1882–1914*. Berkeley, CA: University of California Press.

Shapiro, F. (2006) *Building Jewish Roots: The Israeli experience*. Montreal: McGill-Queen's University Press.

Sharoni, S. (1995) *Gender and the Israeli-Palestinian Conflict: The politics of women's resistance*. Syracuse, NY: Syracuse University Press.

Shaviro, S. (2011) 'No subject experiences twice'. *Concentric: Literary and Cultural Studies* 37(2): 7–28.

Shelach, O. (2005) 'One afternoon'. *Mita'am* 1 (Hebrew).

— (2013) 'Opening speech at the inaugural meeting of the 19th Knesset'. Available at: http://yeshatid.org.il (accessed 8 July 2013) (Hebrew).

Shemesh, E. (2013) 'The alternative tour guide for Al-Shaykh Muwannis and Ein-Hawd'. *Haaretz*, 24 March. Available at: www.haaretz.co.il/literature/ study/.premium-1.1968800 (accessed 15 July 2013) (Hebrew).

Shenav, Y. (2006) *The Arab Jews: A postcolonial reading of nationalism, religion and ethnicity*. Stanford, CA: Stanford University Press.

Shiran, V. (1991) 'Feminist identity vs. oriental identity'. In B. Swirski and M. P. Safir (eds), *Calling the Equality Bluff: Women in Israel*. New York, NY: Teachers College Press, pp. 303–11.

Shohat, E. (1988) 'Sephardim in Israel: Zionism from the standpoint of its Jewish victims'. *Social Text* 19/20: 1–35.

— (1996) 'Mizrahi feminism: the politics of gender, race and multiculturalism'. *News from Within* 12(4): 17–26.

— (1999) 'The invention of the Mizrahim'. *Journal of Palestine Studies* 1: 5–20.

— (2003) 'Rupture and return: Zionist discourse and the study of the Arab Jew'. *Social Text* 75, 21(2): 49–74.

— (2006) *Taboo Memories, Diasporic Voices*. Durham, NC: Duke University Press.

Shtul-Trauring, A. (2011) 'The teachers who teach the Palestinian narrative'. *Haaretz*, 10 June. Available at: www.haaretz.co.il/news/education/1.1176682 (accessed 18 August 2013) (Hebrew).

Slyomovics, S. (1998) *The Object of Memory: Arab and Jew narrate the Palestinian village*. Philadelphia, PA: University of Pennsylvania Press.

Smith, B. (1993) *The Roots of Separatism in Palestine*. London: I. B. Tauris.

Smooha, S. (1993) 'Class, ethnic, and national cleavages and democracy in Israel'. In E. Sprinzak and L. Diamond (eds), *Israeli under Stress*. Boulder, CO: Lynne Rienner Publishers, pp. 309–42.

Sperling, D. (2010) 'Commanding the "Be fruitful and multiply" directive: reproductive ethics, law, and policy in Israel'. *Cambridge Quarterly of Healthcare Ethics* 19: 363–71.

Spigel, U. (2001) *Motivation of Youth to Serve in the IDF.* Jerusalem: Knesset Research and Information Centre.

Stein, R. (2008) *Itineraries in Conflict: Israelis, Palestinians, and the political lives of tourism.* Durham, NC: Duke University Press.

— (2009) 'Travelling Zion'. *Interventions: International Journal of Postcolonial Studies* 11(3): 334–51.

— (2010) 'Israeli routes through Nakba landscapes: an ethnographic meditation'. *Jerusalem Quarterly* 43: 6–17.

Svirsky, M. (2000) 'Creating reality by high school exams'. *Haaretz*, 4 June (Hebrew).

— (2001) 'A pedagogic autonomy is needed'. *Haaretz*, 26 September (Hebrew).

— (2002) 'Education for citizenship, tolerance and multiculturalism'. *Kesher Ain: The Monthly High-School Teacher Journal* 115: 22–5 (Hebrew).

— (ed.) (2010) *Deleuze and Political Activism.* Deleuze Studies Special Issue: Volume 4. Edinburgh: Edinburgh University Press.

— (2011) 'Captives of identity: the betrayal of intercultural cooperation'. *Subjectivity* 4(2): 121–46.

— (2012a) *Arab-Jewish Activism in Israel-Palestine.* Farnham: Ashgate.

— (2012b) 'The cultural politics of exception'. In M. Svirsky and S. Bignall (eds), *Agamben and Colonialism.* Edinburgh: Edinburgh University Press.

— (2014) 'Settler colonialism and collaborative struggles in Australia and Israel-Palestine'. *Settler Colonial Studies*, Special Issue 4.1 (forthcoming).

— and A. Mor-Sommerfeld (2012) 'Interculturalism and the pendulum of identity'. *Intercultural Education* 23(6): 513–25.

— F. Azaiza and R. Hertz-Lazarowitz (2008) 'Bilingual education and practical interculturalism in Israel: the case of the Galilee'. *The Discourse of Sociological Practice* 8(1): 55–81.

Swirski, S. (1981) *Not Backward but Made Backward: Mizrahim and Ashkenazim in Israel – a sociological analysis and conversations with activists.* Haifa: Mahvarot LeBikoret (Hebrew).

— (1999) *Politics and Education in Israel: Comparisons with the United States.* New York, NY: Falmer Press.

— and D. Bernstein (1993) 'Who worked doing what? For whom? And for what? – The economic development of Israel and the constitution of the racial division of labour'. In U. Ram (ed.), *Israeli society: Critical perspectives.* Tel Aviv: Breirot Publishers, pp. 120–48 (Hebrew).

Tauber, D. (2012) 'Keep aliyah on the agenda'. *Haaretz*, 13 January. Available at: www.haaretz.com/print-edition/opinion/keep-aliyah-on-the-agenda-1.407061 (accessed 23 April 2013).

Tilley, V. (2005) *The One-State Solution: A breakthrough plan for peace in the Israeli-Palestinian deadlock.* Manchester: Manchester University Press.

Tzfadia, E. (2006) 'Public housing as control: spatial policy of settling immigrants in Israeli development towns'. *Housing Studies* 21(4): 523–37.

Veracini, L. (2010) *Settler Colonialism: A theoretical overview.* Basingstoke: Palgrave Macmillan.

— (2013) 'The other shift: settler colonialism, Israel, and the occupation'. *Journal of Palestine Studies* XLII(2): 26–42.

Visblay, E. (2012) *Core Education in the Jewish-Orthodox Sector.* Jerusalem: Knesset Research and Information Centre (Hebrew).

Weedon, C. (2004) *Identity and Culture: Narratives difference and belonging.* Maidenhead: Open University Press.

Weitz, G. (2011) 'Shelly Yachimovich – Mrs Mainstream'. *Haaretz*, 19 August. Available at: www.haaretz.co.il/misc/1.1374238 (accessed 4 July 2013) (Hebrew).

Wells, C. (2008) 'Abraham's sacrifice'. In E. Isin and G. Nielsen (eds), *Acts of Citizenship.* London: Zed Books, pp. 75–8.

Weltzer, Y. (2010) 'Nobody teaches a mother how to feel when her son is abducted'. *Globus*, 6 September. Available at: www.globes.co.il/news/article.aspx?did=1000584710 (accessed 2 April 2013) (Hebrew).

Wertheimer, J. (2010) *Generation of Change: How leaders in their twenties and thirties are reshaping American Jewish life.* New York, NY and Jerusalem: Avi Chai Foundation.

Wolfe, P. (2006) 'Settler colonialism and the elimination of the native'. *Journal of Genocide Research* 8(4): 387–409.

Yemini, B. (2009) 'Let the Palestinian refuse'. *Maariv*, 9 May (Hebrew).

Yiftachel, O (2000) 'Social control, urban planning and ethno-class relations: Mizrahi Jews in Israel's "development towns"'. *International Journal of Urban and Regional Research* 24(2): 418–38.

— (2006) *Ethnocracy: Land and identity politics in Israel/Palestine.* Philadelphia, PA: University of Pennsylvania Press.

Yonah, Y. and Y. Saporta (2002) 'Pre-vocational training and the creation of the working class in Israel'. In H. Hever, Y. Shenhava and P. Motzafi-Haller (eds), *Mizrahim in Israel: A critical observation into Israel's ethnicity.* Tel Aviv: Van Leer Jerusalem Institute and Hakibbutz Hameuchad, pp. 68–104 (Hebrew).

Zelikovitz, Y. M. (2009) 'Civic studies are leftist'. *Ynet*, 25 November (Hebrew).

Zemer, E. (2009) 'Change the curriculum of civic education'. *Maariv*, 25 November (Hebrew).

Ziv, Y. (1998) 'To conquer Masada!' *Katedra* 90: 115–44 (Hebrew).

Zuckermann, M. (2002) 'Towards a critical analysis of Israeli political culture'. In J. Bunzl and B. Beit-Hallahmi (eds), *Psychoanalysis, Identity, and Ideology: Critical essays on the Israel/Palestine case.* New York, NY: Springer Science+Business Media, pp. 59–70.

Zuckerman-Bareli, C. and T. Benski (1989) 'Parents against silence'. *Megamot* 32: 27–42 (Hebrew).

Laws and resolutions

Employment Equal Opportunities Law (1988), The Knesset.

Supreme Court of Israel, case 152/03: 'Marcelo Svirsky, Michal Svirsky, and the Association for Civil Rights in Israel vs. IDF'.

The Knesset: Basic Law (1958).

UN General Assembly Resolution 169 (article 66), 1980.

UN Resolution 194, 11 December 1948.

UN Security Council Resolution 237, 1967.

Websites

Abraham Fund Initiatives: www.abrahamfund.org

Adva Center – Information on Equality and Social Justice in Israel: www.adva.org

Breaking the Silence – Israeli soldiers talk about the occupied territories: www.breakingthesilence.org.il

Hand in Hand – Center for Jewish-Arab Education in Israel: www.handinhandk12.org

Israeli Ministry of Foreign Affairs: www.mfa.gov.il

New Profile – Movement for the

Demilitarization of Israeli Society:
www.newprofile.org/english
New Profile exhibition: www.newprofile.
org/english/Exhibition.
Yaffa ODS – For One Democratic State
in Historic Palestine: http://yaffaods.
wordpress.com/2013/04/25/
announcement-on-the-establish
ment-of-the-jaffa-group-for-one-
democratic-state
Zochrot – Remembering the Nakba:
http://zochrot.org/en

Interviews

Udi Aloni, Freedom Theatre: 18 November 2012, Tel Aviv.

Eitan Bronstein, Zochrot: 27 May 2013,
Tel Aviv.
Noam Chayut, Breaking the Silence:
6 November 2012, Haifa.
Diana Dolev, New Profile: 12 November
2012, Tel Aviv.
Ruti Kantor, New Profile: 12 November
2012, Tel Aviv.
Ayelet Kestler, Zochrot: 5 August 2013
(via Skype).
Rela Mazali, New Profile: July 2013 (via
email correspondence).
Orly Picker, The Leo Baeck Education
Centre: 11 November 2012, Haifa.
Shani Werner, New Profile: 13 November
2012, Haifa.

INDEX

guides on hikes, 45 see also 'young guide'
service
guilt, 15, 64, 140
Gur-Ze'ev, Ilan, 94–5, 98–9
gypsies, 22

Haaretz, editorial in Arabic, 193
habitus, 200
Hamas, 145–7
Harel, Amos, 97–9, 152
Hawking, Stephen, 82
Hebraisation of place names, 51
hegemony, 206
Herzl, Theodor, 52
Hess, Amira, 25–6
hidden curriculum: in education system,
93; of voting, 178–81
hiker, figure of, 16, 43–89; varieties of,
59–60
hiking, 96; as nation-building
technology, 49, 54; as part of
subjectivation machine, 86; as
political practice, 17; as proto-
military training, 53; associated
with Mitzvah celebrations, 80;
creates networks of subjectivation,
76; Desert Hike, 84; in the Jewish
fashion, 84; military function of,
53; modes of, 47; perceived biblical
roots of, 87; quasi-mythological
status of, 43; re-creation of, 89;
relation to military training, 75, 88;
significance of, in Zionism, 48–9;
Zionist, 17, 47, 48, 81, 86, 87, 204
(deterritorialisation of, 89; gendered
nature of, 88; refusal of, 79; themes
of, 80) see also tiyul
Hiller, Ruth, 75, 98, 142–3
Hoffmann, Alan, 82, 83, 85
holocaust, ix, 203, 210; as centre of
subjectivation, 21; as medium for
social privileging, 23; as selective
site of belonging, 25; as universal
formative crisis, 25; dissociated from
militarism, 26; manipulations of, 21–
2, 96, 204; militaristic appropriation
of, 28; Mizrahi perspective on, 25;

profanation of name of, 26; 'stealing'
of, 205; Zionist culture of, 26
home, sense of, 29
house demolitions, 128
human rights: accountability of Israeli
commitment to, 186; protection of,
115

'I prefer not to', 163
Ichilov, Orit, 106
Independence Day, commemoration
of, 66
indigenous populations, 174
individualism, 141
informing, 139; against children, 135;
against neighbours, 133–4
Institute for Zionist Studies (IZS), 118–19
Intifada, 159, 188
irrigation systems, 46
Islamic Movement, 191
Israel: academic boycott of, 83; as liberal
democracy, 182; as 'only democracy
in the Middle East', 204; as pariah
state, 19; as perceived democracy,
183–6; as system of anti-life, ix;
Declaration of Independence, 111,
131 (as messianic, 123); decline of
social policies in, 41; definition of,
119 (as Jewish and democratic state,
105, 109, 112, 113–14, 120, 128, 198,
208); established as state, 1; four
governed populations in, 174–9, 187;
promotional programmes of, 83;
Racist Age of, 108
Israel Defence Forces (IDF), 50, 72, 74,
88, 90, 100, 132, 144, 155, 171, 204; as
Israeliser, 153; as moral army, 114–15;
classification of new conscripts,
156; Conscience Committee, 169;
Education Corps, 75; obligation
to serve in, 102; Preparatory
Programme, 100–2; war crimes of,
alleged, 114
Israel Democracy Institute, 182
Israel National Trail (INT), 79–81
Israel Nature and Parks Authority (NPA),
56, 59